Presented to

_____

_____19_____

by

_____

_____

_____

The
BELIEVERS
HANDBOOK

Library of Congress Catalog Card No. 82-72686

ISBN 0-934874-03-4

Printed in the U.S.A.

The BELIEVERS HANDBOOK

A
GUIDE
TO
THE
CHRISTIAN
LIFE

By
Gerard Berghoef
Lester DeKoster

Previous Publications by the Same Authors:
The Elders Handbook, Third Printing, 1981
The Deacons Handbook, Second Printing, 1981
God's Yardstick, 1982.

TO THE READER

The textbook for the Christian life is the Bible.

Through faith you make yourself available to the Bible.

We write this *Handbook* to help you do that by pointing to the means which God provides for this fruitful union.

We come in the spirit of Paul's approach to the believers at Rome: "...that we may be mutually encouraged by each other's faith, both yours and (ours)" (Rom. 1:12).

Come, let's walk a while together!

With appreciation to our wives,
Audrey Berghoef and Ruth DeKoster,
for wise counsel and enduring support, and to
Pastor William D. Buursma, Kalamazoo, Michigan, for
constructive criticism and encouragement.

TABLE OF CONTENTS

THE AUTHORS

Mr. Gerard Berghoef is a native of the Netherlands, who emigrated to the United States early in the 1950s. He is presently a furniture manufacturing executive, and has served the Christian Reformed Church as an elder for twelve years.

Dr. Lester DeKoster is a native of Michigan, and has been professor of speech and director of the library for Calvin College and Seminary, Grand Rapids, Michigan. He retired in 1980 as Editor of *The Banner,* official weekly publication of the Christian Reformed Church.

The authors have previously published *The Elders Handbook,* A Practical Guide for Church Leaders, *The Deacons Handbook,* A Manual of Stewardship, and *God's Yardstick.*

PROLOGUE:
GOD ALWAYS TAKES THE INITIATIVE

GOD'S INITIATIVE

"In the beginning, God..." (Gen. 1:1).

The initiatives in the Christian life are never ours.

The opening move is always God's!

At the dawn of creation: God!

At our conception and birth: God!

At our rebirth through faith: God!

In the Providence that guides our lives each step of the way: God!

All begins with Him. All is ever within His love and care.

His the initiative.

Ours the response.

God plants the seed; we produce the harvest — though in truth He is at work in that, too: "...work out your own salvation," St. Paul writes, "with fear and trembling" (this to us) "for God is at work in you, both to will and to work for his good pleasure" (this for us) — Phil. 2:12-13.

In the Christian life, God first liberates so that we can freely work out the salvation He undergirds and provides.

To Israel, and to us, He says: "I am the Lord your God, who brought you out of the land of Egypt, out of the house of bondage..." (Ex. 20:2) — and then follow the Ten Commandments, God's guide to our use of the freedom He wins for us. First the divine liberation, and then our response according to the divine will.

In a precisely parallel way, Jesus says to the New Testament Church: "Go into all the world and preach the gospel" (Mark 16:15) — the "good news" that by His self-sacrifice He has liberated believers from the burden of guilt and sin. Then follows the duty which the Church must require of the liberated ones: "teaching them to do all that I have commanded you" (Matt. 28:20). First, again, the divine initiative and liberation; then our response according to the divine will.

Always, the initiative is God's; always the response is to be assumed as ours, not as we try to define it, but as God's will requires.

All is in fact God's; yet we are to live as if all were in fact ours.

We have structured this *Handbook* according to this revealed pattern of God's initiative and the believer's response.

11

We begin with God's "call" to the believer: to repent, to believe, to follow, and to grow. We do so after the model of New Testament preaching, which always calls first for repentance and then enlarges upon the consequences of repenting.

Next, we turn to the means God Himself provides us for responding to His call: His inspired Word, Christ's Body the Church, prayer, Biblical models for good behavior (with some as warnings against misbehavior), and the indispensable gift of the Holy Spirit.

Then we listen to what the Bible teaches about the "fruits" which follow upon God's call and our response: humility, forgiveness, stewardship, work, the obedient family, love, and the required witness to the work of God in our lives.

Finally, we rejoice in the blessings with which God surrounds the believer: hope, joy, triumph over adversities and short-comings, and entrance even now upon life eternal.

We prefix each chapter with a brief summary of its contents, in three parts: first, the teaching of the "Truth"; then the kind of practical "Response" required by that teaching; and then the forms of "Distortion" which sometimes pervert the doctrine and life under discussion. These are interwoven into the fabric of the chapter. Each Chapter ends with questions designed to promote reflection and discussion — for self- and group-study.

This is, in short, a *Handbook* drawn from the Scriptures to serve the Christian life, the only life worth living.

INTRODUCTION
GOD INVESTS

Life and time are God's gifts to each of us.

We can guarantee neither for ourselves.

Life and time are special gifts. They are God's investment in our futures.

Like all investors, God seeks a return of interest upon principal.

That return is our living the truly Christian life.

GOD REWARDS

God richly rewards the return we make Him on His investment of time and life in ourselves.

"Eye has not seen, nor ear heard, nor the heart conceived," the Apostle Paul tells us, "what God has prepared for those who love him" (I Cor. 2:9).

That future is for you, and for all who choose to use God's gifts of life and time to serve Him.

SERVING GOD

What *is* serving God?

That is what the Bible is all about — *how* to make God a return on His investment in each of us.

And, therefore, that is what this *Handbook* is also about — what the Bible teaches concerning our "love," that is our service, of God.

To serve God is to obey His will rather than our own.

To serve God is obedience to His commandments.

We obey His commandments when they govern our choices — all our choices!

CHOICE

To live is to choose.

Time is God's gift of opportunity for right choosing.

Shall I do this? or that? or nothing (for doing nothing is also a choice!)?

Shall I say this? or that? or nothing?

Shall I think on this? or that? (It is impossible to think long on nothing.)

Shall I smile, frown, criticize, encourage, praise? Shall I give? or keep? Shall I fight for, or against? Shall I work or loaf?

Indeed, living is choosing. That's what God's gifts of time and life come down to: choice.

SCULPTING SELVES

We become who we are, day by day, through the choices we make.

We become who God wants us to be through choices guided by His will as revealed in His Word, the inspired and Holy Bible.

Obedient choice is the means through which we return to God interest upon His investment of life and time in us.

By choosing (and, remember, to live *is* to choose!) we gradually sculpt our selves. Or, just say that we add each new day further touches to the portrait which we are inescapably painting of our true selves — with paint that will not rub off!

No art museum in all the world houses sculptures or paintings that endure forever. But the selves we are forming, through choices, are eternal. Never, therefore, underestimate who you are — a self destined to live forever!

The work of art that each of us is engaged in creating, day by day, is without measure and without price — who can weigh the worth of one self?

SALVATION

The world will one day pass away: "But the day of the Lord will come like a thief, and then the heavens will pass away with a loud noise, and the elements will be dissolved with fire, and the earth and the works that are upon it will be burned up" (II Pet. 3:10).

Against this universal dissolution, God has made provision for "saving" all who believe.

Christianity takes its name from Jesus the Christ, only begotten Son of the living God.

The Bible reveals how and why God sends His Son into the world. It is "to save sinners" (I Tim. 1:15).

Salvation has to do with God's rescue of His investment in all who hear His Word and believe in His Son.

The Bible is the book of salvation. In it God reveals that the Christ came to "save" believers from all that robs Him of return upon His gifts of life and time in us. Through the Christ, and by the indwelling power of His Spirit, we can sculpt selves that are more and more formed through obedience to God's will.

Jesus thus "saves" all who believe from futile pursuit of false goals, fading hopes, terminal prospects.

Jesus liberates all who believe from the tyranny of the Devil, the whims of self, the fads of the hour.

By faith, in short, we paint self-portraits destined for eternal blessing. This is what "salvation" means!

This *is* salvation!

WAY OR WAY

God's Word sets before us every day anew the basic choice which underlies all other choices: "Enter by the narrow gate, for the gate is wide and the way is easy, that leads to destruction, and those who enter by it are many. For the gate is narrow and the way is hard that leads to life, and those who find it are few" (Matt. 7:13-14). So Jesus Himself says.

Choose: use life and time for right choices! Take the narrow way of obedience to the divine will.

Reject: the easy way of self-indulgence! Beware especially of whatever and whoever represents the narrow gate as broad and the hard road as easy. The truly Christian self is sculpted only along the way of difficult, self-denying choice. So God says!

These two roads end, finally, at different sides of the Lord's throne: "When the Son of Man comes in his glory, and all the angels with him, then he will sit on his glorious throne. Before him will be gathered all the nations, and he will separate them one from another as a shepherd separates the sheep from the goats, and he will place the sheep at his right hand, but the goats on the left" (Matt. 25:31-33).

The "sheep" are those whose selves have been sculpted by choices made in obedience to God's commandments, which are the expression of His will for our behavior. Their destiny is eternal reward: "...inherit the kingdom prepared for you from the foundation of the world!"

The "goats" are those whose choices robbed God of return on His investment of time and life in them. Their destiny is also eternal: "Depart from me, you cursed, into the eternal fire prepared for the devil and his angels" (Matt. 25:34, 41).

FOCUS

It is the aim of this *Handbook* to aid in focusing the light of God's Word upon the ways of choice that open before each of us every moment.

For to live is, indeed, to choose.

But only one kind of choice sculpts a self destined to enjoy divine blessing now and forever. It is the choice of willing obedience to God's revealed will.

We must not suppose, of course, that by ourselves we can make such choices and can work our way through that narrow gate. All the initiatives in the Christian life are God's! None-the-less, the responsibility for acting upon the power that God graciously provides is, as seen from our side, our own. We are not "saved," then, *by* our choices, but we are "saved" *to make them in obedience.*

It is God who provides power to sculpt true selves.

It is by faith that we receive such power.

And it is by faith, then, that we are saved.

God's initiatives are combined with our obedience this way: "...work out your own salvation with fear and trembling; for God is at work in you, both to will and to work for his good pleasure" (Phil. 2:12-13).

Let us hear together how the Bible spells that out.

For Reflection And Discussion

1. *What in essence does serving God mean?*
2. *Why does living come down to constant making of choices?*
3. *Describe how the Bible points to the two ways open to us.*
4. *Give some examples of each "way" from daily living.*
5. *How are we all responsible to act upon the power that God provides?*

PART I

GOD CALLS

Chapter 1.

REPENT

In those days came John the Baptist,
preaching in the wilderness of Judea,
"Repent, for the kingdom of heaven is at hand."
Matthew 3:2

REPENT

TRUTH:
To repent involves recognition of one's own sinfulness, acknowledgement of personal responsibility, confession to God, and plea for forgiveness in Christ, with resolution to do better — as illumined by the parable of the Prodigal Son.
RESPONSE:
Make repentance a daily exercise, done always in the light of the Scriptures.
DISTORTION:
Losing awareness of the need to repent daily, by thinking that to repent once is enough.

Repent!

"Repent" is the first command the Christian really *hears* as faith takes hold of his life.

"Repent" is, no less, first order of the Christian's day as Christian life matures.

What is it to "repent"?

We have from experience a "feel" for what repentance involves. From far back in childhood we know that mixture of shame, sorrow, and determination to do better that together comprise repentance.

We know, too, that repentance relates to persons. What moves us to

19

repenting is the recognition that something we have done has hurt someone else — perhaps directly, or perhaps because our behavior has fallen short of what the other expected of us. Repentance thus differs from regret.

We may regret harm done ourselves, damage done to things, or opportunities ignored. But of these we are not said to "repent".

And we may suffer remorse over harm done ourselves, or others, even done to things. But remorse is not repentance.

To repent is to know, and to acknowledge, that we have hurt another without occasion or excuse — and that this "other" in truth deserved the opposite from us.

In a word, "repent" uniquely belongs to the Christian vocabulary. For repentance goes beyond all we have said so far to include admission that the "other" whom we have offended *knows* our inner motives and our hidden selves. Excuse will not stand up. Evasion, if tried, becomes itself reason for further repentance.

"Repent" sets us before God, aware that from Him nothing is hidden, and that before Him no one is justified in himself.

At the beginning of the consciously Christian life we acknowledge before our Creator that we have done that which we ought not to have done, and have left undone that which we ought to have accomplished. And this is true, not only at the outset of our Christian journey; it is true on every day of that journey.

The command to "repent" always echoes in our ears.

Happily we can do so in the firm assurance that genuine repentance, that is "repent" coupled with re-determination to do better, attains forgiveness and liberation.

First

We place repentance first on the Christian's agenda because that is where the Bible places it.

Have you ever noticed that New Testament preaching seems always to have begun with "repent!"?

Consider these models of what preaching ought to be:

1) John the Baptist, forerunner of the Christ: "In those days came John the Baptist, preaching in the wilderness of Judea, 'Repent, for the kingdom of heaven is at hand'" (Matt. 3:2).

2) Jesus: "Now after John was arrested, Jesus came into Galilee, preaching the gospel of God, and saying, 'The time is fulfilled, and the

kingdom of God is at hand; repent, and believe the gospel'" (Mark 1:14-15).

3) The first disciples: "So they went out and preached that all men should repent" (Mark 6:12).

4) St. Peter, on Pentecost: "Now when they heard this they were cut to the heart, and said to Peter and the rest of the apostles, 'Brethren, what shall we do?' And Peter said to them, 'Repent, and be baptized every one of you...'" (Acts 2:37-38).

5) St. Paul, to the sceptics at Athens: "God...now commands all men everywhere to repent..." (Acts 18:30).

6) Paul's summary of his missionary message: "Wherefore, O King Agrippa, I was not disobedient to the heavenly vision, but declared first to those at Damascus, then at Jerusalem and throughout all the country of Judea, and also to the Gentiles, that they should repent and turn to God and perform deeds worthy of their repentance" (Acts 26:19-20).

7) And the Lord, risen and speaking from glory through the pen of St. John: "...so be zealous and repent" (Rev. 3:19).

The testimony is unanimous: repent!

Of Everyone!

There are no exceptions among the New Testament witnesses. All say: repent!

There are no exceptions, either, among those addressed. All, each and every one, get the same order: repent!

Be you old or young, rich or poor, male or female, weak or powerful, adult or child, white or black, red or yellow, ignorant or learned, churl or sophisticate — no distinction: repent!

Not: repent you sinners — as if some were perhaps excepted.

Not: repent you proud — as if some were already sufficiently humble.

Not: repent you lustful — as if some were already pure.

Not: repent once, and be done with it — as if thereafter nothing repentable would occur.

No, always the first word, always spoken to everybody: repent!

Meaning

What does "repent" mean, exactly?

Fundamentally, it means: get yourself a new Boss!

To understand that, we must recall what has already been said about God's gift to each of us of life, and of the time to live it.

To live, we've said, is to choose.

And by our choices, we've already noted, each of us slowly defines the self each is becoming.

We can now ask why this is so — why is a self built, day after day, out of the choices he or she makes?

The answer: because choice is "free". You forge a new step, into new territory, with every choice — and the territory you thus occupy becomes one bit added to your self. Yesterday's choices cannot be done over. Tomorrow's choices cannot yet be made. We choose *now*. That, indeed, is what "now" means: the moment of choice. And no other person can govern, now, what each choice shall be. That is our decision. Others may threaten, and we may yield to the threats. Or others may tempt, and we may yield to the temptation. But at the moment of choice neither threat nor temptation governs. We do! The threat may well be carried out, or the temptation taken away — but these are the risks of choosing, not its causes.

We are free in the act of choosing. But freedom is not anarchy.

Free choice is not unconditioned choice.

At work in our choices is the whole framework of our lives — what we aim at, what we live for, the hierarchy of our desires, the voice of conscience, awareness of others, and, for the believer, awareness of God. Our choices are strung like beads on the thread of purpose and commitment which binds life for each of us into some kind of unity.

The Bible thinks of this binding unity as citizenship — in one of two kingdoms. Or as allegiance, to one of two "masters".

We may not "see" life so perceptively. We may not trace the factors which influence our choices back to their sources. But God does!

God knows that the string on which the beads of choice are strung is woven in one of two kingdoms. Or, to change the figure, God knows whether the new territory the self acquired from each day of choosing is in His kingdom or the Devil's!

And God knows that our natural disposition is to govern our choices by lures originating in the kingdoms of this world, not in the kingdom of heaven.

By nature we serve the wrong ruler. We bow to the wrong boss. We are citizens of the wrong community.

Therefore: *repent*!

Repent the very first time you see, and acknowledge, this.

The Lord's Adversary, the Devil, garbs himself in countless attractive guises; he appears as any one of many idols: wealth, power, prestige, culture, learning, fun.... He may come to us as "an angel of light" (II Cor. 11:14). He may disguise himself as your very own *self!* Nothing is more common than choice made in obedience to self-interest, in pursuit of self-realization. He tempts us to think: what's wrong with my becoming all that I have it in me to be — even at another's expense?

Repent!

Get the right Boss! Take out citizenship in the right kingdom.

Repent, for that right kingdom is here, *now* — choose according to its laws!

Repent means that: "No one can serve two masters; for either he will hate the one and love the other, or he will be devoted to one and despise the other" (Matt. 6:24).

Repent!

Daily!

Requiring

Genuine repentance requires:

1) Accepting responsibility for who *you* are!

Repenting thwarts passing the buck.

It means that you cannot blame the self you now are — by choice! — onto anyone else.

What you are is all yours! And that's true of each of us. You wrote the story of your life to date. Your choices added every bit of selfhood you have acquired. (We are not forgetting that "in Christ" the self becomes "new" — see Chapter 3, below.)

Blaming someone else for what wrong choices make of us began 'way back in the Garden of Eden with our first parents; it was their second sin:

a) Adam blamed Eve for his eating of the forbidden fruit: "The woman whom thou gavest to be with me, she gave me fruit of the tree and I ate" — he blames God besides (Gen. 3:12).

b) Eve blamed the serpent: "The serpent beguiled me, and I ate" (Gen. 3:13).

c) The serpent said nothing. The Devil knew that God knew that the Devil sins on purpose.

God knows that we sin freely, too. That's why His first word to each of us is "repent"! Quit! Break the habit!

2) Repentance means, also: evasion is out!

What sometimes works in courts of law will not succeed in the court of heaven.

"Repent" means that there is no getting by with excuses like:

a) Not guilty — by reason of ignorance!

b) Not guilty — because victim of discrimination!

c) Not guilty — by reason of parents-too-strict!

d) Not guilty — by reason of parents-too-lenient!

e) Not guilty — because of circumstances!

f) Not guilty — thanks to childhood deprivations!

And so on.... All brushed aside!

Nothing stands up! That's what "repent" declares.

Repentance accepts the whole load: guilty! The buck stops with you.

For Obvious Reasons, Really...

1) No one can be forgiven for what he will not acknowledge as his own misdeed. We cannot repent for anyone else. No one can repent for you.

2) No one can be forgiven for what he will not repent of. Backsliding there may well be, perhaps often. But at the moment of repentance there is full confession *and* determination: no more!

3) Blame you will not shoulder cannot be lifted off your conscience — it simply festers there, eroding peace of mind, burdening confidence with despair, inducing weariness of mind and body. How lonely psychiatrist's offices would become if "repent" were more commonly practised — and advised!

4) Refusal to face reality leaves it unchanged and unchangeable. "Repent" is gateway to "believe" because it is the first step toward shifting the load of sin and guilt from our shoulders on to the Lord's. For that can only happen after we acknowledge our sin and guilt as solely our own!

Swineherd In A Tuxedo!

Jesus tells a well-known parable to illustrate what repentance is, and does. It is the parable of the Prodigal Son, swineherd in dinner clothes.

And he said, "There was a man who had two sons; and the youngest of them said to his father, 'Father, give me the share of property that falls to me.' And he divided his living between them. Not many days later, the younger son gathered all he had and took his journey into a far country, and there he squandered his property in loose living.

And when he had spent everything, a great famine arose in that country, and he began to be in want.

So he went and joined himself to one of the citizens of that country, who sent him into his fields to feed swine. And he would gladly have fed on the pods that swine ate; and no one gave him anything.

But when he came to himself he said, 'How many of my father's hired servants have bread enough and to spare, but I perish here with hunger. I will arise and go to my father, and I will say to Him, "Father, I have sinned against heaven and before you; I am no longer worthy to be called your son; treat me as one of your hired servants."'

And he arose and came to his father.

But while he was yet a distance, his father saw him and had compassion, and ran and embraced him and kissed him.

And the son said to him, 'Father, I have sinned against heaven and before you; I am no longer worthy to be called your son.'

But the father said to his servants, 'Bring quickly the best robe, and put it on him; and put a ring on his hand, and shoes on his feet; and bring the fatted calf and kill it, and let us eat and make merry; for this my son was dead, and is alive again; he was lost, and is found.'

And they began to make merry" (Luke 15:11-24).

*   *   *

The essence of repentance is revealed in this story.

The erring son comes "to himself".

What is that?

It is the recognition that he, and he alone, is responsible for being "in a far country". His was the choice to separate himself from his father, and to waste his money on lush living and fickle friends.

Repentance is more: it is the discovery that life away from the Father descends to the level of the animal. But the pods that sustain the animal do not feed the needs of man.

Still more: repentance is turning back with contrite confession upon the lips: "I have sinned...."

And more: repentance is the acknowledgement that in hurting each other we sin first against God: "I have sinned against heaven and before you...."

The point is important: we do evil against each other, but we can "sin" only against God. For it is God's law that we violate in every choice that does ill to our neighbor, or that omits to do our neighbor good.

And finally: repentance is admission that given our just deserts we have claim upon nothing: "treat me as one of your hired servants...."

What a different young man, this subdued swineherd, from the brash and jaunty chap who set out on the road to self-discovery away from his father.

When we see ourselves as having been just such a person, one just so sure that he "knows" what he needs and feels quite able to take care of himself, then we are prepared to "repent".

And if we foolishly suppose that one act of repenting is all that it takes to make us, thereafter, sinless and beyond repentance — ah, if we make that mistake, then we will need to repent more than ever before!

Happily, we need never fear that the confession of sin which accompanies repentance will in fact alienate the Father from us, or ourselves from Him.

On the contrary, the parable teaches that God comes running to meet us whenever we turn again home!

See how He waits, longing...looking...!

Repent!

Incentive

There is an incentive to repentance.

A "kingdom" waits upon our turning back toward home.

Indeed, our home is in that kingdom.

Why "repent"?

"For the kingdom of heaven is at hand!" So Jesus says.

That is not, obviously, the kingdom where we dwell, or we would not be told that this new kingdom has come to hand.

We are by nature, by inheritance, and by disposition citizens of another, rebel kingdom.

We are there in bondage to the tyranny of self, the tug of desire, the lure of "success," the idols of fashion and power. We are like Israel in Egypt, but bound to the whim of one worse than Pharaoh, God's Adversary, the Devil — out of whose kingdom there is but one gate, labeled "repent"!

And through that gate we step into the Father's kingdom, to find Him waiting, forgiving, loving, and ready to reinstate us among His children.

A kingdom exists where the laws of the king are known and obeyed.

The kingdom of heaven, then, exists wherever believing citizens hear and heed His Word, determined to do His will.

And for such service God gladly equips those who enter by way of repentance. All becomes new. What was left behind beyond the repentance-gate is not missed.

As we shall see.

Not Enough

The first step in learning to swim is to find water.

But finding the lake, or stream, or pool is not all there is to swimming. It is just a good beginning.

So it is with repentance.

Indispensable, but not enough. Just a good beginning!

Repentance ushers us out of Satan's kingdom, and introduces us to the kingdom of heaven. Repentance lifts off our shoulders the burdens of guilt and despair for which the world's idols offer no cure.

But to repent is like cleaning a cupboard. What then? Do we leave it empty? Or sharpening a saw — never to use it? Or clearing an acre of ground — but never planting it with anything?

"Repent" is immediately coupled with a consequence: believe!

Jesus tells a parable to stress the point that repentance is not enough:

When the unclean spirit has gone out of a man, he passes through waterless places seeking rest, but he finds none.

Then he says, "I will return to my house from which I came."

And when he comes he finds it empty, swept, and put in order.

Then he goes and brings with him seven other spirits more evil than himself, and they enter and dwell there; and the last state of that man becomes worse than the first (Luke

27

11:24-26).

To evict, by way of confession, what has led us into choosing disobedience is halfway house to assuming citizenship in the kingdom of heaven. We are, so to speak, at customs. But unless we hasten on, now, to exercise the opportunities of citizenship in God's kingdom, the vacuum left by exorcising one set of evil spirits but tempts others to take up residence — and our feet turn back again to the far country.

The first word is never the last.

Repent!

And....

For Reflection And Discussion

1. *What does "repent" mean, and how does it differ from regret and remorse?*
2. *Why does the Bible place so much emphasis on repentance?*
3. *How is repentance like choosing another "master"?*
4. *What does genuine repentance require?*
5. *Why does repentance require our accepting full responsibility for our own conduct?*
6. *What incentive did the Prodigal Son — and do we — have for repenting?*
7. *Is repentance by itself enough for the Christian life? Explain.*

Chapter 2.

BELIEVE

And without faith it is impossible to please God.
Hebrews 11:6

BELIEVE

TRUTH:
Belief, or faith, is focused on the gospel, conveyed to us by the Word of God. Gospel means "good news," the only truly good *news* available to us. Faith displays a passive and an active side, and is illumined by the miracles of Jesus and the story of the woman who washed His feet.
RESPONSE:
Develop faith through persistent attendance upon the Word preached, faithful study of the Scriptures, and determined effort to obey the will of God revealed therein — it is failure to be perfect here which calls for daily repentance.
DISTORTION:
To set faith against good works, as if the one excluded the other.

What Is Believing?

Believing is not an option.
It is a command!
This means that belief is more than a feeling. Why? Because feelings are not really under our control. We may rise above them, or may seek to stimulate them, but they come and go mostly on their own.
A belief has content. We not only believe, but we believe *something*. We can give an account, more or less, of what we believe. And we know already the belief that leads us to repentance. Indeed, we would not be

prepared to repent if we did not already believe the "good news" (gospel) that repentance would be rewarded by a cleansing of sin and guilt.

Yes, the content of Christian belief is the *gospel*: "Repent and believe the gospel!"

We will turn to what the gospel is in a moment, but first: what is believing?

Belief governs behavior.

We hang our actions upon pegs of belief.

We string our choices upon threads of what we believe.

People who believe that banks are unreliable hide their money somewhere else. We use streets and highways because we believe that most drivers obey traffic regulations most of the time. You accept a check on the belief that the signer has money in his account; the merchant takes your credit card on a similar belief.

A city is an intricate network of human relations all based on beliefs, or their absence. Take a few moments to think of how much of your own behavior derives from beliefs, perhaps from many you did not know until now that you entertained.

Beliefs form the channels through which our choices emerge into behavior. Belief governs what we do, and don't do. Just as the contours of a river are shaped by the banks along which it flows, so our choices are formed along the channels of what we believe. As the dough is squeezed into one shape or another through the cookie mold, so the way we live conforms to the beliefs we hold true.

Tell us what you believe and we can surmise how you will behave; or, tell us how you behave and we can infer what you *really* believe.

The stress, you notice, is on the word "really". The beliefs we proclaim with our lips may not be those which in fact govern our choices. We may fool others who do not know us well in this way, and may even fool ourselves. But the fact remains that beliefs do shape behavior, and therefore our conduct (that is, all we think, say, and do) reflects what we *really* believe. For this reason, the Bible not only tells us *that* we must believe, but also *what* we must believe!

Jesus stresses the intimate relation between belief and behavior in several ways.

He says, for example, "Are grapes gathered from thorns, or figs from thistles? So, every sound tree bears good fruit, but the bad trees bear evil fruit. A sound tree cannot bear evil fruit, nor can a bad tree bear good fruit...Thus you will know them by their fruits" (Matt. 7:16-

18, 20). Belief cannot be disguised. What the tree really *is* will be revealed by its fruit.

Again: "Not everyone who says to me, 'Lord, Lord,' shall enter the kingdom of heaven, but he who does the will of my Father who is in heaven" (Matt. 7:21).

"Believe the gospel," means, then, simply: govern your behavior by the content of the gospel. Make the gospel the channel through which your decisions take shape.

And now we can ask: what is the gospel?

"Good News!"

The term gospel means "good news"!

We know well enough what "news" is. We are bombarded with it every day. TV, radio, newspaper and news magazines all want to tell us the latest news — usually throwing in someone's interpretation of it besides, lest we come to an opinion of our own!

The term "news" is simply "new" in the plural. Our interest in the *new(s)* reflects our craving for a break in the routines of life; we want something novel, something exciting.

We have grown used to the difference, too, between good and bad news. Jokes are created on the distinction: "First, the good news...; now, the bad news...."

And so it is natural that we fit the meaning of "gospel" into an old category: well, well, some *good* news for a change! Like a report of declining interest rates or rising levels of employment!

But doing this robs "gospel" of its real import.

Why?

Because the daily news is not really "new"! It is old stuff in different dress. The actors change, and the sets are remade, but it's always the same human nature in the monotonies of sin: theft, murder, deceit, brutality, lust, greed, pride, the thirst for power. The world seems to move faster, and stories get around more quickly, but it's only another cast of characters repeating the same old drama. Solomon is right about it: "What has been is what will be, and what has been done is what will be done; and there is nothing new under the sun. It has been already, in the ages before us" (Eccles. 1:9-10). And he wrote that a long time ago.

Strange as it may at first seem, in our age of moon-landings and computers, there is nothing new *under* the sun. Man invents new forms for his toys, but uses them like the old ones. What is called "the news" ought better be called "the novel" — just another re-arrangement of pieces and players on the world's stage. The ingredients of the plot change not, nor the real selves of the players.

Not, that is, until the "gospel" comes to govern choices and to produce a really *new* fruit in God's vineyard.

Nothing new *under* the sun, did the wise king say? Yes, but God, who rules *over* the sun, has done a *new* thing! A thing so new that a word is coined to designate it: GOSPEL!

What could not emerge from within the world, out of the shattered resources of the world, is sent into the world by its Creator: gospel!

God promised such new(s) from the very beginning. Immediately after man's taking the Devil as his master, there in the Garden of Eden, God condemns the serpent whom the Devil used as temptor, saying: "I will put enmity between you and the woman, and between your seed and her seed; he shall bruise your head, and you shall bruise his heel" (Gen. 3:15). The promise of gospel, here in embryo!

The Devil who, through the serpent, had seduced mankind, does indeed bruise the human heel — the world overflows with the pain and agony of that bruising, and on Calvary even the Son of God suffered such bruising unto death itself. But the Devil is dethroned as "head" of a kingdom by the very Christ he bruises on the cross. And the Lord establishes a "new" kingdom in the world which the Devil thought to make all his own.

This is NEW! No rehearsal of old stuff in different garb. No repetition of ancient evils as new crimes. Not even the duplication of historical religions in improved form.

The Lord God has, in Jesus Christ, established a kingdom in the midst of earth. It is a kingdom not far from any of us: "...the kingdom of heaven is at hand!" Repent, and come in — via *believing*!

Believe the gospel means believe the Word! Believe the Scriptures!

Believe the gospel means let the Word govern your choices henceforth. Daily "repent" of all choices not governed by that Word, those of yesterday, of today and always.

We have said that belief has content, has substance. Yes, the content of the gospel is the Bible.

The function of this *Handbook* is to help us together hear, and confess, and do all that the Bible sets before us.

The Biblical term most commonly used for such belief is "faith". We will use belief and faith interchangeably hereafter.

Repent and believe the gospel!
This is the response God requires to His initiatives.

What Is Faith?

We have already pointed out that belief governs behavior. What we do demonstrates what we believe. What you do speaks so loudly, as the old saying goes, that I cannot hear what you say. The test of what we believe is what we do, and what we do becomes who we are. This we have so far observed.

Using, now, the Biblical term for believing, *faith*, let us ask further what precisely that means for the Christian life.

It is a question we can never fully answer. Only living by faith reveals faith's dimensions. We learn, from experience, the deepest meanings of faith through "faithfulness," that is faith-governed behavior.

But we can learn about faith from various Biblical points of view.

To begin with:

1) Faith relates to words, and words to persons. At least that is true of Christian faith. God comes to us in His Word.

And we, hearing and believing the Word, find ourselves in communion with God Himself.

Faith fastens on persons, via words. Christian faith unites us to God, via His Word.

2) God's Word speaks our language. As Moses said long ago, "For this commandment which I command you this day is not too hard for you, neither is it far off. It is not in heaven, that you should say, 'Who will go up for us to heaven, and bring it to us, that we may hear and do it?' Neither is it beyond the sea, that you should say, 'Who will go over the sea for us, and bring it to us, that we may hear it and do it?' But the word is very near you; it is in your mouth and in your hearts, so that you can do it" (Deut. 30:11-14).

The language to which we were born, and in which we were brought up, is the language of the Bible through which God speaks His Word to us. We have no excuse for not listening.

3) Language is, when you begin to think about it, mysterious. How do these black marks on the page you are now reading succeed in joining your mind to ours? How do the words of God's inspired Word join our selves with Him? Where did human language come from in the first place? (No one really knows the answer to that question — but

Christians believe that God Himself made us language-using creatures by endowing us with His image.)

In short, and first, the content of faith lives in words, a Word that establishes communion with the Speaker of the Word — God Himself.

Aspects of Faith: Passive

Faith displays two faces to our scrutiny.

Not that there can be two kinds of faith. Faith is always one!

But we can "see" it from two points of view.

First, there is *passive* faith, the faith that accepts.

The initiative in the Christian life is, remember, always God's.

Faith, as passive, simply receives what God does. Theologians compare passive faith to the open mouth of a jar into which God pours the content of belief, and the power of His Spirit.

Faith, as passive, is the recognition that we receive — not extract! — meaning from God's Word. *We* listen! Faith enables us to *hear.*

Faith, as passive, implies that we are searched by God's Word before we can search it. Passive faith means that God's Word masters us before we can think about mastering it.

Faith, as passive, feels the piercing power of the Word which faith admits to the inmost self: "For the word of God is living and active, sharper than any two-edged sword, piercing to the division of soul and spirit, of joints and marrow, and discerning the thoughts and intentions of the heart" (Heb. 4:12).

Passive faith lets the Word find us where and as we are. No facades. No put-on. No fronts. Faith just lets the Word in.

This faith hears the Bible as God speaking, here and now — not as a recording of what He once said, then and there. This faith makes God contemporary — or rather, God uses our passive faith to make Himself present to us, by means of words we hear and understand.

Faith, seen as passive, forms the bridge from the Devil's kingdom — which we have left via the doorway of repentance — into the kingdom of heaven. By faith, viewed as *active*, we become true citizens of the Kingdom of Heaven.

Aspects of Faith: Active

Remember: not *two* faiths, passive and active.

One faith: viewed under two perspectives.

Faith, active, is celebrated all across the Bible as the power that makes the believer triumphant over temptation and weakness, as the strength in which the believer stands, as the grip with which we clasp firm the promises, as the channel through which our acts of obedience emerge as the behavior which sculpts the self after the Image of God. This is the picture, for example, of active faith so vividly drawn by the eleventh chapter of Hebrews.

Faith, active, leads the believer into that obedience which the Bible calls "love". Jesus says: "If a man loves me, he will keep my word..." (John 14:23).

By faith, passive, which opens the self to divine intrusion, through faith, active, which shapes the self's choices in channels molded by the Word — this is the course of the Christian's day. This is how faith becomes the root of fruit-bearing in the Lord's kingdom.

His Word is sown, the Lord says in His parable of the sower, on human ears of various capacities; those who hear the Word in faith are, "...those who hold it fast in an honest and good heart, and bring forth fruit with patience" (Luke 8:15).

One faith, two functions in the Christian life.

More Light On Faith

Because our faith is at the center of our Christian lives, the Bible sheds light upon it in many ways.

For example, we can see the power of faith by studying the miracles of our Lord.

Jesus' miracles teach us many things. They show us His compassion upon those who suffer, and thus stimulate our own. Matthew reports that on a typical occasion, "As he went ashore he saw a great throng; and he had compassion on them, and healed their sick" (Matt. 14:14). Jesus combined speaking the Word of truth with doing the deeds of love — a pattern we must never neglect ourselves.

The Lord's miracles also demonstrate, to our great joy, His triumph over the power of the Devil. Thanks to Adam's fall, all mankind is born under Satan's grim tyranny. The Devil claims authority over "all the kingdoms of this world" when he tempts Christ in the wilderness (Luke 4:6). But Jesus' miracles demonstrate that the ultimate power of this demonic rule is shattered. "When a strong man," Jesus says, "fully armed, guards his own palace, his goods are in peace; but when one stronger than he assails him and overcomes him, he takes away his armor in which he trusted, and divides his spoil" (Luke 11:21-22). The Christ means Himself! He comes to invade the Devil's ill-gotten realm. He comes to liberate from Satan's kingdom everyone who turns to Him in faith. And this is evidenced, we repeat, in Jesus' miracles, as He Himself points out.

Jesus says so when he heals a woman "who was bent over and could not fully straighten herself." The healing was done on a Sabbath day, and there were those who complained that Jesus was "working" — something forbidden on the holy day. The Lord replies, "And ought not this woman, a daughter of Abraham whom Satan bound for eighteen years, be loosed from this bond on the sabbath day?" (Luke 13:11, 16). Yes, the miracles show that "one stronger" than the Devil has entered history (also our own history!) and "divides his spoil" taken in the Garden of Eden. Rejoice, believer; rejoice!

But let us focus, now, upon the miracles to illumine the power of faith. For faith and miracles are correlative. Jesus pauses, now and then, to point this out, saying to those whom He heals, "Your faith has healed...or saved...you" (Matt. 9:22, Mark 5:34, Luke 8:48, etc.). That is why unbelief blocks the way to miracles. St. Matthew says this in explaining why Jesus did not perform many miracles in His own home town of Nazareth: "And he did not do many mighty works there, because of their unbelief" (Matt. 13:58).

The birth and the power of faith, then, is illustrated by the miracles of our Lord. Consider these:

1) Faith brings life out of death:

Lazarus, a friend of Jesus, was dead. He had been buried, as the custom was, in a tomb hewn out of rock and sealed with a stone rolled before the entry way. Jesus comes to the tomb. He cries "with a loud voice, 'Lazarus, come forth!'" And what happens? "The dead came out, his hands and feet wrapped with a cloth. Jesus said to them, 'Unbind him, and let him go'" (we are quoting John 11:43-44 — be sure to read the whole story).

Lazarus was dead. Lazarus was made alive by a Word called to him by his Lord.

But Lazarus returned, in due season, to the grave. Did his death, then, cancel out the miracle that had been performed upon him?

Not at all!

The story is written for us! Who knows if Lazarus really wanted to return from "the bosom of Abraham" as heaven is called (Luke 16:23)? Of course, those who mourned him rejoiced, as did others to whom

Jesus returned their dead, but all died again. The miracle is recounted far more for its symbolic than for its natural value.

What symbolic value?

This, that the raising of the physically dead points to our being enlivened out of spiritual death.

By inheritance from Adam, all of us are born in the alienation from God called spiritual "death" by the Scriptures. So were you born; so were we.

And how was Lazarus brought out of death and into life?

Through the power of a Word, the call of Jesus: "Lazarus...!"

God's Word does not go out aimlessly into the world. The Bible at your elbow does not speak at random to mankind. So long as the Word seems to us to speak general truths, spiritual principles, and the like, just so long we do not even hear it as the living Word of the living God! Via the Scriptures, God is speaking to you, prefacing what He says with your name: "Lazarus...," you who are spiritually *dead*, "come forth!"

Lazarus comes. Bringing with him all the bindings, all the bondages, that still tie him to the realm of death. And the Lord tells others to loose him (that is the work of the Church).

So we!

The enlivening Word is prefaced with a name — yours! ours! every believer's! Read your Bible, hear it preached, as addressed just to you: "Lazarus...!"

"Faith comes," St. Paul teaches us, "by hearing the word..." (Rom. 10:17).

The miracle of the raising of Lazarus strikingly portrays the miracle of implanted faith. The faith each believer has came out of God's call when we were as yet spiritually dead. So we learn from Lazarus, and the others Jesus re-called to life — for our instruction.

The faith we are now called upon to exercise in the light of other miracles is God's initial gift. So the Lazarus account teaches us.

Do we want to know where such miracle is to be experienced?

Where the Word is, in the holy book where it is on deposit. Where that Word is preached, for St. Paul adds this: "Faith comes by hearing the word, and what is heard comes by the preaching of Christ" (Rom. 10:17).

Direct your steps toward the Church! Move your hand toward your Bible!

The miracle of a living faith is illumined by the miracle of Lazarus' return from the tomb. That miracle was done once and for all, but it serves to teach us that the miracle of spiritual rebirth is ever done by the same Word spoken by the same Lord through the Scriptures inspired for that purpose.

There is more to be learned about faith from Jesus' miracles, like this:

2) Faith makes the spiritually blind see:

"The people who walked in darkness have seen a great light;" the prophet tells us, "those who dwelt in a land of deep darkness, on them has light shined" (Is. 9:2, quoted in Luke 1:79).

Once again, a vivid picture of life in the Devil's dominions. The dim light shed by experience and the best of human wisdom only etches out the shadows hovering over our future. Guided solely by their own reason, men stumble as in the dark. The way of tomorrow is obscure, and edged with anxiety.

But Jesus again and again performs the miracle of giving sight to the blind.

Why?

Out of compassion, of course, but far more than that, to teach unmistakably that His Word illumines. In its light we walk by faith. There is striking illumination resident in the Bible — *for all who believe!*

Faith receives power to *see*. So the Lord's healing of the blind teaches us.

And what can the believer, healed of spiritual blindness through faith, be learning ever better to "see"?

We learn more and more to "see" the witness of creation to its Creator, as the Psalmist teaches us to see it: "The heavens declare the glory of God, the firmament shows his handiwork" (Ps. 19:1). By faith the believer sees what unbelievers are blind to, as St. Paul says: "For what can be known about God is plain to them, because God has shown it to them. Ever since the creation of the world his invisible nature, namely, his eternal power and deity, has been clearly perceived in the things that have been made" (Rom. 1:19-20). But unbelief is as wilfully blind as belief must be willingly seeing. Of the unbeliever, Paul says, "although they knew God they did not honor him as God nor give thanks to him, but they became futile in their thinking and their senseless minds were darkened. Claiming to be wise, they became fools..." (Rom. 1:21-22). The foolish live their lives in the light of their own assumed wisdom; the believer lives in the light of the Word of

God. So the miracles of healing the blind teach us.

Believers learn, also, by faith, more and more to "see" Christ waiting their service in those who are in need of what the believer can give — concern, companionship, help of many kinds, money and goods....

By faith we can say with the one born blind whom Jesus healed, "...one thing I know, that though I was blind, now I see" (John 9:25).

Yes, believers know that!

And more:

3) Faith makes the spiritually deaf to hear:

Sin deafens. Unbelief hardens the inner ear to the Word of the Lord, to the cries of the needy, to the appeals for justice raised to the Lord by victims of oppression.

Jesus often stresses "hearing". One of His phrases was, "He who has ears to hear, let him hear" (Matt. 11:15; 13:9, 43; Mark 4:9; Luke 8:8...).

The Lord knows well enough that those standing by were "listening" to Him. Otherwise He would not admonish them to "hear" also. He means, of course, that listeners become hearers only when they attend upon the Word with the determination to obey. He is saying, to them and to us, "Faith listens with the intent of hearing, that is of obeying. Exercise, therefore, your faith — for it is faith that gives hearing where deafness reigned before."

Can we hear before He gives us faith?

No, but we need not resolve the mystery of divine predestination before we resolve to listen in faith.

Let us simply know that the Lord opens the ear by faith. So the healing of the deaf instructs us. Let us live, then, with a solemn determination to listen and obey — and we will find ourselves "hearing" after the pattern set for us by the miracles.

4) Curing the sick, the lame, the crippled:

Time and again, Jesus miraculously cures sick and wounded bodies. In mercy, yes, but to teach us thus, too, the power of faith.

Believers know themselves to be spiritually out of health, as laggard to do the Lord's will as though we were physically handicapped, as slow to help those in need as if feet and legs were crippled or hands were gnarled.

The miracles of bodily healing teach us that faith can cure spiritual ailments, and so enables us to leap to do the Lord's will where by faith we now "see" human need and "hear" the cry of distress or the call of duty.

5) Faith receives a new heart:

The Lord frequently, especially in the Old Testament, speaks in the Scriptures of the birth of faith as the gift of a "new heart".

Through Ezekiel God says to us: "A new heart I will give you, and a new spirit I will put within you; and I will take out of your flesh the heart of stone and give you a heart of flesh" (Ezek. 36:26).

Notice the contrast made by the prophet: God will give believers a "heart of flesh" to replace the natural human "heart of stone". Often the Bible uses the term "flesh" to indicate the old self which the believer is trying to live down. But here a vivid contrast is drawn between the old, dead self and the new, believing self — the contrast as between a heart of rock and a heart of warm, beating flesh.

The cause, and the consequence, of unbelief is a hard heart. How well we know it. How commonly we speak of the calloused, the unmerciful, the uncaring, the ruthless, the unjust as reflecting a heart impervious to need or compassion. Those who are blind to the witness of God's creation, blind to human need, deaf to cries for justice are hard at the very center and core of their being: how aptly called having "a heart of stone"!

And God promises to replace stone with flesh, unbelief with belief, spiritual death with spiritual life, spiritual blindness with spiritual sight, spiritual deafness with spiritual hearing, the spiritual weakness with spiritual strength...to those who come in faith!

Come!

Believe the gospel!

And More Light Still

The power of faith is illustrated, too, in a story which ends with the glowing assurance: "Your faith has saved you; go in peace."

Here it is:

"One of the Pharisees asked him to eat with him, and he went into the Pharisee's house, and sat at table. And behold, a woman of the city, who was a sinner, when she learned that he was sitting at table in the Pharisee's house, brought an alabaster flask of ointment, and standing behind him at his feet, weeping, she began to wet his feet with her tears, and wiped them with the hair of her head, and kissed his feet, and anointed them with the ointment. Now when the Pharisee who had invited him saw it, he said to himself, 'If this man were a prophet, he would have known who and what sort of woman this is who is touching him, for she is a sinner.'

"And Jesus answering said to him, 'Simon, I have something to say to you.' And he answered, 'What is it, Teacher?'

"'A certain creditor had two debtors; one owed five hundred denarii, and the other fifty. When they could not pay, he forgave them both. Now which of them will love him more?'

"Simon answered, 'The one, I suppose, to whom he forgave more.' And he said to him, 'You have judged rightly.'

"Then turning toward the woman he said to Simon, 'Do you see this woman? I entered your house, you gave me no water for my feet, but she has wet my feet with her tears and wiped them with her hair. You gave me no kiss, but from the time I came in she has not ceased to kiss my feet. You did not anoint my head with oil, but she has anointed my feet with ointment. Therefore I tell you, her sins, which are many, are forgiven, for she loved much; but he who is forgiven little, loves little.'

"And he said to her, 'Your sins are forgiven.'

"Then those who were at table with him began to say among themselves, 'Who is this, who even forgives sins?'

"And he said to the woman, 'Your faith has saved you; go in peace.'" (Luke 7:36-50)

Let us pause a moment, and ask how this simple, gripping account leads to the climatic assurance: "saved" by "faith".

What do you "see"?

There are such things as these:

1) Faith enables the believer to "see":

All who were present at Simon's feast behold their guest. Jesus was physically visible to them. But all they "saw," apparently, was a teacher. Of how many who met the Master was this true. Each "saw" only what he had the capacity to see: a teacher, a miracle-worker, an imposter who claimed to be the Son of God, just another man, a nobody.... But the woman "saw" (by faith) the Son of God.

The house was Simon's; the woman knew that. But she goes at once to Him she "sees" as owning all things by right of creation and providence, ignoring Simon just as Simon tried to ignore her.

2) Faith enables the believer to "hear":

All those present at the feast listened to the same words, "Your sins are forgiven."

But Simon and his guests heard only blasphemy; the woman heard the voice of God.

Spiritually deaf Simon wonders, "Who is this fellow! What kind of fanatic is this?"

The believing woman knows whose words she is hearing; does Jesus not say that His sheep know His voice (John 10:4)?

3) Faith is key to knowledge:

Simon smugly marvels at the ignorance he imputes to the teacher he has invited to dinner: "If this man were a prophet, he would have known who and what sort of woman this is who is touching him, for she is a sinner."

But Simon was soon to discover that Jesus knew both him and the woman — as, indeed, he knows you and us and everyone. Did Simon ever discover that, by faith, the woman "knew" the Guest far better than Simon and his scowling friends?

Faith *knows* Him with Whom we have to do.

4) Faith is key to ac-knowledge:

Knowing that she kneels before God, the woman can only ac-knowledge her own unworthiness to receive anything from Him. Her tears bespeak her abject confession. Does Simon call her a "sinner," indeed a notorious "sinner"? The Master knew, and to her who ac-knowledged her sinfulness the Master speaks the Word of salvation.

Simon, lacking the eye and heart of faith, can behold the woman as "sinner," but sees nothing sinful about himself. Thus, as we have already noticed about repentance, Simon's unacknowledged sin is not forgiven; how could it be?

The pattern is familiar; we see the sins of others, while oblivious to our own. So common is this fault that Jesus specifically warns against it: "Why do you see the speck that is in your brother's eye, but do not notice the log that is in your own?" (Matt. 7:3).

The woman does not dispute Simon's description of her. She does not bother. Only one opinion matters; that is the opinion of Jesus. She knows that she can trust Him with full understanding of her wretchedness and of her unspoken confession.

And He forgives her! And us!

Faith gives the strength to accept full responsibility for what we do and what we are making of ourselves.

Faith finds divine forgiveness waiting at every ac-knowledgment of sin and guilt.

5) Faith enters upon forgiveness:

The woman was listening for only one word.

What if Simon drew back? What if the other guests wrote disgust all over their features? What if their eyes spoke hatred? Their lips twisted in malice?

Jesus' lips formed the only word that mattered to her — and to us: "Your sins are forgiven."

Whatever is, by faith, confessed is through faith forgiven!

Whatever is, by blindness unac-knowledged, is unforgiven!

The woman is relieved of her intolerable guilt.

Poor Simon, (yes, *poor* Simon!) is left in the slavery of his pride.

6) Faith liberates:

The woman heard ever more: "go in peace"!

Only the believer knows the joy that floods in upon the wings of these blessed words. Now she knows, as all believers know, "the peace of God, which passes all understanding" (Phil. 4:7).

Two kingdoms met briefly that evening in Simon's house. One, the kingdom of this world; the other the Kingdom of Heaven, region of peace known only to the sheep who are, by faith, its citizens.

"Not as the world gives," Jesus says to us, "do I give you." Not as Simon would have given, did the Lord give to the repentant believer. No, Jesus gives what the world cannot give, but needs desperately to receive: "Peace I leave with you; my peace I give to you." And, *therefore*, "Let not your hearts be troubled, neither let them be afraid" (John 14:27).

The woman is now far away, the dusk of that evening, and of history, shrouding her singing steps, the last faint glow of the sunset touching the clouds above with the color that surges through her soul. She *knows* what only faith can know: "It is God who justifies; who is to condemn?" (Rom. 8:33). The past is dead. The future throbs with promise.

Think a moment of the light in which such a believer walks. Think, too, on the darkness which englooms the house where Simon dwells.

Think...and choose: faith!

Faith Is Not Enough!

But....

Faith is *not* enough?!

Who dares say that?

St. Paul does!

"...and if I have all faith, so as to remove mountains," Paul writes in his First Letter to Corinth, "but have not love, I am nothing" (I Cor. 13:2). Impossible to be less! Nothing is no-thing!

Faith alone is *not* enough!

St. James says it, too: "What does it profit, my brethren, if a man says he has faith but has not works? Can his faith save him? If a brother or sister is ill-clad and in lack of daily food, and one of you says to them, 'Go in peace, be warmed and filled,' without giving them the things needed for the body, what does it profit? So faith by itself, if it has no works, is dead" (James 2:14-17). Just to drive the point home, James repeats it: "For as the body apart from the spirit is dead, so faith apart from works is dead" (James 2:26). Make no mistake. The issue is crucial. It is so crucial that it was because of these two sentences in this epistle that Martin Luther foolishly wished to ban James from the Bible!

We must consider carefully, therefore, the relation between faith and works.

To begin with, note that we only echo the Scriptures when we point to the limitation which is set upon the sufficiency of faith.

To say, however, that faith is not enough is far from saying that faith is unnecessary.

Like repentance, faith is an essential part of the Christian life. But it is *one* of the essentials, not the only essential.

Paul is teaching us that faith must be crowned, completed, by love. And St. James is also affirming that, and suggesting what love is: the doing of good to others!

Paul combines the coordinate roles of faith and works in the Christian life by writing this to us by way of the believers at Ephesus: "For by grace you have been saved through faith; and this is not your own doing, lest any man should boast. For we are his workmanship, created in Christ Jesus for good works, which God prepared beforehand, that we should walk in them" (Eph. 2:10).

What God requires, Paul writes to the Galatians, is simply, "faith working through love" (Gal. 5:6).

It is obvious, by the way, that Luther was mistaken in supposing that James contradicted Paul. Both agree: faith alone is not enough — a living faith flowers in works, that is, in choices governed by love.

The Christian life is the life of love, sustained by faith.

Because believers so frequently get bogged down in dispute over whether salvation is by faith or by works, let us briefly clarify the issues involved.

By Faith Or By Works?

How often Christians have waged this dispute: is salvation by faith or by works?

Let us at once accent the truth that no one is saved by works. The Bible stressed that, and we repeat: "For by grace you have been saved through faith; and this is not your own doing, it is the gift of God — not because of works, lest any man should boast" (Eph. 2:8-9).

So there it is. We are saved by grace — gift — through faith.

To set the relation of faith to works in the light of Scripture, we must move through several steps.

Consider these:

1) *Salvation:*

What is meant by the Biblical term "salvation"?

Salvation means being rescued. "Being saved" *means* being rescued. We use the term "saved" in that way often: *saved* from drowning, *saved* from fire, etc.

Christ came to "save" His sheep. This means He came to *rescue* us from whatever enslaves us — the world, the flesh, or the Devil. To be saved is to be set free.

But freedom is not only *from* some tyranny; it is also *for* another kind of service. And only as we do what we are saved *for* can we demonstrate our being saved *from*. Saved has two sides: from and for.

And what are we saved for?

St. Paul tells us as he continues the passage we have just quoted to the Ephesians — where he says we are saved by grace and not by works — as follows: "For we are his workmanship, created in Christ Jesus *for* good works, which God prepared beforehand, that we should walk in them" (Eph. 2:10).

Saved *from*, by grace through faith, yes!

And saved *for*, by grace and through faith, *good works*!

We are not ever to think of "being saved" only as receiving a heavenly pass which will admit us to the Lord's right hand. No, "being saved" is having our feet planted on the narrow road which leads to the Lord's right hand, by way of doing good.

Being saved is not getting a heavenly guarantee; it is getting an earthly assignment: to do good works!

2) *Good Works:*

What are good works?

Notice, first, that the Bible is everywhere obsessed with our doing them. We take only the teaching given us through St. Paul: "abounding in every good work" (II Cor. 9:8); "fruitful in every good work" (Eph. 2:10); "adorned with good works" (Col. 1:10); "diligently following every good work" (I Tim. 2:10); "being rich in good works" (I Tim. 6:18) — admonitions which might be multiplied from across the Scriptures.

Yes, this is why we are saved: for good works.

And what are good works?

They are not for us to define. It is not we who determine which of our works are good. The Lord says, "If a man loves me, he will keep *my* word..." (John 14:23). Again, "If you keep *my* commandments, you will abide in my love..." (John 14:10).

The good works we are saved to do are those which "God prepared beforehand...." That is, acts which God prescribes from long before we are born, long before (by grace through faith) we are saved.

In short, God defines the works He requires us to do through His Word. God's Word reveals that God's will comes to expression in God's Law, as taught and explained through the Scriptures: "Not every one who says to me, 'Lord, Lord,'" Jesus says, "shall enter the kingdom of heaven, but he who does the will of my Father who is in heaven" (Matt. 7:21).

We, like ancient Israel, have been rescued by God. And we, like Israel, are told: "I am the Lord your God, who brought you out of the land of Egypt, out of the house of bondage..." (Ex. 20:2). God saves. God rescues. No doubt of that. He brought us, too, out of our bondage to world, flesh, Devil.

And why?

So that, being liberated, Israel could do God's will. And so we!

And what is God's will?

It follows immediately upon the prologue we have just quoted: out of bondage, into liberty, to obey the Ten Commandments!

Is this only Old Testament teaching? An era ended by the advent of the New Testament?

No, the Old Testament teaching is repeated by the New. In His Great Commission Jesus first requires that the gospel be preached. And what is the gospel? It is, we have seen, the "good news" that we are liberated, by grace and through faith, just as Israel was, from bondage. And what then? The Lord then requires that those who have been "saved" shall be taught to do "all that I have commanded you" (Matt. 28:20).

In the Old Testament, and in the New: saved to do God's will, as revealed in His commandments. These are *good* works.

Never suppose that Jesus came to set aside the Law given first to Israel as the Ten Commandments: "Think not that I have come to abolish the law and the prophets; I have come not to abolish them but to fulfil them. For truly, I say to you, till heaven and earth pass away, not an iota, not a dot, will pass from the law until all is accomplished" (Matt. 5:17-18). And St. Paul adds, "So the law is holy, and the commandment is holy and just and good" (Rom. 7:12). "Do we then overthrow the law by faith?" he asks, and answers, "By no means! On the contrary, we uphold the law" (Rom. 3:31).

In response to the question, "Teacher, what good deed must I do to have eternal life?" the Lord answers, "If you would enter life, keep the commandments." And when then asked, "Which?" Jesus refers to the Ten Commandments (Matt. 19:16-19).

When asked by a lawyer the same question: "Teacher, what shall I do to inherit eternal life?" Jesus replies in the same manner: "What is written in the law? How do you read?" And the lawyer repeats the summary of the Ten Commandments derived from the Old Testament: "You shall love the Lord your God with all your heart, and with all your soul, and with all your strength, and with all your mind; and your neighbor as yourself" (Deut. 6:5; Lev. 19:18). To which the Lord replies: "You have answered right; do this, and you will live" (Luke 10:25-28).

Eternal life not only hinges upon our obedience to the divine Law, which is the doing of good works, but sharing in eternal life here and now is walking the road which consists of choosing to do good works.

To put it another way: being "saved" *is* doing the Lord's will, day by day. And such being "saved" includes His protection against the ups-and-downs of life. Jesus says, "Every one then who hears these words of mine and does them will be like a wise man who built his house upon the rock; and the rain fell, and the floods came, and the winds blew and beat upon that house, but it did not fall, because it had been founded on the rock" (Matt. 7:24-25). Eternity begins now. Those who do good works build on the Rock which withstands all the assaults of time.

We are saved to obey the Lord's commandments.

Saved, that is, not *by* works of obedience but *for* them!

3) *Judgment:*

To make doubly clear that saving faith inevitably leads to good works, the Bible leaves no doubt that our faith will be judged according to what we have done: "And I saw the dead, great and small," St. John writes, "standing before the throne, and books were opened... And the dead were judged by what was written in the books, by what they had done" (Rev. 20:12-13). And St. Paul, the great apostle of salvation by faith, writes: "For we shall stand before the judgment seat of God...So each of us shall give account of himself to God" (Rom. 14:10, 12). As earlier in his letter to the Romans he had said, "For God will render to every man according to his works: to those who by patience in well-doing seek for glory and honor and immortality, he will give eternal life; but for those who are factious and do not obey the truth, but obey wickedness, there will be wrath and fury" (Rom. 2:6-8).

Notice that the inspired Apostle does not say that "well-doing" *earns* eternal life. No, God "will give" eternal life to those who give themselves to doing His will.

4) *Faith and Works:*

And now we can draw the strands together.

Indeed, St. James does it for us: "But be doers of the word, and not hearers only...he who looks into the perfect law, the law of liberty, and perseveres, being no hearer that forgets but a doer that acts, he shall be blessed in his doing" (James 1:22, 25). Liberated by grace, through faith, we can see God's Law as guide to our exercise of freedom. And in obedience to that Law we are truly free.

But, as we have noted above, the Apostle goes on, "What does it profit, my brethren, if a man says he has faith but has not works? Can his faith save him? If a brother or sister is ill-clad and in lack of daily food, and one of you says to them, 'Go in peace, be warmed and filled,' without giving them the things needed for the body, what does it profit? So faith by itself, if it has no works, is dead" (James 2:14-17).

Faith is not opposed to works. Faith comes alive through them.

The Lord's judgment is passed upon our works, but is executed upon ourselves. Why? Because our works tell who we are. For it is we who believe, or disbelieve. The works only reflect the faith we live by.

Important, then, that this *Handbook* stresses grace: all is, indeed, by grace. God saves; not we.

Important, then, that at another time we stress faith: only through faith do we partake of God's salvation.

Important, then, that at the same time stress be laid on good works, done according to God's Law: striving to keep the Law testifies to the fact of grace and presence of faith within us.

What always matters is, in St. Paul's words, "faith working through love" (Gal. 5:6) — and love is, as we have already heard the Lord say, keeping His commandments.

Grace, faith, and works together constitute the Christian life. They can no more be separated than can the self be divided.

Do not be misled, therefore, by efforts to play grace off against obedience, or faith off against good works. Their union is inseparable.

For Reflection And Discussion

1. *What we believe shows up in many ways in daily life: illustrate.*
2. *What is implied by: "believe the Gospel"?*
3. *How does "Gospel" differ from other "news"?*
4. *When was the Gospel first heard? Explain.*
5. *How has the Gospel affected human history?*
6. *What is the content of the Gospel for us?*
7. *How does God communicate with us?*
8. *Explain the passive aspect of faith.*
9. *Explain the active aspect of faith.*
10. *What is taught us by Christ's combining Word and deed in His own ministry?*
11. *How do Christ's miracles illustrate the power of faith?*
12. *How can "listeners" to the Gospel become "hearers" of the Gospel?*
13. *What is the relationship between repentance and faith?*
14. *What does the Bible mean by "love"?*
15. *Explain why St. James calls faith without works "dead," and St. Paul speaks of the believer who has faith without love as "nothing".*
16. *Is St. James' emphasis on faith-with-works contrary to the teaching of the other Apostles? Explain.*
17. *Is it accurate to say that our good works "earn" eternal life?*
18. *How does God use the Law in our life as believers?*

Chapter 3.

FOLLOW

If any man would come after me, let him deny himself and take up his cross and follow me.   *Matthew 16:24*

FOLLOW

TRUTH:
The believer's calling to follow Christ requires self-denial and cross-bearing — obligations adapted by the Lord, through His Law, to the maturing of each believer. The believer's cross is formed by the Ten Commandments, in their negative and positive applications.
RESPONSE:
Study to learn, and practice to do the will of God as taught in His Word and disciplined in His Church — what life is all about!
DISTORTION:
To view the Law as outmoded or superseded by grace, or to separate following Christ from cross-bearing and self-denial.

What Kind?

On what kind of life do we enter if we choose the Christian life?

You can hear a variety of answers to that question.

Some have it that the believer's life is a triumphant life, a successful life, a joyous life, a cloudless life lived in the radiance of God's love.

And so it is!

But, and we stress that BUT, these characteristics we have mentioned — triumphant, successful, joyous, radiant — must be defined by the Bible, not by ourselves.

One of the things we learn as we walk the Christian way is to let the

Word of God define our words. We may think, for example, that we know from everyday experience what "love" means. Perhaps we do know what is commonly called "love". Jesus, however, defines "love" this way: "He who has my commandments and keeps them, he it is who loves me..." (John 14:21).

We think we know what "success" is, of course; but have we heard the Bible's definition? Jesus says, "You know that those who are supposed to rule over the Gentiles lord it over them, and their great men exercise authority over them. But it shall not be so among you; but whoever would be great among you must be your servant, and whoever would be first among you must be slave of all" (Mark 10:42-44).

Don't forget that Christianity is another language. Our worldly kingdoms are forever Babel — city of the confusion of tongues. The kingdom of heaven introduces another Word — the speech of God, what John Bunyan, in his *Pilgrim's Progress* called "the language of Canaan".

So, yes, Christianity is by all means a guide to joyously *triumphant* and *successful* living — but we must let the Bible define these terms!

And the Bible sets the course of the Christian life with the quotation from Jesus Himself which heads this chapter: "If any man would come after me, let him deny himself and take up his cross and follow me!" This is the way to Christian "success"! Exactly as the Lord defines "success" — becoming a servant of others! Not at all, probably, what we are accustomed to think of as successful?

The Lord adds this requirement for admission to the kingdom of His followers: "For whoever would save his life will lose it; and whoever loses his life for my sake, he will save it" (Luke 9:23-24).

Here our Lord deliberately sets following Him as against the main stream of modern life. As never before in history, "with it" people think themselves entitled to self-realization on their own terms. The watchword of modernity is: "I have a perfect right to become all that it is in me to be!" Make room for countless unguided human missiles zooming by on the thrilling quest of self-discovery!

Against all such forms of self-indulgence Jesus sets His demand for self-*denial*!

Against the ease of doing one's own thing, Jesus sets the hard road of doing His thing! Hear Him: "Enter by the narrow gate; for the gate is wide and the way is easy that leads to destruction, and those who enter by it are many. For the gate is narrow and the way is hard, that leads to life, and those who find it are few" (Matt. 7:13-14).

Following Jesus against the prevailing winds of fad and fashion is never easy, and sometimes risky.

St. Paul is thinking of that when he writes to his spiritual son Timothy, "Indeed all who desire to live a godly life in Christ Jesus will be persecuted" (II Tim. 3:12). It is "through many tribulations," Paul and Barnabas tell the believers in Antioch, "that we must enter the kingdom of God" (Acts 14:22). They are but echoing our Lord: "In the world you have tribulation..." (John 16:33).

In short, as the world counts triumph and success, Christianity sets but a "hard road" before the believer's feet. No detours. No discharge papers until the bitter end.

Is Christ's way, then, a dismal journey? Is the kingdom of heaven a gloomy community?

Not at all!

"In the world you have tribulation," we have quoted Jesus as warning us, true enough. He immediately adds, however, "but be of good cheer, I have overcome the world" (John 16:33).

Christianity does not avoid stress, evade self-denial, or counterfeit worldly success. Christianity triumphs through what by worldly standards is the loss of all that makes life secure, interesting and worthwhile: "whoever loses his life for my sake, he will save it!"

Why Self-denial?

What does God have against self-indulgence, against doing our own thing? Is He some kind of spoil-sport?

Quite the opposite, of course.

The eternal companionship with the Father which every Christian seeks will be joy everlasting, exceeding everything we can even imagine.

What concerns God is that we shall live so as to receive the gift of eternity with Him. And the route to that beatitude is, He says, through self-denial. That is the way through the narrow gate, and over the hard road, to the right hand of the King's judgment throne.

Reflect for a moment on the first step of the Christian life: repentance!

Why repentance?

Because, like the Prodigal Son, we must confess to having "sinned against heaven and before thee," the Father.

Why? Why sin, and sinning?

53

Because we come into the world, at birth, with an inherited disposition to substitute our ways for God's way. We are prone to serve ourselves rather than God and neighbor. By nature we rebel against His commandments and follow after the lure of the Devil's temptations. Sin may be gross and obvious; or sin may be subtle and refined — done by the "worst" or by the "best" people. No matter. Wherever *our* will is lord rather than God's will, there sin occurs! Adam and Eve said, in effect, "Not your will, O Lord, but ours!" That has been sin's pattern ever since.

That's the rule of the road on the broad way which leads to destruction: not God's law, but my own! The broad way is, since Adam's decision to take it, the easy way because it is the natural way. Children find it by themselves. Adults take it with the crowd. We can walk it with our eyes closed and our ears stopped. And it leads inevitably to the left side of God's judgment seat — where are gathered those destined for destruction.

The self that naturally takes the broad way is the self we must learn to deny. Obviously! It is the self that prefers death to life, disobedience to obedience. Unless we deny that self, we are lost! The Lord does not demand self-denial to deprive us of fun; He demands it to spare us eternity in hell!

The self called to repentance by Jesus and His disciples, and by all faithful preachers since, must be "converted" into another self through denial of all that this "old" self desires. Only thus is repentance genuine.

The self disposed to rebellion must be denied so that the self disposed to good citizenship in the kingdom of heaven can mature.

The self blind, deaf, crippled and mortally wounded by an inherited taint aggravated by indulgence in self-will must be transmuted into the self eager to see the witness of God in creation, eager to hear the Word of God through the Bible, eager to do the will of God by living in His kingdom.

The self we must deny stands in the way of the self we must become.

That is why Jesus requires self-denial.

Why Should I?

But why should I — each of us — be the one called upon to deny myself?

Because you are the only one who can!

Just as you are the only one who can endure your toothache, or enjoy your own happiness.

Christ could, and did, die for you.

But only you can believe that for yourself.

Christ could, and does, call you to self-denial.

But only you can do that!

No one can believe for anyone else. No one can sin for anyone else. No one can repent for anyone else. No one can deny himself or herself for anyone else.

In all the important issues of life we stand or fall on our own.

In all the choices of life each is on his own.

"For every one," writes Paul, "shall bear his own burden" (Gal. 6:5).

Some religions, and some philosophies, teach that the individual must seek to forfeit selfhood by disappearing into total forgetfulness. Christianity stands at the opposite pole. Each of us counts, and counts so much that the whole world means less than any one of us: "For what does it profit a man to gain the whole world and forfeit his life?" Jesus asks (Mark 8:36).

"For we brought nothing into this world," says Paul, "and it is certain that we cannot take anything out" (I Tim. 6:7). Nothing, that is, but our *selves* (that is, the "we" Paul speaks of)!

All comes to focus, at last, on what happens to the one possession entrusted to our care that will not pass away at lifetime's end, the immortal "self". What you have become through a life-and-time of choices is what you start with for all eternity. And the fundamental choice underlying all the other choices which sculpt the self is this one: *deny yourself*! That is, submit your will to God's will, your choices to His law.

Only you, only each of us, can do that for the self we are creating. And that is why the active agent in self-denial must be *you*!

My Cross?

The Lord couples self-denial with cross-bearing: "take up his cross daily," we have heard Him say.

Two things here:

1) Cross — "his" cross:

Does that imply that there is a cross for each of us? Each his own personal cross?

No doubt!

We observed just a moment ago that Christianity individualizes. God never deals with us except as individuals, responsible for our selves. We will ask in a moment what the Lord means by a "cross" but for now be it said that to each his own.

The cross assigned each of us is fitted to who we are, where we are, and what in us needs the discipline of cross-bearing.

What self-denial requires of you is *for* you. The cross of self-denial has *your* self-development in view, and your eternal destiny.

This is strikingly illustrated by the Lord's handling of two different persons, both of them rich.

A "ruler" asks Jesus, "Good Teacher, what shall I do to inherit eternal life?" Jesus advises him to keep the (Ten) Commandments. The ruler claims that so he has always lived. Jesus then says, "One thing you still lack. Sell all that you have and distribute to the poor, and you will have treasure in heaven; and come, follow me." This was a cross fitted to that ruler's need — but "when he heard this he became sad, for he was very rich" (drawn from Luke 18:18-23).

The tax collector, Zacchaeus, was also rich. When the Lord paused to pay Zacchaeus an unexpected visit, the tax collector "stood and said to the Lord, 'Behold, Lord, the half of my goods I give to the poor; and if I have defrauded any one of anything, I restore it fourfold.'" What does Jesus say? Half for the poor is not enough? Not at all. He says, "Today salvation has come to this house..." (Luke 19:8-9).

To each his cross.

The Lord commends a poor widow for tossing but a penny into the temple treasury. Yea more, Jesus declares that she "put in more than all those who have been contributing to the treasury. For they all contributed out of their abundance; but she out of her poverty has put in everything she had, her whole living" (Mark 12:42-44). Yet others, like Abraham and King David were blessed in the accumulation of huge fortunes. A cross for each, in a form adapted to each — all for the same purpose: to school the self to the choices of obedience which pave the way to God's right hand.

The cross designed for each of our shoulders is "our" cross, intended to develop *our* citizenship in God's kingdom.

Yes, it is a matter of "take up your cross." No one can do it for you. It has your name on it, and goes unassumed if you try to escape its load.

2) Daily:

There is no release from the necessity of self-denial by way of a cross. No holiday. No recess. No time off for good behavior. Each is "to take up his cross daily...."

Why?

Because life is a "daily" business. We live one day, indeed one moment, at a time. To live is, as we have said, to choose. Our cross is fitted to shape our choices in accord with divine demand. The "old" self is never so completely transformed into the "new" self as to release us from self-denial through cross-bearing. If we did not know that from experience, we could infer it from the Lord's command: "daily"! He would not put it that way if we did not need it that way.

Why A Cross?

Why does the Lord combine self-denial with cross-bearing? What is the significance, for us, of the cross-symbol?

Jesus is not suggesting that our cross is somehow a copy of His. The cross at Calvary stands alone in the midst, and at the turning point, of history. That cross has no duplicates. What God did there is not repeatable, nor need it be. The cross that "towers o'er the wrecks of time" has no offspring.

Why, then, are we required to shoulder a "cross," and what is meant by that command?

For these reasons:

1) To indicate that the "old" self must die! The self-indulgence at which self-denial is aimed must be thorough and merciless — *daily*! A cross is an instrument of execution. Paul has this in mind when he writes, "I appeal to you therefore, brethren, by the mercies of God, to present your bodies as a living sacrifice, holy and acceptable to God, which is your spiritual worship" (Rom. 12:1). We sacrifice ourselves by means of taking up a cross. This is taught by the symbolism.

2) The self-denial which the Lord requires depends upon two closely related gifts, both conveyed through divine revelation:

a) The "light" which sets the "old" self so vividly before us that we perceive unmistakably what must be denied and done away, and

b) A "light" which at the same time illumines the choices we must make to mature the "new" self which is supplanting the "old".

3) The cross symbolizes just such a "light" — namely, the Law of God!

It is by God's Law that Jesus is brought to death, for that is the penalty fixed by God for disobedience: "The soul that sins shall die"

(Ezek. 18:20). Christ is crucified by the Law, symbolized in the cross, because He became, by divine decree, sin for us: "For our sake he made him to be sin who knew no sin, so that in him we might become the righteousness of God" (II Cor. 5:21).

The cross symbolizes the divine Law, written by God with His own fingers upon the tablets of stone entrusted to Moses (Ex. 31:18; Deut. 9:10) — the Ten Commandments to which much of the Bible is inspired commentary.

Does the Law of God illumine precisely those forms of disobedient self-indulgence which must be purged as the believer grows in the faith? Indeed, the Law does just that, for "by the law," St. Paul writes, "comes knowledge of sin" (Rom. 3:20). The Law's repeated "Thou shalt not..." defines the self which must be denied. Indeed, stretches the "old" self out upon the arms of the cross which executes it!

And does the Law of God, at the same time, etch out the kind of self to be sculpted by choices obedient to its commands?

Exactly so!

Jesus stresses this aspect of the Law in response to several inquiries, one of them made by a lawyer: "Teacher," the lawyer asks, "what shall I do to inherit eternal life?" Jesus replies, "What is written in the law? How do you read?" The questioner answers, "You shall love the Lord your God with all your heart, and with all your soul, and with all your strength, and with all your mind; and your neighbor as yourself." This is simply the affirmative summary of the Ten Commandments quoted from Deuteronomy 6:5 and Leviticus 19:18. Jesus says, "You have answered right; do this, and you will live" (Adapted from Luke 10:25-28).

The Law of God, we repeat, sheds double light: 1) upon the "old" self we must deny, and 2) upon the "new" self to which we must daily aspire.

And this Law is aptly symbolized by a cross: "take up his cross daily...!"

We ask, with the "ruler," this question: "Teacher, what good deed must I do to have eternal life?" And we, with him, hear the Lord answer, as clearly this day as then, "If you would enter life, keep the commandments" (adapted from Matt. 19:16-17). That is, we hear Jesus saying, "Take up your cross...!" For the cross symbolizes the commandments.

Deny yourself what the commandments prohibit!

Do what the commandments require!

This is what it means to take up your cross — *daily*!

Symbolizes How?

We can inquire more precisely, now, just how a cross symbolizes the divine Law.

There are several ways:

1) A cross is composed of two parts, beam and crossbar. These readily suggest the two tables of the Law: the vertical to indicate the love we owe God above all, and the horizontal to suggest the love we owe our neighbors as ourselves — both defined by the Law.

2) Looking inward we are aware that the vertical beam points directly at our obedience to idols which must be denied, and the crossbar points to our consequent disregard of others which must be overcome.

3) The vertical beam directs us also to God and His will for our lives; the horizontal arms reach out to embrace all mankind to whom we owe neighborly love — again, both defined by the Law.

4) The cross symbolizes life through death. Through the self-sacrifice of Jesus Christ upon His cross, life eternal opened before all who believe. Through the sacrifice of our "old" selves upon the cross of the Law, life opens for us along the hard road the Law defines as obedience.

5) The cross reminds us that we "sin" against God (the vertical beam) and do "evil" to our selves and to our neighbors (the horizontal arm). After his adultery with Bathsheba, and contrived murder of her husband Uriah, David cries out to God, "Against thee, thee only, have I sinned, and done that which is evil in thy sight" (Ps. 51:4). *Against* God the sinning! *Before* God, who sees all, the evil done another.

6) The cross always symbolizes the intimate relationship between sin and evil, for a cross is the unity of two elements. The evil we do, in violation of the letter and spirit of the Law, against ourselves or others is violence done to God's possessions — for all is His! The self entrusted to our care and maturing is not, strictly speaking, our own. Each of us belongs to God by virtue of creation and preservation. The other whose needs we ignore or whose interests we annul is God's possession, in whom He is defrauded or victimized.

One more question here: because the Lord instructs each of us to take up "his cross," as we have already noted, does this imply that there are many forms of the Law, one adapted to each of us?

Not at all!

The Lord means that His commandments find us where we are. They are fitted, we discover, exactly to our situation. Whatever our particular idol, be it security, or power, or wealth, or fame, and in whatever forms that idol tempts us, the Law cuts at the root of such disobedience: "no other gods before me" (Ex. 20:3).

Now to another question:

Is The Law Outmoded?

There are those who believe that the gospel supersedes the Law.

Paul seems to say so in several places, as for example: "For sin will have no dominion over you, since you are not under the law but under grace" (Rom. 6:14).

What he means, however, becomes clear from what is written to the Galatians: "For all who rely on works of the law are under a curse; for it is written, 'Cursed be everyone who does not abide by all things written in the book of the law, and do them'" (Gal. 3:10, quoting Deut. 27:26).

The believer is not, indeed, "under the law" as a means to his salvation. This we have already seen.

But, being freed from the curse of the Law by faith in the self-sacrifice of Jesus Christ, the believer can affirm with St. Paul that "the law is holy, and the commandment is holy and just and good" (Rom. 7:12). And we are admonished by Paul to love our neighbors *because* "he who loves his neighbor has fulfilled the law" (Rom. 13:8).

As we have already pointed out, the same Law which illumines the "old" self which we must deny also etches clearly the lineaments of the "new" self we must pursue. Jesus says, therefore: "Think not I have come to abolish the law and the prophets; I have come not to abolish them but to fulfill them. For truly, I say to you, till heaven and earth pass away, not an iota, not a dot, will pass from the law until all is accomplished" (Matt. 5:17-18). As St. Luke phrases the Lord's words, "But it is easier for heaven and earth to pass away, than for one dot of the law to become void" (Luke 16:17).

If indeed the Law were no more in effect, Jesus would not have advised questioners after eternal life to obey it. Nor would He have given believers the following summary of the Law to govern their behavior: "Whatever you wish that men would do to you, do so to them; for this is the law and the prophets" (Matt. 7:12).

"Do we then overthrow the law by faith?" St. Paul asks; answering: "By no means! On the contrary, we uphold the law" (Rom. 3:31).

The ten commandments are written by God on the human conscience.

These commandments form the cross which the believer is obliged by our Lord to shoulder if we would truly follow Jesus Christ.

Where He Leads...

Following Christ requires self-denial and cross-bearing. Or, we may say, following Christ is, quite simply, self-denial through cross-bearing. This *is* what being Christian *means*!

The Christian life is, like that of our Lord, a strenuous life. Those who portray it otherwise do not take their models from the Bible. All of the Old Testament saints and prophets suffered in God's service, and few, if any, of the *New Testament* apostles died peacefully — it is believed — in his bed.

"In the world," we have already heard Jesus say, "you have tribulation...."

We may consider the hardships of following Jesus as both "inward" and "outward" — call them tribulation and persecution.

1) Why tribulation?

Because crucifixion is a cruel business. The cross we are required to take up implies the agony of genuine self-denial. God's law frequently indicts our motives, our passions, our desires, our envies, our pride, our self-sufficiency, even the secret pleasure we take in a show of humility or publicized generosity. The "old" self is one with which, on the whole, we have learned to be quite satisfied, thank you — until the law begins, O so painfully, probing it. Then this "old" self reacts to criticism, becomes well aware of its presumed "rights," protects its reputation, and is capable of baring its teeth when cornered. And this is the self we must daily affix to the cross of "Thou shalt not...," and push, over and again, into "Thou shalt...!" Not as we will, but as God instructs. Tribulation all right!

Jesus goes so far as to compare self-denial with losing life itself: "...whoever loses his life for my sake will find it" (Matt. 16:25). The way of the cross is, for the believer, the only way; but no one who tries walking it seriously thinks it easy.

The Church — when true to its calling — prods believers to renewal of laggard self-denial through preaching drawn directly from the Bible and focused immediately upon the life of the congregation. Such preaching penetrates disguises the "old" self so readily adopts, like the lying tongue which drips honey, like the smiling face over greedy hand, like willingness to share faith while hoarding goods, like the thousand facades with which the "old" self mimics self-denial while avoiding it. We will say more about the role of the Church in the believer's life in Chapter 6.

Yes, whoever practices daily taking up the cross of self-denial knows well enough why the Lord speaks of "tribulation".

But Christians live not only with themselves. We live, also, with others, not all of whom take kindly to Christian convictions.

2) Why persecution?

The age of Christian martyrs is never over, in some corner of the world. And more subtle forms of persecution turn up everywhere.

Jesus tells Pontius Pilate why He came: "For this was I born, and for this came I into the world, to bear witness to the truth" by word and deed (John 18:37). And this is why, He had told His disciples, the world hated Him: "If I had not come and spoken to them they would not have sin; but now they have no excuse for their sin. He who hates me hates my Father also. If I had not done among them the works which no one else did, they would not have sin; but now they have seen and hated both me and my Father" (John 15:22-23).

Truth-speaking invites persecution. In totalitarian states, therefore, freely speaking the truth is forbidden — only the party line may be said. But in free states truth also generates reaction. "A disciple is not above his teacher," Jesus tells us, "nor a servant above his master...If they have called the master of the house Beelzebub, how much more will they malign those of his household" (Matt. 10:24-25).

The Christian who presses upon society the "Thou shalt nots..." of his Master's commandments invites retort. The believer who calls for the justice prescribed by the "law and the prophets" generates opposition. And we know why: if the believer's "old" self rages within against criticism, will not unbelievers' selves react even more violently?

Persecution may be open; or it may be in subtler forms — but the believer must not be surprised if his growth in the Christian life is matched by reaction among those once counted among his friends. Cross-bearing is not likely to be a holiday. One of the neatest maneuvers of the "old" self is to suggest that discipleship must be popular, and the Christian life full of celebration and fun, of success and wealth.

Watch out! The Bible nowhere promises that.

An Assist...

St. Paul makes a creative suggestion for the practice of genuine self-denial.

He writes, "Do not be overcome by evil, but overcome evil with good" (Rom. 12:21).

The Apostle's inspired Word offers shrewd advice.

Being creatures of time, we cannot occupy the same moment with pursuits going in quite opposite directions — we cannot at the same moment follow after good and evil, after God and Satan. And if we fix upon the good, time and energy for evil are so far forth diminished.

We are unable to entertain more than one thought, more than one desire, more than one intention, or do more than one act at a given time: "You cannot serve God and mammon," Jesus says (Luke 16:13) — at least not at the same instant.

The hand reaching out to give can hardly with the *same* gesture steal.

The mind cannot at the same time plan good and plot evil.

We are unable to love and to hate the same person at once.

Our thoughts cannot be simultaneously occupied with both the better and the worse.

This is why Paul supplements his advice on overcoming evil with good by writing in another place: "Finally, brethren, whatever is true, whatever is honorable, whatever is just, whatever is pure, whatever is lovely, whatever is gracious, if there is any excellence, if there is anything worthy of praise, think on these things" (Phil. 4:8-9).

O yes! Think on these things — and you will afford evil no place to lodge, no soil to take root, no fruition in sin! Drive out evil with good, because the self is so made that both cannot occupy it at the same time!

For this reason, too, Paul advises: "Rejoice in the Lord always; again I will say, Rejoice!" (Phil. 4:4). The self bent upon rejoicing cannot at the same time be host to despair. Reflect, from this point of view, on the countless admonitions in the Bible, especially in the Psalms, to rest in God, to find joy in His law, to trust Him always, to pray without ceasing, to see His governing hand in all that occurs, to feel His presence close at hand at all times. A self so busied drives out idols, and overcomes evil with good.

But, finally, is there really no "joy" in following Jesus?

O yes, the Bible is full, just overflowing, with promises of delight, not only in union with God at the end of life, but also in the daily assumption of our cross. For the same Lord who lays a cross upon our shoulders declares: "Take my yoke upon you, and learn of me; for I am gentle and lowly in heart, and you will find rest for your souls. For my yoke is easy and my burden is light" (Matt. 11:29)!

Do you know why?

Because He shares it with us!

And what better Companion might we find? Or more accurately, be found by?

For Reflection And Discussion

1. *Does the Bible define some words differently from our common use of them? Illustrate.*
2. *Why is self-denial a critical condition for following Jesus?*
3. *How is self-denial related to repentance?*
4. *Why is self-denial such a personal matter?*
5. *How does the cross symbolize God's Law?*
6. *Explain how each believer's cross is both personal and formed by the commandments which make up the Law.*
7. *Does the New Testament annul the Law?*
8. *If God's Law were not our guide, how would we live obedient lives? How would we know if we were?*
9. *In what forms could tribulation and persecution come to Christians in today's world? In our own experience?*
10. *What is the Biblical way of overcoming evil and practising self-denial?*
11. *How does St. Paul's instruction to "rejoice in the Lord always" comport with cross-bearing?*

Chapter 4.

GROW

But grow in the grace and the knowledge of our
Lord Jesus Christ.
II Peter 3:18

GROW

TRUTH:
The believer who truly follows the Lord grows into ever better citizenship in the kingdom of heaven, through obedience by faith to the will of God the King, especially as that will is taught in the Church, where the believer is also nourished by the sacraments and schooled by the communion of saints.

RESPONSE:
Make daily endeavor to let the Holy Spirit govern through the Word all that you think, say, and do.

DISTORTION:
Assuming that the first awakening of faith is enough, and heaven secure, rather than developing the birth of a new self given life, time, and talent for increasing fruitfulness in God's kingdom.

From Less To More

Christians must grow.

There is no standing still. Either progression or regression.

The Bible is emphatic about it: growth in the Christian life is not an option; it is a mandate!

St. Paul: "Rather, speaking the truth in love, we are to grow up in every way into him who is the head, into Christ" (Eph. 4:15).

St. Peter: "But grow in the grace and knowledge of our Lord and Savior Jesus Christ" (II Peter 3:18).

And the pursuit of growth is guaranteed a reward: "Ask, and it will be given you; seek, and you will find; knock, and it will be opened to you. For every one who asks receives, and he who seeks finds, and to him who knocks it will be opened" (Matt 7:7-8). This is the Lord's own promise!

And His apostle assures us: "Draw near to God and he will draw near to you" (James 4:8).

With growth prescribed, and promised, we must ask what growth in our Christian life is, and how it is to be pursued.

Grow How?

Growth requires nurture.

The Christian life begins in new birth.

Birth brings forth babes, not adults.

Growth is the passage from infancy to maturity.

How do we find, and take, that passage?

The writer to the Hebrews complains that at least some of his intended readers have never left the stage of infancy: "For though by this time you ought to be teachers, you need some one to teach you again the first principles of God's word. You need milk, not solid food; for every one who lives on milk is unskilled in the word of righteousness, for he is a child. But solid food is for the mature, for those who have their faculties trained by practice to distinguish good from evil" (Heb. 5:12-14).

Notice how instructive this passage is, as concerns growth in the Christian life:

1) We are fed by "the first principles of God's word."

2) The stage of infancy, which requires milk, is one "unskilled in the word...."

3) The goal which infancy must seek, in order to attain maturity, is the ability "to distinguish good from evil" — by the Word!

Peter parallels the same thought in this way: "Like newborn babes, long for the pure spiritual milk, that by it you may grow up to salvation; for you have tasted the kindness of the Lord" (I Pet. 2:2-3).

O yes! we have indeed tasted of the kindness of the Lord. For our spiritual rebirth is His gift. Feeding upon the Word we mature that gift into spiritual life.

We have an example — and a warning! — in our natural, physical growth patterns.

The example: growth is the fruit of intake. We cannot command the body to grow. We are obliged to nourish it.

The warning: what we call natural growth is in fact passage from life to death. Spiritual growth reverses the process: passage from death into life eternal. This is the growth believers are commanded to pursue — from rebirth by the Word through faith into sainthood.

Life:

What is the life into which believers are to grow?

The Lord says: "I came that they may have life, and have it abundantly" (John 10:10). This *Handbook* is about that life.

He came to give what we do not, by nature, possess. For if we had life, He need not have come to give it to us. The life He gives, then, is not the life we naturally enjoy, not a multiplication of what we already have.

That abundance is not, either, a vast multiplying of goodies, of possessions, of talents, of learning: "And he said to them, 'Take heed, and beware of covetousness; for a man's life does not consist in the abundance of his possessions'" (Luke 12:15).

Never mistake, then, accumulation of anything whatever as the abundance of which the Lord speaks — unless that accumulation be of good works, which largely consist of giving things away!

Death:

To understand Christ's gift of "life," we must reflect on mankind's loss of it at the beginning.

Man's first parents — Adam and Eve — received both physical and spiritual life at their making: "then the Lord formed man of dust from the ground, and breathed into his nostrils the breath of life; and man became a living being" (Gen. 2:7).

God tested the loyalty of our first parents with the probationary command: "You may freely eat of every tree of the garden; but of the tree of the knowledge of good and evil you shall not eat, for in the day that you eat of it you shall die" (Gen. 2:16-17).

Man ate. The Spirit fled from him. Physically alive, but destined for physical death, man was spiritually dead. So then, so always. As Paul puts it: "Therefore as sin came into the world through one man and death through sin, and so death spread to all men because all men sinned..." (Rom. 5:12).

Adam and Eve fled the presence of God; and He expelled them from the garden of His companionship. The dreary course of human history began.

But at its very beginning was the first promise: the "head" of the evil one would be bruised, even as he, the Devil, bruised the "heel" of mankind. God's Son would wrest the world from the grip of Satan; but only at the cost of dying in man's stead. This is the heart of Christianity. Hope dawned on the very day that man was expelled from God's presence. And in due season that hope was realized in the coming of Jesus Christ, who came to give life — true and spiritual life — to all who believe.

And *growth*, the growing up "to mature manhood, to the measure of the stature of the fulness of Christ, so that we may no longer be children, tossed to and fro and carried about with every wind of doctrine..." (Eph. 4:13-14), becomes what the Christian life is *for*!

How?

And just how do we seek the growth required of us?

Only where, and how, such growth may be found.

Make no mistake: our rebirth is gift. Our growth is no less to be gift. And this gift is given only where and how God wills — and only to those who come seeking for it. God's gifts are never earned, but they must always be sought.

Jesus tells us how and where: "It is the spirit that gives life [how], the flesh is of no avail; the words that I have spoken to you [where] are spirit and life" (John 6:63).

What mankind lost in disobedience — Spirit and life — will be restored in obedience: "Come unto me, all who labor and are heavy laden, and I will give you rest. Take my yoke upon you, and learn from me; for I am gentle and lowly in heart, and you will find rest for your souls. For my yoke is easy, and my burden is light" (Matt. 11:28-30).

Where is the life into which we are to grow?

In Jesus Christ!

How do we receive that life?

By encounter with Him!

And how?

In His Word: "the words that I have spoken to you are spirit and life" (John 6:63).

And where are His words treasured, preserved, vibrant with promise of life and growth to all who seek Him there?

In the Bible, of course!

And where preached?

In the Church, of course!

The prophet cries out in joy: "Thy words were found, and I ate them, and the words became to me a joy and the delight of my heart; for I am called by thy name, O Lord, God of hosts" (Jer. 15:16).

And now we see clearly what nourishment it is that growth thrives on: devouring the Word, plunging into the Word as the starved plunge into food, as the thirsty grasp for drink.

Now we understand the Psalmist: "O how love I thy law! It is my meditation all the day....Thy testimonies are my heritage forever; yea, they are the joy of my heart. I incline my heart to perform thy statutes forever, to the end" (Ps. 119:97, 111-112).

In short, the growth God seeks in us is the fruit of the Word God inspired for us.

And this is God's invitation: "Ho, everyone who thirsts, come to the waters; and ye who have money, come, buy and eat! Come, buy wine and milk without money and without price....Incline your ear, and come to me; hear, that your soul may live..." (Is. 55:1, 3).

Our natural life is nourished by food fitted to its needs. Our spiritual life must be nourished by the food fitted to its needs, conveyed to us by the Word of God.

And one more thing here:

Food nourishes the body by passing through, not by accumulation. Food becomes energy. Energy fires the talents we use to live.

So, too, the Word of God nourishes by passing through into good works, that is into obedience. The Word does not come to be memorized, nor to be debated, nor indefinitely discussed; the Word comes to be heard and done.

Back To The Church

From the perspective we have now acquired, we may consider the Church and our relation to her.

God creates and sustains the Church to promote our growth into life.

"If you would enter life," Jesus says, "keep the commandments" (Matt. 19:17).

And He gives us the Church to school us in keeping them.

Ours is the choice with which the Lord, through Moses, confronts Israel: "See, I have set before you this day life and good, death and evil. If you obey the commandments of the Lord your God which I command you this day, by loving the Lord your God, by walking in his ways, and by keeping his commandments and his statutes and his ordinances, then you shall live..." (Deut. 30:15-16).

The prophet Jeremiah repeats the challenge: "Thus says the Lord, 'Behold, I set before you the way of life and the way of death.'" (Jer. 21:8).

Life is the way of obedience to the will of God as revealed in His Word. The Church exists to proclaim that way, and to disciple believers in walking it.

And the alternative?

This: "But if your heart turns away, and you will not hear, but are drawn away to worship other gods and serve them, I declare to you this day, that you shall perish...." (Deut. 30:17).

The Church exists to utter such warning, too.

From The Church:

What, then, may the believer intent upon growth through the Word expect from the Church?

Two things, really:

1) To be equipped for sainthood, that is to be nurtured faithfully in the truth of God's Word.

2) To be prepared for the service of obedience, both within and without the congregation.

Nurture:

The Church nurtures the believer in three ways:

1) Through preaching.

Be sure to demand, and to support, and to encourage faithful preaching. Preaching which, today, as in the times of the prophets, sets before the congregation both "life and good" and "death and evil." Your concern well may be that the pulpit says too little rather than too much, exhibits too much prudence rather than too little.

70

Abstain from the quest, stimulated by the electronic church, for numbers. Will speaking truth too bluntly drive people away? Will asking too much by way of obedience turn them off? Yours must be the encouragement that blunts such fears, and the reminder, if necessary, that it is the Lord who obliges His Church to teach believers "to do all that I have commanded you..." (Matt. 28:20). And *all* means ALL!

2) The Church also nourishes growth through faithful administration of the sacraments.

In the sacraments the Word becomes visible. We are reached by the truth through senses other than the ear. Use the sacraments that way. So used, they nourish growth in life.

3) And by discipline.

Christ calls upon the Church to "make disciples of all nations" (Matt. 28:19).

The disciple is one who is under discipline, that is under orders from his superior. The Lord is that Superior, and His order to disciples is clear: "If you love me, you will keep my commandments" (John 14:15). Exactly the commandments He calls upon the Church to teach. That is, the commandments taught throughout His Word.

But, as we have observed, food nourishes only when passed through the body. And Lord's Word nourishes only when passed through the believer into obedience. The Church not only preaches, and teaches, the inspired Word, but she also tries through her eldership to encourage its being obeyed by those who hear it. Indeed, it is the obligation of the elders to insist upon believers' obedience, on pain of admonition, censure, and eventual expulsion if the believer declines to heed warnings.

Service:

Obedience begins at home. In this context, it begins with the Church.

We have observed what the believer may expect of the Church.

What can the Church expect of the believer?

In regard to the Church's preaching, and teaching, and obeying:

1) An eagerness to *hear*. Attendance upon the preaching services. Study at home. Participation in Bible study groups.

2) An interest in the Church's confessions. These are the tools created at the time of the Reformation for the purpose of enabling the laity to judge pulpit obedience to the truth.

3) A willingness to be counted. The courageous pulpit comes under criticism. The growing believer does not prudently refuse to get involved. Speak a word for him who speaks the truth — or — against losing the truth in generalities and yielding to pressures.

4) The Church costs money. Give as you have been given, "for God loves a cheerful giver" (II Cor. 9:7).

5) The Church disburses money and goods. Support her diaconate so that they can give generously in the name of the Lord.

(We summarize here what we have discussed in detail in two companion volumes, *The Elders Handbook* and *The Deacons Handbook*, and are obliged to refer the reader to these for the grounds upon which these brief statements rest, as well as to chapter 6 in this *Handbook*).

For Reflection And Discussion

1. *Why is the Bible so intent upon the believer's growing?*
2. *What kind of "abundant" life is the Christian promised? When?*
3. *What kind of "death" did Adam and Eve suffer, and how was the Gospel preached to them?*
4. *How does Christ convey new and abundant life to us?*
5. *What role should the Church play in believers' growing?*
6. *How does the Church accomplish this obligation?*
7. *What can the Church expect from the believer in return?*

PART II

GOD'S MEANS

Chapter 5.

HIS WORD

All scripture is inspired of God, and profitable for teaching, for reproof, for correction, and for training in righteousness, that the man of God may be complete, equipped for every good work. II Timothy 3:16-17

HIS WORD

TRUTH:
The Holy Spirit inspired (breathed) the Scriptures into being for the purpose of evoking true faith, for teaching believers all that we must know and do for good citizenship in God's kingdom, and for use as the Spirit's vehicle for entrance into the human heart — a Word heard in the Church, and read by the believer for understanding through "standing under" its commands.

RESPONSE:
Seek encounter with God through His Word as it is preached in the Church, and as you study it by yourself and with others; strive to understand it better and better by struggling to do all that, through it, the Lord commands.

DISTORTION:
To substitute some form of "hermeneutics" for obedience as key to grasping the meaning of the Bible.

Believer And Bible

We are here:
1) To live is to choose.
2) Our choices gradually make us who we are — and will become.

3) Choices governed by the world, the flesh and the Devil set our feet on the broad way that leads to the hell of separation from God.

4) Choices governed, through faith, by the will of God set our feet on the hard road leading to eternal life in the presence of God.

Now:

1) How shall we know what the will of God is?

As already suggested, we learn the will of God from the Bible which is the inspired Word of God.

Why The Bible?

God tells very plainly why He gives us the Bible: "All scripture is inspired by God and profitable for teaching, for reproof, for correction, and for training in righteousness, that the man of God may be complete, equipped for every good work" (II Tim. 3:16).

In short, God provides us with His Word for the purpose of setting and keeping our feet on the hard road of choices becoming obedient in good works.

What Is The Bible?

We have said that the Bible is God's Word.

But what of the many problems that can be raised about simply receiving the Bible in your hand as *the* Word of God?

How can a book written over many centuries by many writers in terms of *their* times speak to us, now, in terms of *our* times?

What about the errors alleged to be found in the Bible?

What about whole books like, say, Numbers and Leviticus, which no one seems to read? Or Revelation, which few seem to begin to understand? And what about the very difficult passages in many of the Biblical books?

Isn't there a lot of work for us to do *before* we can just glibly talk about listening to the Bible?

These are common questions. We could mention more.

How shall they be answered?

We answer by setting another choice before you — one we have already made for ourselves:

Which Approach?

You must choose between two ways of approaching the Bible.

Why do you come to it? Why take it up? Why read it? Why try to turn listening into hearing?

This is one way, one we do not endorse!

1) Approach the Bible as you would any other book. You are determined to extract meaning from it. You will get hold of its contents, and master them. You will possess the Word. To this end, you will want to know all you can about the author of each book, about those to whom he was writing in his times, and about the circumstances in which he lived. You may outline the book, find errors in it, and study others who have worked it over as you are.

All this is sometimes called scholarship.

The Bible has a way of disappearing in the hands of such scholarship. All of the questions we have raised above, and countless more, shred the Bible's unity and come between listening and hearing.

But this is a way to approach your Bible, all too common a way.

It fails to make *hearing* possible because the Bible is *not* like any other book. And God's Word declines being handled as if it were. That is why this kind of Biblical "scholarship" always develops more questions than answers.

There is another way to approach the Bible, the way we commend:

2) You come to let the Bible do what God gives it to do: that you — and we — may be "equipped for every good work!"

By this choice of approach you stand under, not over, the Bible. Rather than possess it, you want the Bible to possess you. You want desperately to *hear*; for this is the Lord's command: "He who has an ear, let him hear what the Spirit says to the churches" (Rev. 2:7; repeated six times thereafter).

You come, then, with the ear of a believer, not with the eye of a critic. And you will discover that by *hearing*, that is by obeying, the Word you come to under-stand it.

Is there a scholarship that assists us in such hearing?

Of course.

It is the work of those who want to help themselves, and us, to hear better what God says through His Word. Such scholarship has one characteristic method: it lets Scripture interpret Scripture. Not research, not criticism, not shredding the text in search of problems and puzzles — not these, but helping the reader obey through letting the

Bible illumine itself: such scholarship finds the Bible a unity, and hears God speaking through His Word.

The Bible can speak to us, here and now, in words written there and then because the Bible is unlike any other book. We call it the "Holy" Bible. Why? Because the Bible alone, of all the books in the world, was inspired by God the Holy Spirit. The Spirit guided all of the Biblical writers to use their words to convey God's Word. And it is the same Holy Spirit who guides the hearing of all who believe. No need to worry about crossing the historical gap between the times of the Biblical writers and our own; the Holy Spirit does that. He is not bound by time, nor circumstance. No need to wonder how the Word got from *im*pression in one language and culture to *ex*pression in our own; the Holy Spirit managed that. No need, either, to worry over whether one translation or another is the better. The will to obey can *hear*; the Spirit will see to that.

In short, you furnish the determination to let God's Word guide your feet on His narrow way — and you become your own Biblical scholar.

And another thing: because obedience is key to understanding the Word, start always with the passages you do understand by doing them, and let the rest come. Wondering, meanwhile, why so many people want to confess that they understand so little of the Word. Could that be a confession of...disobedience?

In summary:

3) Here, as usual, we face choice: do we come to the Bible in the stance of the critic, determined to "prove" its right to command us? Or, do we come to the Bible in the stance of the believer, determined to hear God's commands for all of our other choices?

We can put the alternatives in another way, a way that will explain an otherwise puzzling teaching of our Lord: do we come to His Word as children, ready to believe and do what we hear Him saying to us? Or do we come as what we think are "adults," determined not to be put upon by this "old" book?

You know what Jesus recommends: "Truly, I say to you, unless you turn and become like children, you will never enter the kingdom of heaven" (Matt. 18:3).

Don't worry about what is said by those who think themselves "adult" enough to criticize the Bible. Your Lord asks you to come ready to hear like a little child. Children don't ask who wrote the stories parents read them, or how those stories got here or hang together. Children listen with rapt attention, ready to let the words take possession of themselves.

Let this be our approach to the Bible.

This choice is so important for all other choices that we want to view it in another way.

Obedience And Understanding

So far:

1) The *will*-to-obey is the key to transforming listening to the Word into hearing the Word.

2) The will-to-obey is also the key to understanding the Word.

This we must explore further.

3) Jesus puts it this way, when He was Himself charged with lacking "scholarly" credentials by critics who said about Him: "How is it that this man has learning, when he has never studied?" That may be said about you if you accept the Bible just as it is. Jesus answers: "My teaching is not mine, but his who sent me; if any man's will is to do his will, he shall know whether the teaching is from God or whether I am speaking on my own authority" (John 7:15-17).

The Lord goes on to explain why these sceptics, who had often listened to the Word but never obeyed it, could not *hear* Him: "Did not Moses give you the law? Yet none of you keeps the law" (John 7:19). They lacked exactly the qualification required for understanding: obedience.

His Word to them is His Word to us: *obey* to understand.

4) What, then, if the Word says things we do *not* understand? Is the key a flurry of research? Hasty trips to the library to pore over commentaries? Maybe even the wistful desire to learn Greek or Hebrew?

No, not if we *hear* what Jesus is saying. The key is a better effort to do what we do already understand.

The best commentaries on the Bible are the lives of saints. There are great saints who amaze us by their obedience. There are lesser saints like ourselves. That is to say, "saints" are all those who will to do the will of God, and come to His Word seeking to know what that will requires. Sainthood is God's gift through our achievement. It is not reserved for special people; it comes along the hard road open to all who have faith. And with sainthood comes the understanding of the Word born of obedience to it. This is always the saint's experience: passages in the Bible which were once dark and mysterious come through living to shine with supernatural light upon our steps: "Thy word is a lamp to my feet," sings the Psalmist, "and a light to my path" (Ps. 119:105).

But *only* so for the believer! Not for unbelief: "The unspiritual man does not receive the gifts of the Spirit of God, for they are folly to him, and he is not able to understand them because they are spiritually discerned" (I Cor. 2:14). And, "Who is wise and understanding among you?" the Apostle James asks, answering: "By his good life let him show his works in the meekness of wisdom" (James 3:13).

5) Because the Bible comes seeking obedience, we can understand an otherwise puzzling question. It is this: how could St. Paul write such complicated letters to such ordinary people? That is, to ordinary people just like us?

Complicated letters? O yes. Library shelves groan under the hundreds of books which are written to take command of Paul's epistles. Most of these commentaries are intended to master Paul; a few aim to help Paul master us. But Paul, and the Holy Spirit who guided his pen, intended his epistles to master believers just as he found them. And this is his description: "For consider your call, brethren, not many of you were wise according to worldly standards, not many were powerful, not many were of noble birth...." He might be talking about most of us! And to such Paul writes his epistles!

So what? So this: "But God chose what is foolish in the world to shame the wise; God chose what is weak in the world to shame the strong, God chose what is low and despised in the world, even the things that are not, to bring to nothing the things that are, so that no human being might boast in the presence of God" (I Cor. 1:26-29).

Paul wrote complicated letters. He wrote to very ordinary people. Like you and us! How could he expect us to understand? Because he knew that God the Holy Spirit (who guided what Paul said) intended to illumine with His insight all who come to *hear* Paul by intending to obey.

Even St. Peter found Paul's letters difficult: "So also our beloved brother Paul wrote to you according to the wisdom given him, speaking of this as he does in all his letters. There are some things in them hard to understand, which the ignorant and unstable twist to their own destruction, as they do other scriptures" (II Pet. 3:15-16).

Yes, there will always be much in the letters of Paul, as in the rest of the Bible, that we too will find "hard to understand." But we will avoid twisting our ignorance into our own destruction, by striving stedfastly to obey what we do understand. For Peter goes on to say that those who twist Paul's words are "lawless men" (II Pet., 3:17). The disobedience of unbelief creates the twisted mind of misunderstanding: "For the word of the cross is folly to those who are perishing, but to us who are being saved it is the power of God" (I Cor. 1:18). This "power" is not ours by way of subduing the Bible to our "scholarship" — no, this *power of God*, received by faith, works through us that obedience which alone comes to true understanding. Let us bow before what we can hear; that will show us how far along we are on the road of sainthood. Let us patiently await the day when we can hear more than now we do, because we will have made further progress on the way of obedience. But let us avoid the folly of thinking we can master God's Word in any ways other than by doing it.

6) And now we know, too, why most of the Bible is written to saints. Observe the opening words of Paul's letters: "To the saints who are also faithful in Christ Jesus" (Eph. 1:1). "To all the saints in Christ Jesus who are at Phillipi..." (Phil. 1:1). "To all God's beloved in Rome, who are called to be saints" (Rom. 1:7). And so on. Peter writes to those, "chosen and destined by God the Father and sanctified by the Spirit for obedience to Jesus Christ and for sprinkling with his blood" (I Pet. 1:2). The Word is addressed to those who *can* understand it — saints who *will* to obey!

This is true of both Testaments. The Law and the prophets, which is the name given sometimes to the Old Testament, is obviously addressed to Israel, the people of God — and now comes to the Church, which is the New Israel.

The Bible is a kind of "in" book. That is because it speaks only to those who will to hear it.

With one great exception: the gospels!

The Jesus who appears to us in the four evangelists is to be preached, according to His own command, to "all nations" (Matt. 28:19), or to "all the world" (Mark 16:15). But only to those who hear and believe the gospel is the rest of the Word addressed. Those who enter by the narrow gate of faith into the message of the gospels can walk the hard road of obedience which leads to understanding of all the Scriptures — including the gospels.

7) The Bible has its own name for the understanding arising out of obedience. That name is "wisdom" — "with all your getting, get wisdom" (Prov. 4:7).

Wisdom cannot be learned; it must be acquired. Wisdom cannot be taught; it follows after obedience.

81

The Lord puts it this way: "Every one then who hears these words of mine and does them will be like a wise man who built his house upon the rock; and the rain fell, and the floods came, and the winds blew upon the house, but it did not fall, because it had been founded on the rock" (Matt. 7:24-25).

Do not be misled by shortcuts to building on the rock, that is on Jesus Christ. There are no easy detours.

Wisdom comes from building, day by day, on the rock. That is, by choosing day by day according to the Word of the Lord.

Don't ever confuse such building with talking *about* the Bible, or about its origins, or its translations, or its difficulties. All this St. Paul carefully warns against, saying to Pastor Timothy, "...you may charge certain persons not to teach any different doctrine, nor to occupy themselves with myths and endless genealogies which promote speculations rather than the divine training that is in faith; whereas the aim of our charge is love that issues from a pure heart and a good conscience and sincere faith" (I Tim. 1:3-5).

Summary

The Bible is God's Word.

God's Word seeks incarnation in our choices made in obedience to that Word.

The Bible reveals God's rules of the road for those who choose to walk the hard way of obedience.

As we make progress in obedience so we also make progress in understanding the Bible.

We are helped by Biblical scholars who enable us better to see and do what the Bible asks of true believers.

We do well to avoid Biblical scholarship which undertakes to use the Word for the scholar's purposes, a scholarship which is "ever learning and never coming to a knowledge of the truth" (II Tim. 3:7).

Happily, we are never on our own in trying to walk the obedient way. God unites all believers into the Church for the express purpose of training us in hearing and doing His will.

And so we turn, in a moment, to the Church.

Note: Understanding And Hermeneutics

For those readers who have encountered the studies called "hermeneutics" and "the new hermeneutics" we append this note. Skip it if the issue has no interest for you; you will be none the worse off, as believer, for that.

* * *

We have said that understanding the Bible arises out of obedience to it.

We could call that the hermeneutics of obedience. Because *hermeneutics* means, simply, the method of understanding a text.

If you prefer speculation to obedience, but do not want to put it so frankly, there is an evasion of the hermeneutics of obedience. That evasion is mistakenly justified by the question: how can you obey the Bible unless you *first* understand it?

For example, how does a child know what his mother wants him to do unless he can *first* understand her words of instruction? Until he knows what she means, how can he act? So it may be argued.

From this point of view, obedience is not the key to understanding at all. Obedience is simply *proof* of it. Our obedience to the Bible shows that we do understand it.

How, then, it is said, shall we go about understanding the Bible so that we can obey?

And the answer becomes: master the science of hermeneutics, and apply it to the Biblical text.

Somewhat lately, the new hermeneutics has been added to the prerequisites to understanding the Bible. The new hermeneutics observes that all communication is via words. But it asks, what is a *word*? And how do words relate to the realities they presume to communicate? Is not putting something into words already an interpretation?

So the new hermeneutics drives us yet one step further from the text. We must master the whole theory of language, and then master its use in the particular Biblical passage we are reading *before* we can even begin to obey.

And, because most of us lack time for such preliminaries, we will have to take the "scholar's" word for it that this passage "means" *this* and not *that*! Hermeneutics envelops the Bible in a haze that only the elite think they can penetrate — and if you read them a little, you will discover that no two of the "scholars" see precisely the same thing through the *lenses of their learning*. The hermeneutical bridge may be anchored on our bank, but no one knows if it has firm hold across the hidden river of understanding. Walk it at your own risk.

Must we shoulder the burdens, if not the bondage, of hermeneutics *before* we can obey God's Word?

Think a moment:

1) Do you suppose that the kind of people to whom St. Paul was writing (as we observed above) had mastered courses in hermeneutics before he could give them the instructions in doctrine and obedience that characterize all of his letters?

Of course not!

2) It is recorded of Jesus that, "the common people heard him gladly" (Mark 12:37). Had they been schooled in hermeneutics, do you suppose?

Of course not!

3) The Lord Himself recommends that we receive the Word as little children (Matt. 18:3, as we have noticed above).

And little children have had no work in hermeneutics!

Or — wait just a moment — have they?

Yes, they have. Children *do* hermeneutics from the time they learn to talk. Indeed, this is exactly what "learning" to talk means! It means understanding words, something which hermeneutics desperately tries to explain.

Philosophers have racked their brains across the centuries to account for what children do quite painlessly: learn to use words both to communicate, and to receive, understanding.

Of course, you must "understand" what your mother is asking you to do *before* you can obey her.

And of course, every child *does*! Learning to talk *is* learning to understand!

The use of language is a great mystery. Happily, we do not have to join the hermeneuticists in trying to resolve that mystery before we can *hear* — that is obey — God's Word.

"My sheep," the Lord says, "hear my voice" (John 10:27). We hear His Word, then, not because we study hermeneutics, but because we will to be His sheep.

We can put it this way: by nature we learned to "listen" to words. No problem there. By faith we "hear" through obedience the Word of God. The better we hear, the better we will understand.

On The Beauty Of Words:

We need not know precisely how words perform in communication in order to appreciate what a mysteriously beautiful gift language is.

Just remember that science has never been able to account for the origins of language. We believe it belongs to God's gift of His Image to man.

Consider:

1) We have said that "under"-"standing" the Bible is like "standing"-"under" it.

2) That is picture language, called metaphor.

3) Why use picture language to explain what "understanding" is?

4) Because, in fact, we can only say what understanding is "like." We can only point to illustrations of understanding.

5) Why so?

6) Because you have to understand *before* we can explain to you what "understanding" is. Just as you have to see before anyone can explain to you what "seeing" is. Try telling a person born blind what the color blue is! You will discover that the ability to understand *must* precede receiving any explanation of what "understanding" is. So you point to it with pictures, hoping that in this way we may both "see" what we have been doing, in fact, since childhood, namely exercising the power to understand.

7) And that leads to a fascinating thing: words can shed light!

8) And we think that "understanding" is simply being able to say, "Oh, now I see!"

9) Remember the last time you were puzzled about something? And somebody came along and explained it to you? And what did you say? You probably said, "Oh, now I *see!*" Isn't that odd? Why say "see" when it was what you *heard* that shed the light? Why not, "Oh, now I *hear*"?

10) Well, that is because words shed light. That is, true words shed light. Lies counterfeit light, but leave us in the dark just the same!

11) Words can shed light because they are assigned that function by God Himself. (We said above that He is the giver of language.) Light was first *spoken* into existence by words: "And God said, 'Let there be light'; and there was light" (Gen. 1:3). Long before there were sun, moon and stars, too! Light came from the Word.

12) Now, consider carefully:

    a) Words shed light. This was designed at creation.

    b) God created light and all other things by Word.

    c) That Word is Jesus Christ. St. John teaches us that: "In the beginning was the Word, and the Word was with God, and the Word was God. He was in the beginning with God; all things were made through him, and without him was not anything made that was made" (John 1:1-3).

d) The Word that sheds true light is Christ: "I am the light of the world; he who follows me will not walk in darkness, but will have the light of life" (John 8:12).

e) But what does it mean to "follow" Christ?

f) He tells us, as we have already observed, what following Him means: "If any man would come after me, let him deny himself and take up his cross and follow me. For whoever would save his life will lose it; and whoever loses his life for my sake and the gospel's will save it. For what does it profit a man to gain the whole world and forfeit his life?" (Mark 8:34-36). Which is but another way of saying that to follow the Lord is to walk the hard road of self-denying obedience — as we have been saying.

g) And just how do we walk that road?

h) In the "light" of the Word — Jesus Christ and His Word, the Bible! We have heard the Psalmist say: "Thy word is a lamp to my feet and a light to my path" (Ps. 119:105).

i) Obedience *is* walking in the light.

j) Disobedience *is* walking in darkness.

k) The Lord sends out His Word to shatter our darkness and set our feet in His light, as He said to Paul: "...to open their eyes, that they may turn from darkness to light and from the power of Satan to God, that they may receive forgiveness of sins and a place among those who are sanctified by faith in me" (Acts 26:18).

13) And now all comes full circle: we say, "I see" when we come to understand something because the words that bring understanding do shed light. The sun is a daily illustration of this. We grope in darkness until the dawn; then all things become plain. So in our spiritual lives: we stumble in spiritual darkness, until the Son of God rises through His Word; then the way we should go becomes plain in its light.

14) But we do not walk in the light of the Word by simply talking about it! That is what hermeneutics does. It seeks to explain words by talking about them. That is not the Bible's prescription, as we have already seen. We do not achieve an understanding of the Bible in the same way, in the same form, through the same medium in which it comes to us. It comes as Word. We understand through act!

15) The Bible is a little like a cookbook, or a guide to better golf or hockey. The instruction comes in words, but the understanding comes out of action. You may apply all the hermeneutical principles you like to your cookbook or golf guide; but you will become a better cook or golfer *only* by *doing* what the manual requires. And *how* will you know what the manual *does* require?

By reading it, of course!

Doing what you do with the newspaper. Doing what you learned to do 'way back when you learned to talk. You do hermeneutics every day. It's behind you. Leave it there. Listen to the Word. And you will understand it when, by standing-under it, you suddenly exclaim, "Oh, now I *see!*"

Yes, that is what light is for. To enable us to see.

That is what the Word is for: to enable us to see the narrow gate, to follow the hard road walking in His light.

The only way to improve your cooking, or golf, is by practice.

Let's go on, now, to practicing God's handbook for our behavior!

For Reflection And Discussion

1. *Define, and distinguish, two approaches we can take toward the Bible.*
2. *How does Jesus' comparison of believers with children relate to reading the Bible?*
3. *What is the key to profitable Bible study?*
4. *What principle of understanding the Bible is available to us in reading difficult passages? Can you illustrate from your own experience?*
5. *Why are so many of the Biblical books addressed to "saints" and those within the faith?*
6. *What is the Biblical term for understanding arising out of obedience? Is there any other route to this precious possession? Is it more likely to characterize the old or the young? Why?*

Chapter 6.

HIS CHURCH

The household of God, which is the church of the living God, the pillar and bulwork of truth.
I Timothy 3:15.

HIS CHURCH

TRUTH:
The Church is the Body of Christ, active for Him in history, and is created and sustained by the Word preached for the purpose of making disciples, that is those who through faith come under the discipline of God's will as revealed in the Bible, exercised through the Church and nourished by the sacraments.
RESPONSE:
Develop and sustain a close relationship to the Church in the form of some congregation, supporting it through attendance, the gifts of self and time and money, and yielding to its admonitions when these are due.
DISTORTION:
Thinking it possible to have God for Father without having the Church (in the form of some congregation) as Mother, or forgetting that the Lord has given to His Church the keys to the kingdom of heaven.

You And The Church

We commend to you a very simple and practical view of the Church, one we have already briefly outlined.

We do so because the Bible does.

It is Jesus Himself who defines the unique, and irreplaceable role of the Church. Through St. Paul the Lord defines its structure.

Whenever the Church is less than her Lord commands, the world suffers loss. Whenever the Church attempts to do more, or other, than her Lord requires, she suffers loss.

The obedient Church is the health of civilization, a source of guidance, instruction, and discipline.

The Church's Doing

In His farewell to His disciples, representatives of the New Testament form of the Church, Jesus assigns the Church her role in history: "All authority in heaven and on earth has been given to me. Go therefore and make disciples of all nations, baptizing them in the name of the Father and of the Son and of the Holy Spirit, teaching them to observe all that I have commanded you; and lo, I am with you always to the close of the age" (Matt. 28:18-20).

In accord with its general practice, the Bible is less concerned with telling us what the Church *is* than with what the Church is to *do*.

The Lord commands these things:

1) *Make disciples of all nations:*

A disciple is one under discipline. The Lord's disciples are under His discipline. It is natural, therefore, that the command to "make disciples" climaxes in "teaching them to do all that I have commanded you."

The Church is a disciple-making institution.

And here, in a word, is the purpose for which the Lord ordains His Church: discipling. It is the purpose which makes the Church unique and incomparable among institutions. Join it only if being an ever better disciple of Jesus Christ is your goal.

In St. Mark's account of this farewell mandate, the Lord reveals just how disciples are to be evoked from out of the mass of mankind: "Go into all the world and preach the gospel..." (Mark 16:15).

The unique task of discipling is accomplished only through the unique calling to *preach...the gospel!*

No other institution is designated to *preach.*

No other institution is entrusted with the *gospel.*

From ancient times, thoughtful men have marveled at the power of speech. The Greek philosophers Plato and Aristotle, among others, shrewdly analyzed the nature of verbal persuasion — by speech and by writing — called rhetoric. The Romans Cicero and Quintilian carefully prescribed the most effective forms of public address.

But none of the ancient analyses fits precisely the nature of preaching. It remained for St. Augustine, in the fourth century after Christ, to define the sermon as "homily" — that is, a specific form of Christian discourse — and to signal its uniqueness.

What makes preaching different?

Two things, really:

    a) The preacher's "word" is not entirely his own, and

    b) The preacher's "word" is not altogether just a word.

All speech conveys truth — or lie — through word. And the power of oratory to persuade resides in the dynamic gift of voice to truth — or falsehood — which some do far more effectively than others. Just how this is done is the subject of rhetoric.

The sermon, too, clothes Truth in words. In so far as the preacher slips into falsehood or error, his is not a sermon. But the Truth "preached" is more a "who" than an it, more a Person than a principle. This is in accord with the Lord's own declaration: "I am...the truth" (John 14:6). Preaching brings the living Lord into the midst of the congregation. Provided, of course, that the sermon exhibits its first unique characteristic, namely that it is governed by the Word of God as revealed in the Scriptures. Given this obedience, the faithful preacher enjoys the Lord's own promise: "He who hears you, hears me" (Luke 10:16).

The unique calling of the Church's pulpits, then, is to bring the living Lord into the midst of the congregation via proclamation of His Word. The transformation of Word spoken into Person present is accomplished within the Church by the Holy Spirit, as the Lord promised: "When the Spirit of truth comes, he will guide you into all truth..." (John 16:13).

Even a little reflection on these things will underscore the totally unique role of the Church in the world as the institution designated by her Lord to provide pulpits for preaching the Word.

And the Word is gospel, that is, as we have seen, *good news*! Its content is that of the Bible. Its proclamation is the presence of Him whose birth, life, death and resurrection *is* the gospel. Only the Church has been entrusted with this treasure and its communication to mankind.

Within the Church the syllables of God's Word, vehicles of the living Christ, fall from human lips.

It is not by happenstance, then, that Jesus assigns preaching to His Church. Preaching is what the Church is all about. Remember that the

Church which neglects to preach robs society of encounter with the living God in terms of gospel, while the Church which undertakes to do more, or other, than preach robs herself of devoting full energies to her essential calling.

But preaching is not, as the saying goes, everyone's bag. Even though the air waves and crusade rallies abound with the oral noises of those bent on self-ordination.

The Church which is aware of what preaching involves carefully prepares her preachers and carefully supervises them. Across the centuries the Church screened those who aspired to preach. With the Reformation ecclesiastical control of the pulpit was sometimes relaxed, and today the ability to speak may be assumed license to "preach".

Reformation confessions, however, identify the true Church as established only where the gospel is preached in faithful adherence to the Bible — an obedience overseen within the Church by a watchful eldership, elected for the purpose. Moreover, the pulpits of the faithful Church are open only to those confirmed as capable and called through the Church's process of ordination. We have, in our *Elders Handbook*, entered into the details of ecclesiastical supervision of the pulpit, and preparation for it.

Choose your Church with all this well in mind.

Whenever preaching deteriorates, as it did in the Middle Ages immediately preceding the Reformation, and as it widely languishes in our own time, the Church often seeks vainly to give herself meaning in terms of popular alternatives — companionship, service, counseling, etc. — in which she has successful secular competitors. And whenever preaching is counterfeited outside the Church's own pulpits, emotions may be stirred and false hopes given birth, but the promise "who hears you" never reaches fulfillment in "hears Me"!

You will want a Church, therefore, where preaching is paramount, primary, ultimate, absolutely first priority. Where else will you hear, and thus encounter, Jesus in the words of men? Where else, that is, will faith be evoked, nurtured, guided, corrected, inspired and brought to fruition by the inspired Word of God?

2) The Lord commands, also, that the Church administer the sacraments: "baptizing them in the name...."

A sacrament is a temporal symbol, palpable to the senses, adapted by the Scriptures to express eternal, spiritual significance. Protestantism commonly counts but two sacraments: baptism and the Lord's Supper. Catholicism finds seven sacraments addressed to strengthening faith.

Baptism is the symbol of transition. By it is portrayed escape (salvation) from the Egyptian bondage to sin and the devil into liberation through the service of God — represented in the Old Testament Church, Israel, by the people's passing through the Red Sea on dry ground (Exodus 14).

Bitter and prolonged struggles have characterized the Church's theology of the sacraments. More acrimony has been aroused and more division driven into the Body of Jesus Christ by dispute over these symbols than by any other single issue. The Reformation, for example, began as an effort to reform the one holy catholic Church. But the Reformers themselves divided so stubbornly over the nature of the Holy Supper as to leave Protestantism a hopelessly divisive heritage.

You will have to decide for yourself, if you have not already done so, what the sacraments are, and what they are for. Do they actually convey divine grace? Are the Lord's words spoken at the Last Supper to be taken literally of the broken bread and poured out wine: "This is my body...my blood" (Matt. 26:26, 28)? Or is He speaking symbolically? If literally, as Roman Catholicism holds, then the sacrament is a vehicle of grace, author and nourishment of faith. If symbolically, as Protestantism holds in varying degrees, then the sacraments are but visible forms of the Word of God which conveys grace and ignites faith.

You may want to decide, too, if the Supper is properly termed "eucharist," a word suggesting celebration more than nourishment, pointing more to what *we* do than what we are *done to* in the partaking.

Yes, we have a view on these matters, one we think Biblical:

a) There are but two sacraments authorized by the Word: baptism and the Lord's Supper.

b) Because the Word is chosen vehicle of grace, faith being aroused and nourished by the Word preached and read, the sacraments find their importance for the Christian life as making the Word "visible," that is appealing to senses other than the ear to reinforce the gospel.

c) Faith is genuinely *celebrated* in works of obedience to the Word, that is, to the divine law. Sacraments nurture faith. To this end, then, we gratefully *receive* rather than *celebrate* them.

d) The Lord entrusts the administration of His sacraments to His Church, and obliges her to adhere to the conditions He sets for participation in them.

3) Finally, the Lord reveals why He establishes His Church: "teaching them (disciples) to observe all that I have commanded you...."

The Church is the Lord's school for discipleship. The textbook in that school is the Lord's Word: all that He commands disciples to know and do.

The purpose given the Church is strikingly parallel to that for which the Word which the Church preaches is given, according to St. Paul: "All scripture is inspired by God and profitable for teaching, for reproof, for correction, and for training in righteousness, that the man of God may be complete, equipped for every good work" (II Tim. 3:16-17). In short, the Word is given as textbook to discipling. And the Church is sustained as means through which such discipling takes place — the school of saints.

And these both — Church and Word — find their goal in realizing God's purpose in accepting us as disciples: "For we are his workmanship, created in Christ Jesus for good works, which God prepared beforehand, that we should walk in them" (Eph. 3:10).

This means, of course, that Church membership is a very serious and lifelong thing. How else shall we even learn *all* that the Lord requires of His disciples, let alone mature in doing His commandments? And what less can we require of the Church to which we commit our tutelage than scrupulous adherence to the Word, courageous preaching of the Word, open and integral disciplining of disobedience to it?

The Communion of Saints

The Apostles Creed lays these words upon the lips of believers: I believe a holy, catholic church; the communion of saints....

The Church creates that communion, that fellowship, with its sense of belonging to the family of God universal when the Church does its own business well — as we have been describing it.

This communion begins in the local congregation, and takes many, many forms. The congregation assembles as a family of God. We greet fellow believers as brothers and sisters, all of us through Christ children of one loving Father, who infuses us with love for each other through the Spirit. This fellowshipping in the worship service takes many forms, all intended to accent the unity believers enjoy. The Body shares common concerns, offers prayers for common and special needs. Singing unifies, and lifts hearts to God in praise and adoration. Giving draws the resources of the congregation together and focuses them upon need, through the diaconate, and upon the expenses incurred by staffing and operating the Church.

Communion of saints flowers in fellowship groups, in study groups, in youth programs, in care of the elderly, in concerns for the single, the widowed and widower, and for those in the Church's "parish" who lack goods and other expressions of love.

You will find the congregation which gives what is for you the fullest expression of that familial closeness which Christ creates with His Word and through His Spirit. Be sure to take your part in that loving unity.

Note, too, that the communion of saints binds believers together across denominational lines. It is in such communion, such common effort on many fronts, that the oneness of the Church becomes visible. Thanks to this universal unity, Christians cooperate together on many projects, despite confessional differences and doctrinal problems. In the communion of saints the Church becomes most nearly what God intends His children to be. Such communion is one of the fruits of the Word courageously preached, the sacraments faithfully administered, and discipline carefully exercised.

The Church's Being

The Church's structure is formed in accordance with the Church's purpose.

Making disciples requires preaching. The Church must, therefore, provide for pulpiteers, including their education. The Church must support her ministry, defend and encourage it, and subject it to discipline in faith and life and performance.

Paul instructs Timothy as to the selection of overseers — bishops or presbyters — to supervise the ministry and the congregation (I Tim. 3:1-7). And he provides for deacons to administer finances and charity (I Tim. 3:8-13). We discuss these offices in greater detail in our *Elders* and *Deacons Handbooks*.

In Summary

We take, we have said, a simple and pragmatic view of the Church because the Bible does so. Perhaps much that you have taken for granted as done by, or within, the Church is not here.

But what, then, as required by the Lord of His Church in the charter we have quoted from St. Matthew has been omitted here?

Can the Church which determines on her own to try to be more, or other, than her Lord demands really be an obedient, and therefore approved servant? Or is such a Church foolishly bending to trends of the times under the illusion of being relevant?

Consider what we are saying about the Church in the light of certain Biblical perspectives:

God creates and sustains the Church because:

1) He gathers in citizens for His kingdom: "But seek ye first the kingdom of heaven and its righteousness..." (Matt. 6:33). It is in the Church that such citizenship is offered and schooled.

2) The Lord Jesus looks for a family: "For whoever does the will of my Father in heaven is my brother, and sister, and mother" (Matt. 12:50). The Church exists to enlarge the Lord's family by teaching those who would join it to know and to do the will of God.

3) The Lord desires servants: "Take my yoke upon you, and learn of me" (Matt. 11:29). Through the Church Christ's yoke is laid upon our shoulders.

4) True wisdom is to be found only in discipleship under the Word: "Every one then who hears these words of mine and does them will be like a wise man who built his house upon the rock; and the rain fell, and the floods came, and the winds blew and beat upon that house, but it did not fall, because it had been founded on a rock" (Matt. 7:24-25). The Church teaches such building, and conveys by preaching such wisdom.

When you face seriously what all this involves, what it requires of those who belong to the Church, you will be far from wishing that more was required of the Lord's Body and of members in it. And you will suspect that activisms not directed to discipling are in fact evasions of the Church's primary responsibility.

There is, indeed, just such busy-ness, too: "And every one who hears these words of mine and does not do them will be like a foolish man who built his house upon the sand; and the rain fell, and the floods came, and the winds blew and beat against that house, and it fell; and great was the fall of it" (Matt. 7:26-27).

The building may be gaudy, and done with flourish; it may be so extensive that "great" will be its fall — but the Church which builds outside the divine mandate lays a foundation on sand.

Don't participate in that!

For Reflection And Discussion

1. *What is God's purpose with His Church?*
2. *How is that purpose to be realized?*
3. *What is the Church's unique duty?*
4. *How does preaching differ from, say, lecturing?*
5. *What is the promise given by the Lord to faithful preachers? Does He give it to anyone else?*
6. *How do the sacraments relate to the preaching of the Word?*
7. *Why is the Church at the center of history? Could you believe that if you did not look through the words of the Bible?*

Chapter 7.

PRAYER

*But when you pray, go into your room and shut the door
and pray to your Father who is in secret; and your Father who
sees in secret will reward you.*
Matthew 6:6

PRAYER

TRUTH:
Communion with God through prayer can range from formal petition
to the wordless and habitual "practice of the presence of God" in daily
life. The Lord's Prayer is model for our communication with Him, and
Jesus Himself urges us to persist in making our requests known to
God.
RESPONSE:
The life of prayer grows through constant exercise, based on study of
the Word's teaching and its models.
DISTORTION:
Failure to take prayer seriously, like mouthing words unrelated to
deeds, asking for what one has no intention of participating in achiev-
ing, leaving large areas of the day untouched by the awareness of
God's presence, or praying only out of habit or for show.

Pray Always!

How frustrating it is to be filled with enthusiasm for serving the
Lord, here and now, only to find nothing important to do for Him. Sets
one to thinking that the "ordinary" life offers few opportunities for
Christian service. One may envy, without admitting it, the missionary,

the preacher, the gospel crusader.... They make ripples, and sometimes headlines, for God. But we...? What can I do?

God is well aware of this frustration, and instructed Paul to relieve us of it: "And whatever you do, in word or deed, do everything in the name of the Lord Jesus, giving thanks to God the Father through him" (Col. 3:17).

Taught us here are two things:

1) Catch hold, and never let go, of the difference between the *what* we do and the *how* we do it. *What* measures the quantitative — the seeming size and importance of our doing. We are all caught up in the quantitative, thinking that size alone matters — especially things that catch the eye of others. But Christianity is concerned with the qualitative: *how* we do all that we do. What does Paul mean by doing "everything in the name of the Lord Jesus"? He means, obviously, doing whatever we do in obedience to the commands of the Lord Jesus. That's what counts along the way leading to eternal life. The *what* may be anything; the *how* may only be "obediently". There are no little acts. There are only obedient or disobedient acts, whatever the quantity involved. Christianity is everyone's religion, structured so that *how* we govern our tongues is as important as taking a city in battle. The secular mind sees only quantitatively — and so distributes its rewards. God sees qualitatively — and so distributes His rewards. Nothing to do for Christ? *Whatever* you do, do for — that is in obedience to — Christ. It will be enough.

2) Pray.

Prayer is the immediate answer to the "What can I do now?" asked by faith.

There seem to be no challenges, no opportunities, nothing at hand to go at Christianly?

Pray. It was Saul's first prayer to the Lord who appeared to him on the Damascus road: "What shall I do, Lord?" (Acts 22:10). And Saul the persecutor of the Church became Paul the greatest missionary of the Church.

When in doubt, then, pray.

You need never be immobilized by frustration as to what to do.

Prayer is always at hand. And, as the poet Tennyson has it, "More things are wrought by prayer than this world dreams of...For so the whole round earth is every way bound by gold chains about the feet of God." Add your link to that chain, *always* — as St. Paul commands.

Prayer tills the soil where the seed of the Word has been planted

100

(Matt. 13:8).

Prayer nourishes the good tree which bears the good fruit of obedience (Luke 6:43-45).

Prayer joins us with God in His government of history — for God answers prayer (Barth).

Prayer digs up for us the riches preserved in God's promises (Calvin).

Prayer exercises the muscles of faith: "For whoever would draw near to God must believe that he exists and that he rewards those who seek him" (Heb. 11:6).

How will you know if indeed you have saving faith?

Do you pray?

How will you know how strong is your faith?

Do you pray much?

How will you know if your faith is growing?

Do you want to pray more?

So central to the Christian life is prayer that God the Holy Spirit undertakes to assist us in it: "Likewise the Spirit helps us in our weakness; for we do not know how to pray as we ought, but the Spirit intercedes for us with sighs too deep for words" (Rom. 8:26).

Prayer is the atmosphere in which we inhale the very presence of God.

Prayer transcends time and foretastes eternity.

Prayer arms against the Devil, and sets boundaries to his dominion.

The good citizen of the kingdom of heaven...*prays!*

It is not by accident that the Evangelists recount for us how often and how long the Lord Jesus gave Himself to prayer: "And after he had dismissed the crowds, he went up into the hills by himself to pray" (Matt 14:23; Mark 6:46; Luke 6:12; 9:28).

If *He* needed to pray, how much more we!

So, too, the Apostles devoted themselves "to prayer and to the ministry of the word" (Acts 6:4).

And so the Church across the ages has heeded Paul's admonition: "Pray always" (I Thess. 5:17).

Nothing to do right now for the Lord?

Pray!

What, Then, Is Prayer?

Yes, it may be puzzling to know what to pray for, and how to pray.

The Lord's disciples felt that difficulty: "He was praying in a certain place, and when he ceased, one of his disciples said to him, 'Lord, teach us to pray, as John taught his disciples'" (Luke 11:1).

And in response to their — and our — plea, the Lord taught them — and us — His model prayer. We say "model" because it is not the only prayer that Jesus Himself used; so it need not be our only vehicle of communication with God either. But it is a *model*, not only for how we should pray but also for how we should live. The Lord's Prayer compacts into a few sentences a structure for the Christian life. And in our effort to pray the Lord's Prayer effectively we discover more and more what we need to pray for in order to *do* what He wants us to do.

When in doubt, then, as to what needs doing *right now* — pray!

If in doubt as to what, or how, to pray — repeat the Lord's Prayer. It is, in any case, a good way to start and end the day.

Jesus says: "After this manner, therefore, pray:

> Our Father, who art in heaven,
> Hallowed be thy name.
> Thy kingdom come, Thy will be done on earth,
>   as it is in heaven.
> Give us this day our daily bread.
> And forgive us our debts as we forgive our debtors.
> And lead us not into temptation, but deliver us
>   from evil.
> For thine is the kingdom, and the power,
>   and the glory, forever.
>
> Amen" (Matt. 6:9-13).

This is the Lord's model for our prayers.

This is, too, the Lord's pattern for our lives.

This prayer will stimulate all sorts of praying, for all sorts of blessings, the more we approach understanding its profound importance.

We will make some brief comments on each part of the Lord's Prayer, just to alert you to the scope of other prayers it will inspire and to the range of duties it involves. You can add your own interpretations. Together we will never exhaust the Prayer's full meaning.

The Lord's Prayer: Salutation

Our Father . . .

What a beginning!

"Have you not known! Have you not heard? The Lord is the everlasting God, the Creator of the ends of the earth" (Is. 40:28) — this Lord may be addressed as *our* Father!

Three things about this approach to God — as Father!

1) Remember who He is, and who you are. Come in due reverence. Indeed, come in awe — an awe that never wears off: "...let us offer to God acceptable worship, with reverence and awe; for our God is a consuming fire" (Heb. 12:28-29). Don't ab-use the term "Father" to reduce God to our level, or to elevate us to His. When Moses encountered God in the burning bush, he was instructed: "...put off your shoes from your feet, for the place on which you are standing is holy ground" (Ex. 3:5). And the Christ in Whom we stand to pray "Our Father" is no less holy. In that spirit draw near to — remember — God!

2) But awe is not at odds with joy. Joy flowers out of awe. Awe opens into light, not gloom. The more we are aware of how exalted God is, the more joyous our appreciation of Him as Father. Awe produces joy: "For you did not receive the spirit of slavery to fall back into fear, but you have received the spirit of sonship. When we cry, 'Abba, Father!' it is the Spirit himself bearing witness with our spirit that we are children of God, and if children, then heirs, heirs of God and fellow heirs with Christ, provided we suffer with him in order that we may also be glorified with him" (Rom. 8:15-17). Revel in the comfort; delight in the security; grow serene in the peace of this greatest of all condescensions: the everlasting God is our *Father*, in Jesus Christ His Son. Into whatever "far country" of disobedience we may stray, He awaits our return as did the father of the Prodigal (Luke 15:20); indeed He comes swiftly to greet us. He is even more anxious for our welfare than was King David for that of his wayward son Absalom: "Is it well with the young man Absalom?" (II Sam. 18:32).

3) God is, in fact, twice our Father.

Once by nature through our first parents Adam and Eve.

Again by grace, through faith, through the second Adam, Jesus Christ.

The first Adam is called by Scripture "the son of God" (Luke 3:38). Through him the universal brotherhood of man reflects the universal fatherhood of God. No one comes into the world as human being, save in the line of Adam's descent and from the hand of God. We are God's, and members of God's family by nature.

The first Adam repudiated God, and cast his whole progeny under the pall of sin and death.

The second Adam obeyed God, gave His life to pay for the guilt of all who believe, and restores us to God's family. In Christ, by faith, we pray: our *Father*!

Four things about approaching God as "our" Father:

1) "Our" is inclusive. To affirm God as Father means to affirm all of His children as members of *our* family — and to treat them accordingly. To forget, or ignore the meaning of, the "our" is to lose the blessing of the "Father".

2) The nearer we draw to God as "our" Father, the nearer we must be drawn to all of God's children, twice:

a) We begin to see all members of the human race as of one family with ourselves — and recognize that the gospel requires familial concern and behavior toward all human beings. This, too, is a fruit of faith.

b) We are also taught by the "our" Father to see all other believers as especially kindred to us. Paul sums up our obligations to the two forms of the human family thus: "So then, as we have opportunity, let us do good to all men, and especially to those who are of the household of faith" (Gal. 6:10).

3) We see, now, that claiming God as Father *requires* recognizing God's children as brothers and sisters. The privilege implies an obligation. So it always is with Biblical privileges. We may fool ourselves into mouthing the words as if we said only "Father" without saying "our," but God is not deceived: "Not every one who says to me, 'Lord, Lord,' shall enter the kingdom of heaven, but he who does the will of my father who is in heaven. On that day many will say to me, 'Lord, Lord, did we not prophesy in your name, and cast out demons in your name, and do many mighty works in your name?' And then will I declare to them, 'I never knew you, depart from me, you evildoers'" (Matt. 7:21-23). Unless we mean to act upon the "our," we do not really pray to the Father.

4) The family we affirm, and claim membership in, by using "our Father" in faith, is a family carefully defined by Jesus, its elder Brother: "Whoever does the will of God is my brother, and sister, and mother" (Mark 3:35). There is but one way to validate the "our Father" which we take upon our lips: it is to will, at the same time, renewed obedience to the Father we make bold so to address.

The Lord's Prayer:
Commitment To First Table Of The Law

Hallowed be Thy name . . .

Our first claim: God as our Father.

Our first commitment in return: to hallow His name.

We are asking, that is, God's help in hallowing His name. It's not our pious wish that others may do that. We have no right to lay obligation upon anyone else, least of all an obligation we do not intend to assume ourselves.

Hallow?

To keep holy. To revere. To invoke. To obey. To do whatever brings honor, and to avoid whatever brings disrepute, to God's holy name.

Name?

The name *is* the Person.

God *is* . . . *God*: "You shall have no other gods before me" (Ex. 20:3).

Here we take upon our lips a commitment to the first table of the divine Law: "You shall love the Lord your God with all your heart, and with all your soul, and with all your strength, and with all your mind..." (Luke 10:27).

This is the comprehensive commitment we undertake at this point in the model prayer. Only total dedication truly hallows His name. God's Law is to be our law; God's will is to be our will; God's Word is to be our companion always.

God's priority is the foundation of the Christian life.

Here we pledge ourselves to making that priority ever and always our own.

The Lord's Prayer:
Commitment To The Second Table Of The Law

Thy kingdom come . . .

A kingdom exists:

1) Where there is a king.

2) Where there are loyal subjects.

3) Where the subjects display their loyalty by keeping the king's laws.

This commitment means, then:

1) I pledge my allegiance to God the Father as my King.

2) I will to display that allegiance by obedience to God's Law.

In short, Thy kingdom come, beginning always with me!

And the Law of that spiritual kingdom is framed by the first table already acknowledged, and by the second table focused upon citizens' behavior toward each other: "You shall love...your neighbor as yourself" (Luke 10:27).

Thy will be done on earth as it is in heaven. . . .

Now we know, for sure, where that "kingdom" is. It's wherever God's will is done, the earth around. God's kingdom has no physical geography. It appears on no maps. But it has spiritual dimensions, and is carefully mapped in heaven: wherever His will is done, *there* is His kingdom, for there He is acknowledged as Lord and King.

There is a lot of speculation as to the meaning of the term "kingdom" as used in the Scriptures, be it "kingdom of heaven" or "kingdom of God". The model Prayer removes us from speculation to obligation: we pledge ourselves to be doing in every way whatever we can do to obey, and to have obeyed, the will of God. Wherever this occurs, in whatever forms and actions, there His kingdom appears. This is what the Lord Jesus means by saying: "But seek first his kingdom and his righteousness..." (Matt. 6:33). Here, in the Lord's Prayer, we pledge ourselves to follow just this order of priorities.

The Lord's Prayer: Petition

Give us this day our daily bread . . .

Here begin our petitions.

We ask first for all what is necessary in order to carry out the commitments we have so far made. "Daily bread" covers everything.

There are several matters to observe here:

1) Again the plural: this time "us". Also in the asking there is the recognition of our belonging to the families of God.

2) The petition is limited to the day: "this day...our daily bread...." An echo of the Lord's teaching in the same Sermon on the Mount where the Prayer appears: "Therefore be not anxious about tomorrow, for tomorrow will be anxious for itself. Let the day's own trouble be sufficient for the day" (Matt. 6:34). We are to pray *every* day; no piling

up petitions in advance so as to avoid, it may be, troubling to pray for a while.

3) "Daily bread" reminds us of the daily manna which sustained Israel for forty years in the wilderness (Ex. 16:14-36). Except for a double portion to be collected on Friday for over the Sabbath, only enough was to be taken for each person for one day: "he that gathered much had nothing over, and he that gathered little had no lack" (Ex. 16:18). He who tried to hoard the manna, discovered it spoiled the next morning. We may learn that:

a) God wants us to know, as He wanted Israel to know, that He is the source of our life and whatever sustains it. Like Israel, we turn to Him, asking: "give us *this* day...."

b) Though God no longer rains down manna, His will is obvious: if we mean the "our" and the "us" we are using in the Prayer, then it is up to us to do what we can to see to it that no one in God's family has too much nor not enough: give us, so we can give!

4) The divine economics are not our economics. We do not think of our daily bread as "given." We think of it as *earned*; we say, I ask nothing of anybody; I earn my own way! Perhaps we do, but in fact the Lord instructs us to pray "*give* us...bread."

5) Note carefully the Lord's order: first our pledge, and then our plea. Not "give us" first and then "we will do" afterwards. No, commitment first, and then: *give*. Our right to beg rests on our prior dedication to making right use of what we are given. This is the structure of all human rights: we have a right to whatever we need to perform our duties. Other claims to rights are fraudulent.

Forgive us our debts ...

If we get what we ask for, we are in God's debt. Much more than that, were we not already in His debt for uncountable blessings, we could not even find breath, or right, to pray.

In short:

1) Before our debts mount higher *this day* through the added generosity for which we plead, O God, forgive us what we already owe and can in no way repay: forgive us our debts!

2) Though we know that the bread we request should be used only to strengthen our pursuit of the commitments we have already mouthed, we know from experience that much of it will serve just ourselves. We will not share as we should. We will not obey as we ought. O

God, forgive us...!

3) We rest this plea, of course, upon the sacrifice of Jesus Christ on Calvary. If He had not there paid in full for all our debts, a just God could not simply ignore them. An indulgent Father, who winks at His children's ab-use of His gifts is not the God we serve. And such winking would not reflect "love" but rather sentimentalism. Debts come due — also those we owe God for what we ask Him to give us. In the moral universe no debt goes unpaid. Happily for those who sincerely pray these words, God has provided in advance, and in toto, for the debits we daily incur by accepting more in the way of His gifts than we repay in the way of obedience.

Does this mean, then, that we might carelessly take God's largesse with no real intention of obedience to His will?

Well, this happens. The gifts of life, time, talent and goods which all mankind enjoys are from God's hand. And how much of all that He freely provides is used, indeed, in disobedience? But not so with the believer!

St. Paul writes: "What shall we say then? Are we to continue in sin that grace may abound? By no means! How can we who died to sin still live in it?" (Rom. 6:1-2). And the Apostle adds, "God forbid!" — even the thought of ab-using His gifts.

In Christ, then: *forgive us our debts*!

As we forgive our debtors ...

There are two things to note here:

1) Jesus Himself immediately applies this petition to us, saying: "For if you forgive men their trespasses, your heavenly Father also will forgive you; but if you do not forgive men their trespasses, neither will your Father forgive you your trespasses" (Matt. 6:14-15). Sober warning. One we can hardly misunderstand.

2) Notice, however, that the Prayer uses, "forgive us our *debts*" and the Lord uses "trespasses". There is a difference. A "trespass" is a wrong done someone, a hurt, an injury. And the Lord is saying that we must freely forgive such trespassing against us. Revenge is out! But a "debt" does not imply a harm done. A "debt" means that you have received something on which, or for which, you owe repayment. That is the meaning of the Prayer: first, God, please give us; second, when He does, we are in His debt; finally and quickly we add, God, please forgive us that debt. And *then*: "as we forgive our debtors"! You, God, do it *because* we do it! (Better not say that if it isn't so!)

And how, do you suppose, could we acquire debtors to forgive?

Obviously, in the same way that God makes us His debtors: by doing good to them.

The Prayer goes beyond not repaying trespasses. The Prayer obliges us to forgive debtors as God forgives us our debts. We are, first, to create debtors by doing good to those who cannot repay. Jesus tells us how: "...if any one would sue you and take your coat, let him have your cloak as well; and if any one forces you to go one mile, go with him two miles. Give to him who begs from you, and do not refuse him who would borrow from you" (Matt. 5:40-42). This is how believers acquire debtors. And if we do so, and IF we then forgive the debts owed us, THEN we can pray: forgive us our debts, as we forgive our debtors!

A hard command?

Yes, but the Lord never said that obedience would be easy!

Lead us not into temptation . . .

That seems to be a strange petition. All the more so when we recall that St. James writes: "Let no one say when he is tempted, 'I am tempted by God'; for God cannot be tempted with evil and he himself tempts no one; but each person is tempted when he is lured and enticed by his own desire. Then desire when it has conceived gives birth to sin; and sin when it is full-grown brings forth death" (James 1:13-15).

How can the Lord instruct us to pray, then, asking God not to lead us into temptation?

We can answer that question in several ways:

1) We have just been praying for "daily bread" — that is for all that we need to keep our commitments pledged in the Prayer. God is generous. He answers before we call; He gives before we know how to ask; He is apt to shower us with more than we can handle. And this we acknowledge now: lead us not into temptation through the abundance of gifts showered upon us. We might not use too much aright! Don't tempt our selfishness beyond resistance; don't lure greed beyond our strength to resist. Give, Lord; yes, but prudently!

2) Solomon knew, and succumbed to, the temptations of God's generosity: "...give me neither poverty nor riches; feed me with the food that is needful for me, lest I be full, and deny thee, and say, 'Who is the Lord?'" (Prov. 30:8-9). This is the spirit of the Prayer.

3) Still more, we are praying that God so temper the kind and extent

of His gifts that we never fall victim to pride. We ask; God gives; and we promptly forget asking, and take all the credit for earning "every cent" ourselves! That temptation seems to loom the greater when God has given us many, many cents.

4) Notice, of course, that St. James is careful to point out that the root of all temptation is our "own desire". It is in recognition that this desire does get the better of us, all too often, that we utter this petition.

5) We ought to be thinking here, too, about our first parents, Adam and Eve. God made them free, and surrounded them with every good gift in Eden. And they rebelled. We are saying, in effect, "Don't push our freedom, Father, too far. As they fell, so might we — all the more so because we have inherited the taint of their wilfulness."

For thine is the kingdom, and the power, and the glory forever . . .

1) We acknowledge citizenship in the kingdom of heaven — God's kingdom.

2) We acknowledge that He *can* do all that we have asked — God has the power!

3) We acknowledge that life finds its purpose, and therefore all that we have petitioned finds its proper place, in the obedience which witnesses to the glory, the transcendence, the everlasting priority of the Father.

We end the Prayer on the high note that ought to characterize our lives, the joy that ought to surge through our being: the everlasting God is our Father; recall, as we repeat:

"Have you not known? Have you not heard? The Lord is the everlasting God, the Creator of the ends of the earth. He does not faint or grow weary, his understanding is unsearchable" (Is. 40:28-29).

Yes, this God is Father, in Christ, of all who believe.

The Lord's Prayer is a "model" prayer.

Its petitions cover the whole of the Christian life. It sets the tone for our prayers, and the order of first pledge, then petition.

The Lord's Prayer is not only a model. It is also a prayer we should often repeat, striving each time we do so better to perceive, and to will to obey, all that it implies. Its full meaning, and our dedication to full obedience to its implications, will always gleam far ahead of where we are.

Pray, when?

When should the believer pray?

Anytime!

Where should the believer pray?

Anywhere!

How often?

"Pray constantly" (I Thess. 5:17).

Fixed times for prayer, say on rising, on retiring, at the table, have much to commend them. But never let such scheduled occasions rob the rest of the day of prayer. "The practice of the presence of God" sets us always in the posture of prayer — not in words, but in attitude. To be ever aware of God's eye, of His hand, of His presence is a form of prayer. Such daily sensitivity to His surrounding power and love turns into prayer whenever we put into words the thanksgiving, the needs, the hopes, the fears of the hour.

God is ever present.

We may ever converse with Him in prayer.

The saint is always a person of prayer.

The world is bound to the feet of God, we have heard the poet say, by the prayers that rise from the hearts of the faithful.

Add your links to that chain every day!

For Reflection And Discussion

1. *Why does God place so much emphasis on prayer in the Scriptures?*
2. *How does the Spirit assist believers in praying?*
3. *What are some of the implications of addressing God as "our Father"?*
4. *What does the Lord imply by teaching us to pray "our" rather than "my"?*
5. *How does the Lord's Prayer relate to the two tables of the Law?*
6. *Why do we ask only for "daily" bread?*
7. *Can you explain the relation between debts forgiven us and our forgiving debtors?*
8. *What are we taught by "lead us not into temptation"?*
9. *What do we confess by the doxology which ends the Lord's Prayer?*
10. *How does the Lord's Prayer model the Christian life?*

Chapter 8.

MODELS

For to this you have been called, because Christ also suffered
for you, leaving you an example, that you should follow in
his steps.
I Peter 2:21

MODELS

TRUTH:
The Bible is a gallery of portraits, a collection of dramas, a portfolio of sketches — intended to serve the believer with models of behavior both recommended and warned against, on the sound premise that truth is caught as well as taught.
RESPONSE:
Make firm and lasting "friends" of Bible characters, and learn from each what the Lord intends to teach by having portrayed him or her in the Scriptures, never supposing that any is 'there' by accident — each is in the Word for you!
DISTORTION:
Reading Bible stories as if they were out-dated, perhaps half-mythical accounts of persons long dead and no longer relevant.

Imitators

St. Paul tells us, "Be imitators of me, as I am of Christ" (I Cor. 11:1).

There is always a subtle struggle going on within ourselves between the urgent desire to be ourselves and the temptation to pattern ourselves after what are commonly called "role models". We want to act like someone, hoping thus to achieve the success or fame that person enjoys.

Wanting to be oneself is a healthy desire — apt to take a wrong turn.

Healthy because there are, in fact, no duplicate human beings. You *are* you! No one else is; no one else can be — ever! But apt to take a wrong turn because so likely to fall into the latest fad for self-expression. Have you ever observed how conformist many would-be non-conformists become — all the same careless dress, long beards, long hair, often thoughtless in behavior and deliberately flouting moral standards and responsibilities? And they all look and act alike — just what each is desperately trying to avoid!

Perhaps you cannot make yourself an individual?

Ah, but you don't have to!

God has individualized us already! We've just pointed that out. Careful observers say that no two snowflakes are ever exact duplicates; and if that's true of the snowfall, how much more true of the family of mankind! No doubt the infinite variety among snowflakes is meant to teach us a lesson: you need not make yourself into "you" — God has provided for that in your birth.

What each of us needs to realize is that we become the unique person we are meant to be only by putting ourselves under the discipline of God's will — as revealed in His Word. Then, and only then, can we be truly, uniquely, permanently *our*selves!

Portrait Gallery

To give us an assist in becoming ourselves, God the Holy Spirit has hung the Bible, as it were, with a host of portraits of selves, sketched in the form of stories.

All kinds of children's story books are drawn from the Bible. And children listen to these stories with rapt interest. What adventures! What suspense! What battles and narrow escapes! How vivid and alive are the heroes and the heroines.

Why? Why so many stories?

To teach us something about becoming ourselves. As role models, yes; that is as models to imitate and also, sometimes, as models of what to avoid.

And more than role models, too. To teach us something about the way in which God has structured His universe.

Still more, the Biblical portrait gallery is not hung at random. As we tour the spacious rooms, pausing again and again before this and that picture of God's saints and heroes, we discover that we are following a thread — two threads, really, intertwined, one of red and one of gold.

The red thread joins the Biblical models by one characteristic: they point to the One who is coming, the fulfillment of promise, the Lamb of God whose self-sacrifice atones for sin. Again and again, we realize that strikingly powerful figures foretell the Christ: Adam, the Patriarchs, Moses, Joshua, Gideon, Samson, David — and many others illumine one aspect or another of the coming One, whose Person and deeds sum up them all. This is the red line of revelation illumined by the Biblical portrait gallery.

There is also the golden line, that of the divine Covenant. Between God and man there has ever been reciprocal relation, always structured in the same form: God will be to man all that only God can be, source of life and all good; man, in exchange, will use all that God gives in accord with God's commandments. This relationship is called "covenant". The probationary command, not to eat of one tree in the Garden of Eden, was the first test of the divine covenant — a test that man failed. God renews the covenant with fallen Adam, with Noah, with Abraham, with the liberated Israel under Moses, with David, in Christ. Always the form is the same: God is the giver, the liberator, the restorer, the guarantor of life both temporal and eternal; man is the recipient, the beneficiary, the blessed on condition that he use God's gifts and promises in accord with God's will as revealed in His Word.

The Biblical portrait gallery is hung with the dominant figures in covenantal history, those with whom God negotiated face to face and the prophets God sent to illumine the implications of His covenant.

Together, these threads bind the Biblical gallery into a unique display of God's ever active role in the history of mankind, of the Church, and of each believer — including ourselves.

We may add that a thorough study of these twin threads, running through the Bible from end to end, would constitute a volume larger than this *Handbook*. We only allude here to the obvious unity they give to the galaxy of models the Bible presents us.

Science And The Story

Let's compare science and the story as ways of getting at the truth about the world and ourselves.

Science digs into the universe, including the human body, and derives information which is marvelously useful. Most of what we call progress roots in science, at least what we call material progress.

But notice that science always deals with natural law. Science "explains" events by subsuming them under a pattern of cause and effect. The scientist "understands" what he is studying only when he has traced it back to its causes, and can predict with some accuracy its future.

The universe as explained to us by science is bound by cause and effect. The goal of science is to fit all happenings into a web of natural law.

Efforts are persistently made to subsume human behavior also under the governance of natural law. The school of psychologist B.F. Skinner, for example, formulates educational theories on the assumption that children can be "programmed" for predictable behavior on the basis of scientific theory.

No doubt one of the grounds for some of the non-conformity of our times is an unconscious reaction to being viewed as just a statistic for scientific manipulation. No one wants, instinctively, to be treated as only another cog in the great, universal web of cause and effect. For this is what science always makes of the individual — just another cog, just another nameless factor, just another item. Science dissolves the particular in the web of the universal.

Human beings wish to be treated as what they in fact are: *free!*

Science And Freedom

Science allows no scope for freedom. An atom which could go its own way would only frustrate science — and this is one of the problems with which theoretical physics has struggled since Einstein. A tree which resisted classification would be scientifically dismissed as a freak. A sun that rose off schedule has no place in the world as known to science.

And a human being who insists upon the right, indeed the obligation, to be thought of as an independent agent — as *free* — slips right through the scientific net.

Freedom and science do not mesh.

For scientific purposes, freedom is an illusion. And on this assumption theoretic science has furnished mankind with countless practical results. Nature is every day being more and more subjected to human exploitation, usually to our benefit.

It is natural, therefore, for us all to believe that science could solve problems in human relationships as it resolves puzzles in the world of nature. *If*, then, our behavior could also be subsumed under patterns of natural law.

You are welcome, of course, to believe — but don't forget that it is an act of belief, not of demonstration — that we human beings are, in fact, subject to natural laws not yet discovered. But Christianity denies that. On the simple ground that if we were not free, we could not be held responsible for our choices. Something we have already discussed.

And here enters the portrait gallery aspect of the Bible.

The Story And Freedom

What science cannot do, namely lay hold of the truth about each of us as free and particular persons, is done by the story.

Stories deal with their characters as free, as responsible, as both able and obliged to live by choices. This is true of fiction and drama, especially as created by the great writers; and this is why the playwrights of ancient Greece were the moral teachers of their times. All the more does the story lay hold of reality about life when the account is told in the Scriptures, divinely inspired to reveal only the truth.

Stories come, not to lay down laws for behavior, but to sketch in vivid colors models to be imitated, or avoided.

What a gallery of Biblical examples people the minds of those who know Bible stories: Adam, Eve, Cain and Abel, Noah, Abraham and Sarah, Moses and Mariam, Deborah, Lot and his too curious wife and over-anxious daughters, David and Jonathan, Solomon, Mary and Joseph, Paul and Timothy, the Disciples...and on and on!

Why, then, these matchless stories?

To impress our minds with witness to one truth: life is a matter of choice, for which we are ever responsible because we are in fact free.

Still more, to fortify our wills with examples of great strength and fortitude; and to stimulate our courage by observing how others met life's problems and God's challenges. And, also, to curb our despair at our failures as we see how even the greatest of the saints comes short of aspiration. They fall — and rise again! So can we! They dig in; so can we. They speak out; so can we! They show compassion, concern, and exhibit self-denial; so must we! They sometimes sin; that we must, as best we can, avoid!

In short, the characters pictured for us by the Bible were alive — as we are alive. Their times may have differed in detail from our own, but life faced them with the same kind of moral choices, the same commands from the same God, the same tempting Devil.... They can be models, therefore, because in its essentials, living does not change across the ages, nor does the will of God, nor does the basic element of choice as the sculpting agent in becoming who we are.

*   *   *

Treasure the story, especially the Bible story, then, because the story, especially in an age of science, is another avenue to the truth.

The more science trespasses upon our freedom and responsibility, the more precious the story becomes.

Do not foolishly suppose, of course, that the pulp paperbacks ground out by formula to enrich writers and publishers are avenues to truth about life. For instructive insights we must go to the classic writers of all times, and especially to the Bible.

The more some theorists try to foist natural law upon human behavior, the more resolutely must we turn to the Bible as antidote.

We are free because made in God's image. This freedom is the foundation of the Bible story.

True, that image was marred by Adam's fall, but not so marred that we are become but cogs in the universal machine so successfully controlled by science.

The thirst in psychiatry to trace conduct back, a la Freud, to our "subconscious," or to our environment, or to hidden "drives," really aims at reducing persons to things. The tendency, especially in courts of law, to attribute misconduct to causes beyond the culprit's control, really aims to make things out of persons. Beware of that!

As we observed in the discussion of repentance, only those who freely assume full responsibility for their own behavior can hope to find the divine forgiveness when that behavior violates God's will.

The story keeps that crisply alive in our minds.

Make the characters portrayed in the Bible your personal friends; and let those whose lives reflected obedience to the Lord become more and more your role models.

For obedience to the Word of God is the only way in which each of us can become truly him- and herself. All other efforts at non-conformity are counterfeit and self-defeating.

You cannot make yourself unique. You are! God has seen to that.

You can only enter upon your own uniqueness through obedience to the God who already made you that way.

Let Biblical models help you do just that.

For Reflection And Discussion

1. *How can each of us become truly and uniquely him- or herself?*
2. *Why is individualism so tempting?*
3. *Give several reasons why the Bible reports stories about so many persons.*
4. *What is the difference between scientific description and story-telling?*
5. *How is science related to freedom?*
6. *How is the story related to freedom?*
7. *Set some of the Biblical characters in the red thread of redemption culminating in Jesus Christ.*
8. *Trace the golden thread of the covenant through some of the Bible stories.*

Chapter 9.

HIS HOLY SPIRIT

There is now no condemnation to those who are in Christ Jesus, who walk not after the flesh but after the Spirit.
Romans 8:1

HIS HOLY SPIRIT

TRUTH:
The believer is required to walk "after the Spirit," and not "after the flesh," an obligation to be fulfilled only as the Spirit (lost in man's fall) re-enters the self via the Word He has "breathed" for just that purpose. The Spirit displays His presence by motivating the believer to do the "works of the Spirit" listed in the Bible.

RESPONSE:
Test persistently, and often, for the presence of the Spirit in your own life by comparing your behavior with the "works of the Spirit" taught by the Scriptures — knowing that the Spirit will enter your life via the Word, if you attend to its preaching and study.

DISTORTION:
Never disjoin Spirit from Scripture, nor presume yourself given special revelation or gifts through the Spirit unless you can validate these by the Word — nor agonize over the "sin against the Spirit".

The Spirit-Filled Life

"There is, therefore, now no condemnation to those who are in Christ Jesus," St. Paul writes, "who walk not after the flesh, but after the Spirit" (Rom. 8:1-2).

What does the Apostle mean to teach us when he says, "walk...after the Spirit"?

He explains it this way: "But you are not in the flesh but in the Spirit, if so be that the Spirit of God dwells in you" (Rom. 8:9).

Our interest, then, is receiving the indwelling of God the Holy Spirit. For it appears that the dividing line between the life of belief and the life of unbelief is the inner presence, or absence, of the Holy Spirit.

Paul writes to believers: "Do you not know that your body is a temple of the Holy Spirit within you, which you have from God? You are not your own; you were bought with a price. So glorify God in your body" (I Cor. 6:19-20).

We are not — if we want to be the Spirit's temples — our own! The way of the Spirit is not our way, but His way!

It is evident that we are either temples indwelt by God's Spirit through whom we are building upon the Rock which is Christ, or we are houses of clay built according to our own blueprints, footed upon the sand and always threatened by destruction.

On these alternatives hinges a destiny of eternal beatitude, or a destiny of eternal suffering.

Let us learn what we can, then, of the Power of the Holy Spirit in the life of the believer, with an eye to His finding in each of us a temple in which to dwell — and through which to act!

Executive Agent!

God reveals Himself to us as Trinity — one Being in three Persons, each Person no less God than the others, and the Unity as one God, not three.

The triune God reveals Himself as Creator, called Father.

The triune God reveals Himself as Redeemer, called Son.

The triune God reveals Himself as Executive, called Spirit.

In theological language this is called the "divine economy," or "economic Trinity," meaning the division of labor (economics) which God imposes upon Himself.

God acts through the Spirit:

1) Genesis opens this way: "In the beginning God created the heavens and the earth. The earth was without form and void, and darkness was upon the face of the deep; and the Spirit of God was moving over the face of the waters" (Gen. 1:1-2). The triune God acts through the Spirit. Then God speaks: "And God said, 'Let there be light;' and

there was light" (Gen. 1:3).

To Whom, do you suppose, was God speaking?

Well, who was there?

The Spirit!

Observe that already, in the first lines of Genesis, the Trinity is in action. God, the Father, initiates. He does so by speaking. Speech employs words. God, the Son, is called God's "Word" — and, St. John adds, "all things were made through him" (John 1:1-3). God the Father, then, addresses, through God the Son, commands to God the Spirit — and all is accomplished as God the Trinity wills.

2) God creates in this manner until man is made. God makes man in a unique way. We are not "spoken" into existence like all other created things. Genesis reports that "the Lord God formed man of dust from the ground, and breathed into his nostrils the breath of life; and man became a living being" (Gen. 2:7). "Breath" and "breathes" are Biblical terms for the Spirit — God gives man "life" by the gift of His Spirit.

3) But man enjoyed "spiritual" life on condition; God says, "You may freely eat of every tree of the garden; but of the tree of the knowledge of good and evil you shall not eat; for in the day you eat of it you shall die" (Gen. 2:16-17). But man does disobey! Adam eats! And man loses the indwelling presence of the Spirit. God's Spirit flees him. The sentence of spiritual death is executed! The Spirit remains busy in the creation as God's agent, still; He works in and among mankind to make civilization possible against the rage of the Devil. But both man and creation suffer the agonies of alienation from their Creator. "We know," Paul writes, "that the whole creation has been groaning in travail until now..." (Rom. 8:22).

4) Fallen man, bereft of the indwelling Spirit, comes short in every respect of the status in which he was made. Created capable of knowing the truth (Col. 3:10), and able to live as righteous and holy (Eph. 4:24), fallen man loses the light of truth, is unable to do the right which God requires, and exchanges the holy service of God for slavery to the Devil and the kingdoms of the world. In such depravity is each of us born.

5) God's plan of redemption is executed by His Spirit. The incarnation of the Son, the "Word" of God, is foretold by the Scriptures. The Spirit is agent of the Trinity in bringing the Scriptures into existence: "All scripture," writes Paul, "is inspired by God..." (II Tim. 3:16). "Inspired" means "breathed." The "breath" of God is the Holy Spirit.

6) When "the time had fully come, God sent forth his Son, born of a woman..." (Gal. 4:4). And representing the Trinity in this incarnation of the Son of God was — of course — the Holy Spirit! The angel Gabriel, sent to Mary of Nazareth, to announce to her that she shall bear God's Son, says: "The Holy Spirit will come upon you, and the power of the Most High will overshadow you; therefore the child to be born will be called holy, the Son of God" (Luke 1:35). The Spirit is Author of incarnation.

7) And when Jesus is ready to assume His ministry among men, and is baptized by John in the river Jordan, "the heaven was opened, and the Holy Spirit descended upon him in bodily form, as a dove, and a voice came from heaven, 'Thou art my beloved Son; with thee I am well pleased'" (Luke 3:21-22). Thereafter, Jesus is "full of the Holy Spirit" (Luke 4:1).

8) The Spirit serves the Son as "Executive" in Jesus' earthly ministry: "...it is by the Spirit of God that I cast out demons..." (Matt. 12:28).

9) And after God completes the Son's sacrificial role in our redemption by raising Jesus from the dead (Rom. 8:11), it is the same Holy Spirit who serves the Trinity as Executive in bringing about our salvation, as already indicated by St. Paul.

Saving Agent

"Work out your own salvation," Paul writes to us, "with fear and trembling; for God is at work in you, both to will and to work for his good pleasure" (Phil. 2:12-13).

And we may be sure that it is through the Holy Spirit that God "is at work" in us.

How, then, do we share in this divine working? For we, too, are told to be at work: "Work out your own salvation...!" How?

We have already noted that the Spirit "breathed" the Scriptures into being through the pens of those chosen to inscribe the Word.

Would it be surprising, now, to discover that the Spirit did "inspire" the Scriptures just so that He could use the Word to create faith in us, and through that faith enter upon making His temple out of ourselves?

God's purpose in using the Spirit to "breathe" the Bible into existence now becomes clear: *in this way* the Spirit provided Himself with a vehicle for entering and taking possession of the self.

God "inspired" — that is, breathed the written Word into being. We do not really know how, nor can we trace out the course of its providential preservation over the centuries. But this we can know: God "inspired" the Bible so that by means of this Word the inspiring Spirit can enter and go to "work" in the self of those who truly *hear* it! More than that we need not know!

Would you receive the faith which admits the Holy Spirit into the self?

Hear the Word! Receive precisely the vehicle which God the Spirit breathed for the express purpose of creating faith.

It is St. Paul who writes: "So, then, faith comes by hearing; and hearing by the word of God" (Rom. 10:17). The Spirit-breathed Word pursues the end for which it was "inspired" by the creation of faith in the believer. And out of faith — through faith — the Spirit works obedience.

But how is this "hearing" accomplished?

Paul tells us that, too: "How, then, shall they call on him in whom they have not believed? And how shall they believe on him of whom they have not heard? And how shall they hear without a preacher?" (Rom. 10:14).

Faith, the root of the Christian life, is created by the Spirit within the believer through the Word of God — *preached*!

This is the beginning of God's work in us.

"And how shall they preach," the Apostle goes on, "except they be sent?" (Rom. 10:15). And we recall from Chapter 6 what this means. Preaching is the primary task of the Church. She "sends" preachers into the world by means of ordination. Preaching is the unique mark of the Church, one she shares with no other institution.

And it is through the Word preached that believers acquire faith, and enjoy the ingress of the Holy Spirit.

Now we can understand an otherwise puzzling act of Jesus done on the evening of the first Easter.

The shaken band of His disciples was gathered behind closed doors. Suddenly the risen Lord was among them. "The disciples were glad when they saw the Lord," St. John records. Then Jesus said to them, "Peace be with you. As the Father has sent me, even so send I you." (John 20:21). The Lord "sends" — that is, commissions His Church, of which the disciples were representative. To do what? To preach! This is later confirmed by St. Mark: "Go into all the world and preach the gospel to every nation" (Mark 16:15).

Then Jesus does a strange thing: "And when he had said this, he breathed on them, and said to them, 'Receive the Holy Spirit'" (John 20:22).

There is something familiar about that "breathing" isn't there. There was such a "breathing" at the dawn of man's creation. Remember? "Then the Lord God formed man of dust from the ground, and breathed into his nostrils the breath of life; and man became a living soul" (Gen. 2:7). Just as spiritual life was first "breathed" into Adam at his creation, so the Holy Spirit is "breathed" into the Church by her risen Lord on the first Easter. The Holy Spirit is given once again to work among men. Christ "breathes" the Spirit into the Church so that the Word preached by those ordained in the Church can "breathe" the faith to work with the Spirit a new spiritual life in all who believe.

How then, do we receive the Spirit?

Through the Word which the Spirit inspired, preached by the Church!

One more thing: Jesus adds more to what He has already said: "If you forgive the sins of any, they are forgiven; if you retain the sins of any, they are retained" (John 20:23).

This is commonly understood to authorize the Church's discipline. And so it does. But it also relates to the Word preached. Only the Word of God truly preached, in strictest obedience to the text, conveys the Spirit. This is the Word which generates the faith which receives forgiveness of sins: "they are forgiven!" But when the preacher neglects the Word, discourses from other sources and other texts, the impoverished listeners receive no release from their sins: "they are retained!"

The Spirit In The Church

We have called the Holy Spirit the "Executive" of the Trinity.

He is not an independent agent.

The Lord makes this clear.

Jesus says: "When the Spirit of truth comes, he will guide you into all truth; for he will not speak on his own authority, but whatever he hears he will speak, and he will declare to you the things that are to come. He will glorify me, for he will take what is mine and declare it to you" (John 16:13-14).

Note how carefully Christ as the "Word" of God limits the activity of the Spirit to what "is mine"! The Spirit is bound by the written

Word! It is the Word which He Himself, of course, "inspired"! The limitation is not, therefore, a restraint upon the Spirit; it is a restraint upon us!

Why?

Because the Church is hereby taught that all claims to personal "revelations" or "Spirit-led" behavior must either be validated by the Bible — or must be rejected by believers!

Take careful note of that!

Both within and without the Church there arise those who claim "new" communications from above. Such "prophets" add that they must be true to the leading of the Spirit within them. And they claim a "liberty" unrestrained by the Scriptures or the Church. But we are instructed by Jesus that all such "revelations" are to be tested by the Bible, and rejected unless they are confirmed by the teaching of the Word.

Jesus adds that the Spirit will "bring to your remembrance all that I have said to you" (John 14:26) — indicating, no doubt, how the gospels were "inspired" and the rest of the New Testament "breathed" into existence.

But there remains no room for claims to spiritual insights or discoveries which are not clearly derived from the Word.

The centrality of the Word in the work of the Spirit is displayed on Pentecost, when the Holy Spirit is audibly and visibly given to the Church as represented by the Apostles.

The disciples are gathered in one place, and suddenly there is a sound "like the rush of a mighty wind" — reminding us once again that the Spirit comes as the "breath" of God. "Tongues of fire" rested upon each disciple — reminding us that the tongue speaks the Word, and that the Word of God is "light" in the darkness of disobedience.

Then another strange thing happens.

The sound of the wind and the glitter of the tongues of fire drew a crowd: "devout men of every nation under heaven," Luke tells us. And to their surprise these visitors to Jerusalem each heard the Apostles "speaking in his own language".

"For they were amazed and wondered, saying, 'Are not all of these who are speaking Galileans? And how is it that we hear, each of us in his own native language?'" (Adapted from Acts 2:5-11).

We must not miss the import of the miracle. The disciples were not learned men. They were speaking in the only language they knew, their own. But they were being heard in the languages of many nations. The one Word of God penetrated and shattered the divisions among men caused by diversity of tongues. The worldwide unity of the Church was thus foretold.

Note:

1) The vehicle which the Spirit uses here is the word spoken by the Apostles — the "mighty works of God" are come alive in speech. Always, in the Church, it is the word that enlivens, the "Word" that mediates between God and men, through the agency of the Holy Spirit.

2) God's Word is addressed to all mankind after Pentecost — to each in his own tongue. This worldwide mission goes on to this day!

3) Man's disunion in sin and pride were vividly displayed in the confusion of tongues at Babel (Gen. 11:1-9). Men's reunion with God, with self, and with each other is as vividly displayed at Pentecost, when the one language spoken by the Apostles was heard in languages of the world.

How Do We Get?

How do we open ourselves to entrance by the Holy Spirit, so that each of us, also, may become His temple?

This is each believer's sincere desire.

We already know the answer.

The Spirit's chosen vehicle is the Word, the Holy Scriptures truly preached, humbly searched, carefully read, thoughtfully absorbed, and understood, finally, through obedience to them.

The Spirit comes via the way the Trinity has chosen: the Bible.

Just as the ark of the covenant, containing the stone tablets of the divine Law, was centered in the heart of the Jewish temple, so the Bible upon the pulpit radiates the central fire in the Christian church. From here Pentecost is ever renewed in the Word faithfully preached.

The burden thus laid upon the Church is obvious: the Bible *must* be courageously, continuously, thoroughly exposited and applied. For only *this* Word is the Spirit's means of access to the believer's listening self.

The burden thus laid upon the believer is equally obvious: God gives to those who seek! The Spirit waits "within" the Word, as it were, upon the faithful coming of those who truly desire His "invasion" of the self. And those who really seek the Spirit's presence will not only attend upon the Word preached, but will never long be without reading and studying it by themselves. Remembering, always, why they take up the Bible: not to increase their knowledge, nor to harmonize apparent flaws in the text; but only to open themselves more and more to the flow of the Spirit along the channels He has already "inspired" for just this purpose.

Happily, God Himself assists in the true believer's seeking of His Spirit. Jesus promises: "If you then, who are evil, know how to give good gifts to your children, how much more will the heavenly Father give the Holy Spirit to those who ask him!" (Luke 11:13). This is said by the same Lord who declares: "Ask, and it will be given you..." (Matt. 7:7).

But we must remember the divine economy: God gives to those who themselves strenuously work at seeking; do not be among those who think that to "ask" is sufficient substitute for their own doing. Wishes are not the kind of horses that Christian beggars can ride.

God will do more, however.

The very Spirit, as we have noted before, for whom we ask will Himself improve upon our prayer: "...for we know not how to pray as we ought," St. Paul says, "but the Spirit himself intercedes for us" (Rom. 8:26).

The mystery of the indwelling Holy Spirit is not hidden from those who truly seek His presence. The more diligently we seek, the more certainly will He find us!

How Will We Know?

The more ardently we desire the indwelling of the Spirit, the more eager we are to "know" whether or not He chooses to live in our poor quarters.

How can we be sure?

Will we "feel" His presence?

No doubt, but the warmth of His indwelling will be an effect, and not a guarantee, lest we take the fervor of our own over-wrought emotions as evidence of His working. Nothing in the Bible suggests that the shoutings, and wailings, and swoonings induced at "charismatic" encounters do in fact testify to the active presence of God's Spirit. Self-induced psychoses counterfeit the true believer's Pentecost. It is not recorded that the Apostles themselves displayed charismatic symptoms.

Will we enjoy glossolalia, the speaking in unknown tongues, if the Spirit takes up His abode in us?

129

There are those who think so, but the Bible does not make glossolalia the *proof* of the Spirit's indwelling.

No, the Bible has its own measure, one we can easily apply to ourselves (not, mind you, to others lest we fall afoul of God's prohibition against judging others — Rom. 14:10-13).

How shall we know if the Holy Spirit is making us, more and more, His temples?

Easy, really.

God inevitably reveals His presence. The living Spirit is never without living fruits.

Question: does the Spirit dwell in me?

Answer: does my behavior display the "fruits" of His active presence?

What are these "fruits"?

The Bible carefully lists evidences of the indwelling Spirit. If we find them in our behavior, we may joyfully know that He lives within us.

Paul writes, "But the fruit of the Spirit is love, joy, peace, patience, kindness, goodness, faithfulness, gentleness, self-control..." (Gal. 5:22-23). The discovery of these in ourselves, and in our behavior, is the witness we seek for the presence of the Spirit. And not only the reality of these virtues, but the ardent desire to practice them the more, for we, like Paul, do not always succeed in living as we desire (Rom. 7:14-25).

You will observe that this list of Spirit's fruits opens outward, one evidence leading to another. For in the list quoted, Paul sets "love" as first fruit of the Spirit's presence. And elsewhere Paul expands "love" into behavior like this: "Love is patient and kind; love is not jealous or boastful; it is not arrogant or rude. Love does not insist on its own way; it is not irritable or resentful; it does not rejoice at wrong, but rejoices in the right. Love bears all things, believes all things, hopes all things, endures all things" (I Cor. 13:4-8). Again, the Sermon on the Mount with which St. Matthew opens his account of the ministry of Jesus lists still other fruits of the Spirit we are to seek in ourselves — if He truly dwells within us (Matt. 5-7).

It will soon be clear that the "fruits" of the indwelling Spirit form the ethical content of the whole Bible. And our passionate desire for assurance of His presence once again turns us to the Word of God for guidance to the obedient life. And even the eagerness with which we turn to the Word will be itself evidence of the work of the Spirit deep in our selves.

130

"A sound tree cannot bear evil fruit," Jesus says, "nor can a bad tree bear good fruit" (Matt. 7:18).

This is the Biblical test we must apply to ourselves when we wonder if indeed God the Holy Spirit dwells within us.

No other tests will do. This is the Word of the Lord: "Beware of false prophets, who come to you in sheep's clothing but inwardly are ravenous wolves. You will know them by their fruits. Are grapes gathered from thorns, or figs from thistles?" (Matt. 7:15-16).

Is this, then, a command to "judge" others?

Not at all. It is a command to avoid all "teachers" who point us anywhere but to the Word of God as access to the indwelling Spirit, and to any "fruits" but those specified by the Word as evidence of His coming.

"The words that I have spoken to you," Jesus says, "are spirit and life" (John 6:63).

There alone will we find, and receive, and test that we have God's Holy Spirit.

The Sin Against . . .

The Lord warns us that there is only one unforgiveable sin, the sin against the Holy Spirit.

"Therefore I tell you, every sin and blasphemy will be forgiven men, but the blasphemy against the Spirit will not be forgiven. And whoever says a word against the Son of man will be forgiven; but whoever speaks against the Holy Spirit will not be forgiven, either in this age or in the age to come" (Matt. 12:31-32).

This frightening language has given rise to much speculation. Precisely what does the Lord have in view here as the "sin against the Spirit"?

The context suggests that Jesus means the sin of attributing to the Devil what is really the work of God's Executive. For it was while Jesus was casting out demons that the Pharisees dared to say that it was "by Beelzebul, the prince of demons that this man casts out demons" (Matt. 12:24).

Observe that these stiff-necked teachers paid Jesus no respect. "This man" they called Him. It is with reference to this slur, no doubt, that He graciously grants that a word spoken against Him is forgiveable.

But not, He says, a word spoken against the Spirit.

Why not?

Because, as we have seen, the Holy Spirit is God's Executive. How could God "get in" if that Agent is barred because His redeeming power is deliberately attributed to His adversary, the Devil?

Demon-worship makes God-worship impossible: "You cannot," says Paul with reference to the Lord's Supper, "drink the cup of the Lord and the cup of demons" (I Cor. 10:21). The Devil is a dark reality in human history. Attributing the work of the Spirit to the power of the Devil is an awesome sin; once committed, it re-focuses a man's relation to the world in such a way that the activity of God is no longer perceived anywhere. This is characteristic of the secularism of our times, and of all times. Avoid it!

When we attribute to other powers the work that is really done by the Spirit, we cut ourselves off from the Spirit's own power. God has been made alien, His Executive means of acting upon us, and access to us, having been denied. And not only denied, but confused with the spirit of the age, the Devil himself.

We may believe, therefore, that the unforgivable sin is of man's own creation. Not that God, thereafter, ceases to seek entrance to our lives. No, His love never cools. But that man can cut himself off from the Agent whom the Trinity uses to instil divine love within the human self. Such a man has joined forces with the Devil who, in the poet Milton's words, declared in his original rebellion: "Evil be thou my Good!" Against such rebellion God reveals His love in vain.

The unforgivable sin has haunted some believers, who wonder all their lives if perchance they are guilty of it. Such a man was the father of Soren Kierkegaard, the Danish philosopher. But no doubt those who are in fact guilty of that sin are least concerned over it, for the admonitory whisper of the Spirit through the conscience has been stilled.

We are not to worry ourselves about the sin against the Spirit. But we are to beware of attributing to other sources all His mighty working in the world, and in ourselves.

Consider that the glory of the creation, the joy and beauty of natural life in its countless forms are the working, right now and always, of the ever-active Spirit. Receive the seasons, the wind and the rain, the snow and the storm as His doing. View the beauty of the mountain and the intricate tracery of the tiniest flower as His witness. Consider the order which makes society possible as His work. Hear the beauties of music and see the loveliness of the arts as of His inspiring. Accept the bounties of the soil, and fruits of human labor, as His empowering.

Never will we "see" enough of His inexhaustible activity; never will we think enough on His omnipresent working; never will we thank the triune God sufficiently for the executive action of God the Spirit.

Let such meditations, such thanksgiving, be our own antidote to fear that we may have thoughtlessly committed the unforgivable sin.

God will know, and understand, and bless!

For Reflection And Discussion

1. *What does the Bible mean by speaking of our bodies as temples of the Holy Spirit?*
2. *How do you understand the Trinity in terms of the divine "economy"?*
3. *How was the Holy Spirit active in creation?*
4. *What does St. Paul mean by saying that "the whole creation has been groaning in travail until now"?*
5. *What does it mean that upon the Fall man became spiritually "dead"?*
6. *How was the Holy Spirit involved in the birth and ordination to ministry of Jesus?*
7. *Was the Spirit active in Christ's earthly ministry? How?*
8. *What role did the Spirit play in bringing God's Word to man?*
9. *How is it possible for the spiritually "dead" to become living believers?*
10. *What use does the Spirit make of the inspired Word of God?*
11. *What was the Spirit's role in Pentecost?*
12. *What did the Apostles mean by "the mighty acts of God" in their sermons after Pentecost?*

PART III

THE BELIEVER'S FRUIT

Chapter 10.

HUMILITY

For every man who exalts himself will be humbled, and he who humbles himself will be exalted.
Luke 14:11

HUMILITY

TRUTH:
The believer must strive daily to forego being a self on his own terms, so that God can re-model us on His terms — only humility makes this possible.

RESPONSE:
With one eye always on the Lord who humbled Himself to take our flesh and die on a cross, nip every spark of pride in the bud, and learn through daily practice to follow Jesus in His teaching of humility as recorded in the gospels.

DISTORTION:
Pride — especially pride in our humility, as neatly revealed by the Lord's parable of the Pharisee and the publican.

Humility

Society is pestered, we have noted, by numbers of misguided humans recklessly bent on being all that is in them to be — bent, that is, on self-discovery through self-expression.

"Being yourself" is in fashion. Those who decline to pursue every whim are thought to be timidly out of style. Some work at self-development as if life were not time enough to get the job even decently begun. They make an eleventh commandment: "To your own self be true!" Or, better: "To your old self — if you can locate it — be always obedient!"

It happens that "to your own self be true" is the advice which Shakespeare puts in the mouth of old Polonius, a character in the play *Hamlet*. But Shakespeare's Polonius is in fact a fool.

Why does the dramatist have "be yourself" mouthed by a witless old man? Could it be because such advice is nonsense until it is clear which self is in view?

The self which we may so desperately serve is worth the finding only if it is *not* the self we are born to.

"Being yourself" is a theme which any number of people obviously should not play. The result can only be sour notes. Think of how many enemies of social order should be discouraged in every possible way from being themselves and acting according to their inclinations! "Be *not* yourself" should be their watchword.

While that may be easy to see as concerns the lawless, we ourselves walk in darkness until we ask, "Should *I* work at being *my*self?"

The answer will be "No!" unless you mean trying to be the *new* self born through faith and nurtured by the Spirit of God's Word.

And here we encounter the Biblical demand for humility: "Humble yourselves before the Lord and he will exalt you" (James 4:10). The true key to self-discovery: we — humble! God — exalting!

What Is Humility?

Humble? Humility? What's that?

Is it wringing our hands, not lifting our voices, cringing in a corner out of sight? Is it bowing and scraping before "important" people, smiling with the face, and never being heard?

No, these are characteristics of the timid, not the humble. The "your humble servant" image coming down from the days of kings, queens, and cringing courtiers is a pose. No doubt the maid often secretly despised the mistress and the valet sneered privately at his master. The obsequious are not the humble.

Humility is sparked by the Bible's call to "Repent!" Humility can enter only when its opposite, Pride, departs.

Humility, then, is the discovery that "in me (that is in my flesh) dwells no good thing" (Rom. 7:18) — by "flesh" Paul means the natural self.

If this be all, humility seems to be an easily attainable virtue. Where do we go from here?

But mouthing Paul's words in confession of total depravity is far easier than believing them — that is, acting upon them.

We deal here with one of the trickiest aspects of the believer's life and experience. We are born proud. It's an inheritance from Adam. That is to say, we are born with the "after me, you're first" attitude. We want to paddle our own canoe, steer our own ship, chart our own course — as did the Devil before his fall from heaven, and as did Adam and Eve by their sin in the garden. Thus we live, and think well enough of ourselves besides, until God's "Repent!" penetrates our smugness.

Then we may resolve to expel Pride from our premises. Now! At once! Out!

We dust off our hands. Pride has vanished!

Until we are aroused, one day, by "Repent!" to realizing that now we take pride in our humility! Pride has slipped back disguised in the cowl of the humble.

Jesus has a neat way of alerting us to this subtle invasion by Pride. He tells a story. Watch your own reaction as you read it once again:

> "He also told this parable to some who trusted in themselves that they were righteous and despised others: 'Two men went up into the temple to pray, one a Pharisee and the other a tax collector. The Pharisee stood and prayed thus with himself, "God, I thank thee that I am not like other men, extortioners, unjust, adulterers, or even like this tax collector. I fast twice a week, I give tithes of all that I get." But the tax collector, standing far off, would not even lift up his eyes to heaven, but beat his breast, saying, "God, be merciful to me a sinner!" I tell you, this man went down to his house justified rather than the other; for every one who exalts himself will be humbled, but he who humbles himself will be exalted'" (Luke 18:9-14).

Did you keep watch on yourself as you read?

And discover that you, of course, think of yourself as like...the tax collector!

No one, but *no* one, thinks himself the Pharisee.

And so we look down on the Pharisee just as he looked down on the tax collector! Which means that we, in fact, act like the Pharisee, and think ourselves as superior as did he!

Only if the parable takes our eyes off others, and leads us also to say, "Lord, be merciful to me, too, a sinner!" are we really en route to true humility.

The parable is a booby trap. Spring it on yourself from time to time to see if you are improving.

Notice that the choice which the Lord presents us in the parable is sharp and clear: either we do humble ourselves in this life, or God will humble us on the Last Day.

When the Reformer, John Calvin, was once asked what was, in his judgment, the first requirement for the Christian life, he replied, "Humility." When asked for the *second* requirement, he said, "Humility!" And the *third*? "Humility!!"

Long before Jesus told the parable quoted above, His prophet warned: "The haughty looks of man shall be brought low, and the pride of men shall be humbled; and the Lord alone will be exalted in that day. For the Lord has a day against all that is proud and lofty, against all that is lifted up and high..." (Is. 2:11-12).

When the disciples ask Jesus, "Who is the greatest in the kingdom of heaven?" He once again warns against Pride: "And calling to him a child, he put him in the midst of them, and said, 'Truly, I say to you, unless you turn and become like children, you will never enter the kingdom of heaven. Whoever humbles himself like this child, he is the greatest in the kingdom of heaven'" (Matt. 18:1-4).

"Pride," says Proverbs, "goes before destruction, and a haughty spirit before a fall" (Prov. 16:18).

Why?

Why humility?
Or, why *not* Pride?
Among other things,
1) Pride holds God away!
Humility lets God in.
Pride is the *root* of sin. Humility of repentance.
And, again, Pride is the *fruit* of sin. Humility of repentance.

Isaiah records that Lucifer, "Day Star, son of Dawn," prince among the angels, fell from heaven to become God's arch-enemy, the Devil, thanks to Pride: "How you are fallen from heaven, O Day Star, son of Dawn! How you are cut down to the ground, you who laid the nations low! You said in your heart, 'I will ascend to heaven; above the stars of God I will set my throne on high; I will sit on the mount of assembly in the far north; I will ascend above the heights of the clouds, I will make myself like the Most High.' But you are brought down to Sheol, to the depths of the Pit" (Is. 14:12-15).

Tempted by the fallen Lucifer, Adam and Eve sinned in their Pride (Gen. 3:1-19) and cast all mankind under the shadow of death.

Thereafter were all their descendants born with the same disposition to foreclose God from the counsels of the heart. Pride brooks no equal, admits no competitor.

Pride is not only "Me first!" but no less "Me alone!" Pride picks and chooses among the rules it wants to obey, and bends even them when necessary. Pride has no ear for the still, small voice of conscience and God's Law; Pride pays little mind to the pleading of others. Pride strides through history, trampling all in its way.

Yes, Pride holds God away — far away.

Pride's trademark is thus unchanged from Lucifer's rebellion to our own.

Until the spirit is broken by "Repent!" — and we see ourselves for the brazen rebels that we are — faith is impossible. How can they believe in *An*other who feel no need to be other than themselves?

This is the deadly delusion of the natural self: I do well enough on my own, thank you!

The gospel is at first too easy: *only* believe? And then it is too hard: *obey*, too?!

2) But Pride is not necessarily bested by our first encounter with "Repent!"

Pride will gladly take God or Christ on as a partner, even nominally a senior partner, so long as in fact Pride quietly runs the show.

We may make God chairman of the board, so far as decision-making is concerned — provided that in fact the old self is, say, *executive* vice-president.

God goes along for the ride, and for the front! Our language is spiced with pious talk, while our decisions are made on hard-line self-interest. We claim that God makes all the choices in our lives, but we hardly ever search His Word to find out what His will really is. Moreover, we are sure that the Bible only lays down very general precepts, which each must — and may — work out in detail for himself. That leaves the field pretty clear for whatever ventures in self-realization we want to undertake (*old*-"self"-realization, that is). We once turned everything over to Jesus, but He seems somehow to have returned it all to us — and our behavior is hardly distinguishable from an unbeliever's! What if God sees no difference at all?

Pride is back- in humility's clothes! In fact, Pride never left. We only mouthed the words, "I believe...," and "it is now no longer I that live...!"

The Pride/humility axis underlies the Christian life.

Pride is very subtle. Its temptation to set self above God will never depart us.

The Evidence

What, then, is the evidence we can look for in ourselves to see if humility has found a foothold, and Pride is being overcome?

Things like these:

1) We see that we will never make it on our own.

2) All that we most want, peace and love and security and hope, are unattainable through our most strenuous efforts. When we do grasp one or the other on our own, it quickly fleets away again.

3) Only God is the answer.

4) And He is only within the reach of faith.

5) Faith secures all that we truly need in this life and the next only when we are humble enough to wait on God for it.

6) But the faith that subdues Pride is genuine; not the pseudo-faith which in fact quickly makes — or thinks it can make — God our obedient servant. Jesus came to disciple (that is to discipline) us; not that we might ride to "success" on His shoulders!

7) Humility, then, turns us to the Bible for nourishment, for direction, for Law, for guidance. The disciple does His Master's bidding — and to do that must seek to know what the bidding is.

8) Humility not only gives God entrance, but humility keeps His Word our ever-guiding star.

How?

And how is humility achieved?

The last trick of Pride is to let us suppose that we can acquire humility on our own.

So, you want to be humble?

Good! Just go out and *be* humble!

Still making it on our own.

No, humility is a gift, too.

Seek it. Ask for it. Covet it. Pray for it. Search the Word for keys to it, and examples of it. Listen long, and often, to Jesus, who invites us so to set aside all pretension, all self-assertion, all self-interest and patiently to wait on Him for all the gifts we need — including humility.

What?

Do not, however, expect humility to reveal itself as cowardice.

The heroes of faith are not cowards (read Hebrews, chapter eleven).

Do not, either, expect humility to reveal itself as timidity, especially as to speaking out for truth, right and justice. Jesus teaches us that the world hated Him because He spoke truth to sinners. And that the world will hate His disciples for doing the same (John 15:18-23).

It is Pride that leads to bravado, to braggadocio, to violence — all covers for its emptiness.

It is humility that lends strength, courage and initiative — all because humility admits to the self the *power* of the Word and the Spirit.

Expect *real* courage from humility. Its quiet strength will make show and pretense quite unnecessary: "If God be for us, who can be against us?" says St. Paul; and adds that in all things "we are more than conquerors through him who loved us" (Rom. 8:31, 37).

The humble win!

The proud lose!

It may not look that way, from the brief perspective of time alone, but as seen from the perspective of the Word, in its light of eternity, so it really is!

Seek humility!

Seekers are finders in the kingdom of heaven (Luke 11:9).

For Reflection And Discussion

1. *How should the Christian try becoming him- or herself?*
2. *What is the difference between humility and timidity?*
3. *Why is humility so difficult to practice?*
4. *What is the challenge in applying Christ's parable about the tax collector and the Pharisee to ourselves? Does it trap you?*
5. *What did John Calvin list as primary requirements for the Christian life? How does this relate to repentance and self-denial?*
6. *Why is pride at the root of sin? Can we take pride in our humility?*
7. *What are some of the fruits of true humility?*

Chapter 11.

FORGIVING

*For if you forgive men their trespasses, your heavenly Father
also will forgive you; but if you do not forgive men their
trespasses, neither will your Father forgive your trespasses.
Matthew 6:14-15*

FORGIVING

TRUTH:
The degree of our forgiveness of those who deliberately wrong us indicates how much of God's forgiveness of our sins against Him and our neighbors we enjoy, and this includes our ability to forgive violations of "rights" we think we own.
RESPONSE:
Determined growth in the ability to forgive wrongs done us, by assuming the hurt ourselves and stedfastly declining to seek revenge.
DISTORTION:
Forgiveness of wrong does not imply timid sacrifice of the exercise of a right, nor does it mean permitting the wronging of others to avoid "getting involved".

Forgiving

The disciple Peter has a question.

He asks it for us, and the answer he received was recorded for our instruction.

Listen:

"Then Peter came up and said to Jesus, 'Lord, how often shall my brother sin against me, and I forgive him? As many as seven times?'"

The number "seven" holds a special place in the Scriptures.

Some believe that it represents completeness, perhaps because it combines the number for the Trinity — three — with the number for man — four (body, mind, will, emotions), or the number for the Trinity combined with the four elements thought to underlie all creation — earth, air, fire and water. This is, however, speculative.

Seven does figure more than any other number in Biblical symbolism: seven days in the week, the seventh day holy to the Lord, Israel's feasts scheduled in multiples of seven, seven weeks between Passover and Pentecost, the seventh year as the Sabbatical year and the forty-ninth year (7 x 7) as the Year of Jubilee. The Hebrew term used to signify "swearing" allegiance to a treaty (Gen. 21:28) implies "to do seven times", etc.

Peter does not, therefore, choose "seven times" at random. He is thinking of a long cycle of forgiveness. The injured person ought to go, Peter is thinking, the full round of forgiving sins done against him: "seven times". But, after that...! Watch out!

What does Jesus say?

He replies: "I do not say to you seven times, but seventy times seven" (Matt. 18:21-22).

Peter was no doubt astonished.

The Lord is obviously saying to him — and to us — that there should be no limit to our willingness to forgive wrongs done to ourselves. Moreover, Peter had used the term "sin against" to indicate deliberate, and knowing, wrong-doing. How often are we to forgive those who harm us or our interests *on purpose*?

Jesus says, in effect, "every time" and no less!

Who is capable of such long-suffering?

St. Luke records these words: "Take heed to yourselves; if your brother sins, rebuke him; and if he repents, forgive him; and if he sins against you seven times in the day, and turns to you seven times, and says, 'I repent,' you must forgive him."

Here is added something that helps: if he who wrongs us can say, "I repent," *then* we owe him forgiveness. Though, obviously, if he turns right around and does it all over again, we will be wondering how sincere the repentance is. Which leaves us at about the same place: *forgive*! No questions asked.

Luke adds: "The apostles said to the Lord, 'Increase our faith!'" (Luke 17:3-5).

That had better be our own reaction to the Lord's ideal! Or we will never make it! Never even want to, probably! "Lord, increase *my* faith!"

But why "such a thing" about forgiveness?

A Story

Jesus tells one of His stories to illustrate why He makes so much of our being forgiving:

> Therefore the kingdom of heaven may be compared to a king who wished to settle accounts with his servants. When he began the reckoning, one was brought to him who owed him ten thousand talents; and as he could not pay, his lord ordered him to be sold, with his wife and children and all that he had, and payment to be made. So the servant fell on his knees, imploring him, 'Lord, have patience with me, and I will pay you everything.'
>
> And out of pity for him the lord of that servant released him and forgave him the debt.
>
> But that same servant, as he went out, came upon one of his fellow servants who owed him a hundred denarii; and seizing him by the throat he said, 'Pay what you owe.'
>
> So his fellow servant fell down and besought him, 'Have patience with me, and I will pay you.'
>
> He refused and went and put him in prison till he should pay the debt.
>
> When his fellow servants saw what had taken place, they were greatly distressed, and they went and reported to their lord all that had taken place. Then his lord summoned him and said to him, 'You wicked servant! I forgave you all that debt because you besought me; and should not you have had mercy on your fellow servant, as I had mercy on you?' And in anger his lord delivered him to the jailers, till he should pay all his debt.
>
> So also my heavenly Father will do to every one of you, if you do not forgive your brother from your heart (Matt. 18:23-35).

We begin to see the importance of our being forgiving. At most, it will be but a slender return upon all that the Lord God forgives us. Still more, in order to forgive us our sins, God had to surrender His own Son to the death we so richly deserved. God paid all so that He can forgive us! Shall we try to get by with less?

The extent of our willingness to forgive others who sin against us, at whatever cost of self-discipline and refusal to take revenge, mirrors the extent of our appreciation of what it cost God to forgive ourselves. If He could give so much, can't we even give what is by comparison so little? This is suggested by the huge debt the first servant owed his master, in contrast to the small debt the second servant owed the first. This, no doubt, lies behind the Lord's "seventy times seven" — when it comes to "Forgive us our debts," the Lord sets us no limits — IF, we try to imitate Him!

Forgiveness of our sins, following upon our repentance of them, is first step to our communion with God. God can deal with us only as we are "in Christ," that is, have found forgiveness in Him. His obedience, His self-sacrifice, His resurrection must become ours — through faith — before we have access to God, and God will be Father to us. The roadblocks have to be cleared away before normal traffic between heaven and ourselves can begin, or be resumed after our sins once more interfere. Forgiveness sweeps away hindrances to communion.

Not only so as between God and the believer. Also as among believers themselves.

We cannot hold a grudge, seek revenge, plot retribution, nurse a grievance against another and at the same time enjoy fellowship together. The roadblocks have to go. From the side of the sinner there must be the confession of fault; from the side of the sinned-against, there must be wholehearted forgiveness. Then the traffic of love, conveyed by good works, can flow again as between them.

The Lord's obvious concern about being forgiving is with an eye to the "communion of the saints" — possible only when forgiveness is practiced.

Sharing

There is a kind of "pass along" character about the Christian life.

"We love," writes St. John, "because he first loved us" (I John 4:19).

The initiative is always God's!

The imitative is always to be ours!

He loves us.

And we?

We are to love Him and our neighbors in reflection of His love.

And if not?

"If any one says, 'I love God,' and hates his brother," John warns us, "he is a liar; for he who does not love his brother whom he has seen, cannot love God whom he has not seen. And this commandment we have from him, that he who loves God should love his brother also" (I John 4:20-21).

Similarly, we have been warned that if we do not forgive, freely and from the heart, those who sin against us, then God does not forgive our sins against Him.

Pass along God's gifts!

We have learned already (see Chapter 2) that the measure of the love we display reveals the weight of sins lifted from our shoulders. So it was with the "woman of the city" who anointed Jesus' feet with her tears and wiped them with her long hair. The Lord says, "Therefore, I tell you, her sins, which are many, are forgiven, for she loved much; but he who is forgiven little, loves little" (Luke 7:47).

If we, then, nourish our passion for getting even, let us perceive that this desire bears witness to sins we bear, unforgiven.

Not that the Lord suggests a kind of double entry bookkeeping as between heaven and the believer. If you, God, then I...!

No, Jesus portrays reality.

Because we enjoy forgiveness, *therefore* we are forgiving. No calculation at all. We rejoice in that we find ourselves being forgiving when we learn that willingness to forgive testifies to our having already been forgiven of our sins in the sight of the Lord.

And we are instructed by finding ourselves unwilling to forgive that we had best hurry to repentance! Perhaps confession and repentance of sins of which we have been unaware because we slight the study of God's Word.

Yes, Christianity is a religion of sharing.

Share God's love. Share God's forgiveness.

Or never really enjoy them for ourselves.

What Forgiveness Is

What does it mean to "forgive"?

It means more than just to forget. Let bygones be bygones is often good advice, but it is not forgiveness — though it may follow after forgiving.

Understanding "forgiveness" involves catching a glimpse of the moral nature of God's creation.

149

God makes His universe without flaw, and creates man without sin. We do not know why. All we know is that so God does because so God is.

Among the perfections God grants man, made in God's image, is freedom. God chooses that man shall love God freely, because any other giving of allegiance would not be love. Love can only be asked for, and given — or withheld. The love, manifest in obedience, which God asked of man was to be freely given.

But man used his God-given freedom to serve himself, in obedience to the temptation of the Devil.

The sin of disobedience, of taking another 'god' than the Creator, rent the perfection of the creation and alienated the creature from the God who had made him free.

Now what?

In God's universe every sin has consequence.

Violation of divine Law exacted its own punishment. Man loses the indwelling of the life-giving Holy Spirit, who cannot abide where an idol is also served. God cannot share sovereignty.

The Creator might have permitted His creation to dissolve. He could have decided to start it all over again. But the risk would be the same, if He made man free by sharing with him the divine Image.

There was another way.

What if God Himself assumed the penalty of death laid upon sin, and thus opened to man re-access to community with Him and eternal life?

We know that this is what God did.

In Jesus Christ the Trinity paid the price for man's defection. The death of the Son removed the penalty imposed upon sin, and all who share in the Son's self-sacrifice through faith are born to newness of life in the Spirit.

And to these the command comes to forgive sins done against themselves. What God did, His children are asked to do, namely to assume the hurt and the pain of sin done to themselves rather than to return it in kind.

Ours is the kind of creation in which sin cannot lightly be brushed aside. Sin hurts. It hurts the sinner. If the sinner is a believer, sin raises a barrier between God and himself which must be removed through confession and repentence. If the sinner is not a believer, sin adds to the burden of guilt which will on the Last Day drag him down into eternal alienation from heaven.

Sin also hurts whoever is sinned against.

And this confronts the believer with a choice. Shall we try to return the hurt in whatever form it was received or in some other way? Or shall we forgive it, meaning that we will bear the hurt, suffer the pain, endure the loss, swallow the pride — because God so commands us?

St. Paul answers this way: "Do not be overcome by evil, but overcome evil with good" (Rom. 12:21). Revenge promotes the progress of evil in the world; it multiplies sinning. The one sin becomes two. We who are warned against sinning cannot choose that way!

The Christian is under other orders: "But I say to you, Love your enemies and pray for those who persecute you, so that you may be sons of your Father who is in heaven; for he makes his sun rise on the evil and on the good, and sends rain on the just and on the unjust..." (Matt. 5:44-45).

The Lord who says this to us does not take evil lightly. He knew, above all, what payment sin exacts, and that no sinning ever goes unpaid for in God's world. When someone sins, someone pays.

But the Lord can ask the believer to be forgiving just because in Him the believer himself is forgiven — at the expense of Jesus' own life! He therefore asks less of us than we need from Him.

But this does not mean that God winks at the sins of those who seem to get away with doing evil in His world or to His children. For those who never do repent the evil done others, and the sin done therefore to the Creator, there remains a day of reckoning. The Christian who endures the suffering of evil done wrongfully to himself need not fear that the scales of right shall forever remain unbalanced.

Paul is thinking of that: "Beloved, never avenge yourselves, but leave it to the wrath of God; for it is written, 'Vengeance is mine, I will repay, says the Lord'" (Rom. 12:19, quoting Deut. 32:35).

We can forgive because the guilt of all sin and evil has already been assumed by God Himself. And we can endure, without striking back, the hurt of injustice because God will one day recompense all the sinning not confessed to Him and forgiven because He has paid for it.

This does not mean that the Christian may ever be indifferent to social or judicial injustice. The command to forgive is personal. God's demand for social and political justice is never relaxed.

What Of My Rights?

This is a good place to take note of a term on everyone's lips these days, "my rights!"

The phrase "rights of man" not only titled one of Tom Paine's inflammatory pamphlets, and appears in the Declaration of Independence, but has for centuries been stimulus to political revolution. Men revolt to secure their "just rights" for themselves and their posterity, as our Constitution has it.

The Declaration lists the innate rights of each person as "life, liberty, and the pursuit of happiness," among others not mentioned.

From these people derive innumerable "rights" which each is likely to assign himself.

There is a reason for this self-justification by way of claiming an inherent *right*.

The reason is conscience.

The human conscience records the divine Law, which comes to verbal expression in the Ten Commandments.

And the conscience sits in quiet, but intense, judgment upon human behavior. Indeed, the term conscience means "to know" (science) "with" (con). The conscience "knows" what we do, "with" — in comparison to — God's Law. And, like it or not, believe in conscience or not, each of us is constantly being put in the dock for examination of our behavior.

And the easy answer to such unpleasantness, when our wish is to do violence to God's Law, is the assertion of "right".

"I have a right," I say, when conscience indicts me for what violates divine Law. And by "right" I mean, then, an authority higher than God and His Law — an authority which rises out of the necessity to live, to succeed, to do my own thing — however I choose to define these.

I claim a "right" by virtue of necessity, or survival, to define my own traffic laws, to define my own conception of property, to define my own business ethics, to put myself ahead of everyone else. And, in the context of this chapter, I seek revenge, I decline to forgive, because the sin against me has violated my "rights". How can I forgive that? And remain true to myself?

It is evident that we deal here with an idol, the self, decked out with the trappings of innate "rights". How common an idol that is!

But what are "rights," really?

Rights are always dependent, never independent.

If we have a "right" to "life, liberty, and the pursuit of happiness," it is because we need these to perform the duties incumbent upon being human and a member of human society.

Indeed, our "rights" derive from the duties which God lays upon us in the service of Himself and the doing of good works toward our neighbors.

It is, as the Declaration says, our "Creator" who endows us with rights — and He does so because the exercise of these rights is essential to the life He prescribes for us.

There is no "right" aside from a correlative duty, which requires that right. For example, a school teacher has the "right" to demand quiet from her classroom. Why? Because the teacher has the duty to teach — and teaching requires an orderly context.

Parents have the "right" to discipline their children. Why? Because parents are held responsible by God for their childrens' upbringing.

Duty validates "right". Nothing else does.

And the duties of mankind toward God and themselves are defined in the Law (written on the conscience) by Him who "creates" us, the Lord God Himself.

God's Law reflects precisely the behavior which the duty of obedience requires of us, and limits exactly the "rights" we have. Those "rights" we assign ourselves carry no weight in heaven, and bring no lasting good upon earth.

We, therefore, can never justify refusal to forgive another on the ground that he has violated our "rights". The same God who gives us "rights" requires that we always, and willingly, forgive those who violate them by sinning against us.

The duty to forgive supersedes the status of "rights" we claim for ourselves.

For Reflection And Discussion

1. *Is there a limit which the Bible permits to the number of times we forgive wrongs done ourselves? Why or why not?*
2. *How does an unforgiving spirit compare to a traffic roadblock?*
3. *Why does God lay such emphasis on our being forgiving?*
4. *Does God's stress on forgiving imply His winking at sin? Or our winking at it?*
5. *What is the relation between "rights" and "duty" as applied to forgiving?*
6. *Are we to forgive those who do not repent of wrongs done us?*
7. *When, and how, may we revenge wrongs done ourselves? Done others?*

Chapter 12.

STEWARDSHIP

As each has received a gift, employ it for one another, as good stewards of God's varied grace.
I Peter 4:10

STEWARDSHIP

TRUTH:
All that each of us has — life, time, talent, goods, success, power, etc. — is on loan from God for the purpose of use in obedience to His will. Such obedience is blessed in the Bible as "good" stewardship, and it is by such stewardship that the conduct of believers shines as a witness to God before the world and wins divine approbation on the day of judgment.

RESPONSE:
The challenge is, first, to recognize God's hand in what we take to be our own achievements; second, to be ever thankful; third, to seek from His Word, without respite, how God wants His gifts to be used; and, finally, to strive for such obedience, and to repent of failure.

DISTORTION:
To take life, time, and talent for granted, and whatever we accomplish as done on our own; to live willingly in ignorance of God's will for the use of His gifts; and to substitute pride for charity.

Stewardship

Life, time, talent and all that each of us has are God's gifts.

How we use God's gifts in sculpting ourselves also defines what kind of stewards we are.

To all who believe, God has a Word on stewardship, just quoted from the Apostle Peter: "As each has received a gift, employ it for one another...."

Stewardship summarizes what Christian life is all about.

The Bible is textbook to good stewardship.

The school for instruction in the Bible is the Church.

The power to become good stewards is the indwelling Spirit of God, who comes into our lives via the inspired Word.

Good stewards bear fruit — that is the Biblical term for good works. That is to say, good stewards use God's gifts for the performance of good works.

Bad stewards are, from God's point of view, fruitless.

In a word, good stewards have found the narrow gate, and walk the hard road of obedience. Bad stewards have found the broad gate, and walk the way of disobedience.

As we have observed before, fruit-bearing stewardship is *not* the key to salvation. We are saved only by grace, received by the faith which grace itself creates. But fruit-bearing salvation is the *proof* of salvation, of the presence of the Spirit.

We improve on our fruit-bearing potential, then, by constant recourse to the Word of God, especially as that Word is faithfully preached in the Church we attend. And we happily observe the steady ingress of the power of that Word in a growing desire to be ever better stewards of all the gifts God entrusts to us.

The basic form of stewardship is work, and we devote a whole chapter to it.

Here let us consider the believer as God's steward, or manager, from a more general perspective.

What Is A Steward?

A steward manages another's goods. Eliezer was steward over the vast household of Abraham. That is to say Eliezer was in charge of all that Abraham owned (Gen. 24:1).

The steward owns nothing, and yet manages everything.

So it is with the believer.

We know that we can claim absolute ownership of nothing, even life itself.

All that we have is on a lease coming due at our death.

The Psalmist asks, Who is man? And answers: "Thou hast made

him little less than God, and dost crown him with glory and honor. Thou hast given him dominion over the works of thy hands; thou hast put all things under his feet..." (Ps. 8:5-6).

To us, God entrusts His temporal household. Jesus talks about that in parables of the talents and of the pounds (Matt. 25 and Luke 19).

But stewards are not independent agents. A day of reckoning is fixed for each of us. In the Lord's parable: "When he (the King) returned, having received the kingly power, he commanded those servants to whom he had given the money, to be called to him, that he might know what they had gained by trading..." (Luke 19:15).

To be a steward means facing a day of reckoning.

Such stewards we are. The Last Day, Day of Judgment, is coming. And on that Day each shall give account to the Master of his stewardship of the Master's goods.

One day we will each be asked for an accounting of our stewardship. What kind of manager are you?

Basic Principles

The Bible teaches us certain basic principles of stewardship:

1) All things are made and sustained by God: "The earth is the Lord's and the fulness thereof; the world and those who dwell therein..." (Ps. 24:1). Both the steward, and all that he has to manage, belong to God.

2) Life itself is God's gift: "In his hand is the life of every living thing and the breath of mankind" (Job 12:10).

3) God alone terminates the life He gives: "Thou turnest man back to the dust, and sayest, 'Turn back, O children of men'" (Ps. 90:3).

4) God decides on the distribution of goods which we are called upon to manage under His Law: "The Lord makes poor and makes rich; he brings low, he also exalts" (I Sam. 2:7). It is so hard for us, especially if we are materially successful, to credit God with our wealth that the Lord goes out of His way to stress His role in our accumulation of goods: "Beware lest you say in your heart, 'My power and the might of my hand have gotten me this wealth.' You shall remember the Lord your God, for it is he who gives you the power to get wealth" (Deut. 8:17). The unbeliever does not acknowledge this; as God says of faithless Israel: "And she did not know that it was I who gave her the grain, the wine, and the oil, and who lavished upon her silver and gold which they used for Baal" (Hos. 2:8). Those who do not steward God's

gifts in obedience to His Word are putting them into the service of an idol!

5) Because He is Creator and Master, God decides how we are to use His gifts aright: "Listen to my voice, and do all that I command you. So shall you be my people, and I will be your God" (Jer. 11:4).

6) God's voice is heard speaking through His Word. And His will for our management of His gifts is summarized in the Ten Commandments and all the commentary upon them spread across the Bible. The Bible is the good steward's manual.

7) Finally, all managers come to judgment: "And I saw the dead, great and small, standing before the throne, and books were opened. Also another book was opened, which is the book of life. And the dead were judged by what was written in the books, by what they had done" (Rev. 20:12).

8) Paul sums up the Biblical pattern of stewardship this way: "Do not be deceived; God is not mocked, for whatever a man sows, that he will also reap. For he who sows to his own flesh will from the flesh reap corruption; but he who sows to the Spirit will from the Spirit reap eternal life" (Gal. 6:7-8).

Mandate

Stewardship in the form of good, that is obedient, works is never optional nor incidental to the Christian life.

Fruitful management of God's gifts *is* the Christian life.

It may be that the believer becomes aware of the centrality of good management of God's gifts in a series of steps, like these:

1) At first our stress is all on "being saved".

Our concern is with salvation and the assurance of heaven.

If we think of good works at all, it is in the knowledge that no good works of our own can — or must — earn our eternal security for us.

As to doing good works, we will consider "sharing the faith" as most important, and will think of charity as something alongside the faith, coming after it.

2) Reflection upon salvation by grace, and the sacrifice made by Christ for our redemption stimulates feelings of gratitude.

The believer begins to wonder how he can act in such a way as to "show" God how thankful he is.

We give to charities, perhaps even tithe faithfully in support of the Church — to put flesh on our prayers of thanksgiving.

3) We come to see, however, that works of obedience are in fact required of believers. Stewardship is not an afterthought, or appendage to salvation. It is commanded of all who think themselves saved: "Let your light so shine before men, that they may see your good works and give glory to your Father who is in heaven" (Matt. 5:16).

Good works are now perceived as in themselves a form of witness to our faith. We obey, that is we practice good stewardship — and God gets the credit!

How the believer stewards the gifts received from God sets him, as it were, up front!

4) And this soon leads to the discovery that the Bible *equates* faith with good works. To believe *is* to obey. To disobey is *not* to believe.

Jesus asks: "Who are my mother and my brothers?" And He answers: "Whoever does the will of God is my brother, and sister, and mother" (Mark 3:33, 35). If, by faith, we are members of the Lord's family, then we are good stewards of the Lord's gifts. It is not, first faith and then obedience; no, it is *both* faith and obedience together. It is not, first being saved, and then turning to good stewardship. No, being saved and good stewardship are twins, are indeed one and the same as seen from two perspectives.

"And by this we may be sure that we know him," writes St. John, "if we keep his commandments" (I John 2:3). Jesus Himself says, "If you love me, you will keep my commandments" (John 14:15). To love the Lord is the same as to obey Him.

St. James adds: "Be doers of the word, and not hearers only, deceiving yourselves..." (James 1:22).

And St. Paul: "Owe no one anything, except to love one another; for he who loves his neighbor has fulfilled the law" (Rom. 13:8).

As to witness: "By this all men will know that you are my disciples, if you have love for one another" (John 13:35).

Looking back, now, we can see that experience with the Word leads the believer a long way from the first steps in the faith.

From viewing good stewardship as something almost incidental to salvation by faith, through perceiving it as desirable, and then as mandated, the faithful steward comes finally to understand that to believe *is* to obey, to love *is* to do good works, and being saved is precisely being good managers of God's gifts.

Forms Of Stewardship

We will observe in the next chapter that the largest single block of our lives, that devoted to our daily work, is the primary form of stewardship.

But the talent employed in our work is not the only gift the Lord entrusts to our management.

There are countless forms, really, of managerial service; among them:

1) The simple things:

How well do you steward your ability to smile, to wear a cheerful countenance, to be affirmative, to see the best in others, to lend the boost of a kind word...?

Life is full of little things — so full that together these "little" things add up to very important facets of character and experience.

The believer gradually learns to say the kindly word instead of the critical one, to take the bright view instead of the dark side.

We see as we mature that behavior in private is more revealing than what is done as deliberate show, and that true character may emerge in times of frustration and stress. That's when stewardship of lip and emotion and the exercise of self-control stand out.

You might make a useful survey of all the seemingly unimportant incidents of a day or a week — examining as you do just how well your "light" was shining in each one.

Consider that the Lord teaches us through wise Solomon: "He who is slow to anger is better than the mighty, and he who rules his spirit than he who takes a city" (Prov. 16:32). Reflect on this inspired comparison: what an accomplishment in time of battle for a general to direct an attack that takes a city! Ah yes, says the Lord — but *not* as impressive as taking command of your own unruly self! Not as important, that is, in the sight of heaven! Could it be that fewer people control their tempers than do "mighty" deeds of one kind or another? Easier to be famous for some achievement than to master flares of anger?

In short, stewardship begins at home, with the self, and with all those we meet in the course of the day.

Remember: note well how you manage the "little" things — God doesn't seem to think they are so unimportant!

2) Goods and money!

We think readily enough of managing goods and money.

160

And the way we steward our money *is* a test of obedience.

From ancient Israel onwards, the Lord asked for the tithe — one tenth — and offerings. The tithe — plus, then. And He lets us know, through St. Paul, that "God loves a cheerful giver" (II Cor. 9:7).

The Bibles gives no more precise measure than the tithe of what the good steward must give away of God's gifts to him in goods and money. But there are suggestions:

There is the story of Jesus at the temple treasury. He observes that a poor widow tosses into the collection box a matter of a few pennies. He calls His disciples to Him, to pass a lesson on to us: "Truly, I say to you, this poor widow has put in more than all those who are contributing to the treasury. For they all contributed out of their abundance; but she out of her poverty has put in everything she had, her whole living" (Mark 12:41-44).

You notice the measure the Lord uses — then and now: the amount we give is weighed in heaven by contrast to the amount we keep for ourselves. And, measured that way, the gift of a few pennies can amount to far more than the gift of great sums.

There is the story of a rich young man who wanted to know what he should do to inherit eternal life. Jesus tells him to "keep the commandments." The young man replies that so he does. Jesus then adds this: "If you would be perfect, go, sell what you possess and give to the poor, and you will have treasure in heaven; and come, follow me" (Matt. 19:16-22). This is obviously not a general rule, for the Lord did not require such divestment of Abraham or of David or of Solomon, all of whom were very rich. But if wealth becomes an idol — the message is clear!

Money represents goods.

We may sometimes have goods we can spare more easily than money. The Lord accepts that, of course.

The point always is the same: share! That is stewardship!

3) Time and self:

It is often easier to steward goods or money through sharing than it is to find time to spend with those who need our attention. But time and self are also to be managed for the good of others.

That includes a call, a card, a letter.

When you consider that most things have a price, but time is priceless because not for sale, you will conclude that stewarding the gift of time by sharing it with the lonely and bereaved is important stewardship indeed.

So is sharing yourself. No one can do that for you.

4) In short, where there is a need for something you could share, there is stewarding to do. You have no talent, no gift, for which there is not some need, somewhere. Keep eyes and ears alert for such needs.

The good steward is on the lookout for such opportunities.

And now we turn to the basic form of stewardship: work.

(We have discussed good stewardship in greater detail in both our paperbound volume entitled *God's Yardstick* and in our hardbound *Deacons Handbook*).

For Reflection And Discussion

1. *What does the Bible mean by "stewardship"?*
2. *Is there a difference between ownership and stewardship? How might this apply to the Christian life?*
3. *Unless stewardship is an important key to salvation, would the Bible place such stress upon it?*
4. *While talents and gifts obviously vary, what do all stewards share in common? Is this God's answer to both envy and pride?*
5. *What are the basic principles of Biblical stewardship? How do these apply to daily economic life?*
6. *How is stewardship an important form of witness?*
7. *What are some forms of stewardship beside our daily work?*

Chapter 13.

WORK

If anyone will not work, let him not eat.
II Thessolonian 3:10

Work

TRUTH:
Work is the highest form of stewardship, because it is the form in which we make ourselves useful to others. Therefore daily work gives meaning to life when done with the conscious intent of adding our little thread to the fabric of civilization. Still more, for the believer, daily work becomes service to the Christ, as illustrated in Jesus' parable of the Last Judgment.

RESPONSE:
Doing our daily work, whatever and wherever, at our best as service of God in the neighbor, where God waits to receive the work of our heads and hands.

DISTORTION:
To view daily work as done only for the pay check, only for satisfaction of personal interests, only for the amassing of wealth or power, thus blinding ourselves to the far larger dimensions of even the humblest occupations and robbing ourselves of divine blessing.

What Is Work?

The largest single block of our lives goes into our daily work.

By "work" we mean what anyone does to "earn" a living. We are thinking of the "work" of those who lead and manage business, industry, and politics; of those who staff the professions and the arts;

of those who do the manual and routine jobs of every kind; of those who are home-makers, of those who work the land and are on the road. We are thinking of work done anywhere by any one — including you!

How do you look at your work?

Enjoy it? (You are probably in a minority among workers in the world).

Endure it?

Despise it? Seems as if you work to live, and live to work?

Always hoping for another, and better, job?

Whatever your attitude toward your work, ask with us: what *is* work?

Our answer is: work is the form through which we make ourselves useful to others — and, therefore, from a Christian perspective, useful to God!

Work gives meaning to life.

We want to repeat that: far from robbing life of meaning, and far from obliging us to find meaning in things we do off the job, we believe that it is work that gives meaning to living. We want to help you find it there!

If you now do not see your work that way, take another a sharper look through the words that follow.

Make The Wheels . . .

Yes, work turns the wheels of civilization. All that we call civilization, or culture, rides on the backs of all the workers of the world.

Suppose, for a moment, that right now all work stopped — yours and that of every other worker. Very soon everything we take for granted would grind to a halt — no food in the stores, no water at the tap, no trucks on the road, no planes in the air, no TV to watch...surprisingly quickly, no-thing at all! Those who survived would, after a while, be huddled around campfires, living in caves and clothed with animal hides.

Or suppose that just you lost your job, or quit.

What would that mean?

To you it would mean all the hardships of unemployment.

And what would it mean to the world?

You may be tempted here to reply, "Nothing much. Who would know, or care, besides myself and my family, if I quit or lost my job?"

That is, of course, the natural thing to say — and because most workers do feel anonymous and unnecessary, their work is a burden and hardly seen as the source of meaning in life. But things are not always what they seem to be.

Consider, for example, a recession, or depression. You see that a very real loss is involved when lots of individual workers are idle. All kinds of goods and services they might be producing are lost to society. That is, indeed, the irony of recession — on the one hand, the energies of labor being unused, and on the other hand, needs for all sorts of goods or services being unmet, plus untold personal suffering. Economists try to explain this irony in various ways, and Marxist revolutions feed upon it. But without entering into the theory of the thing, we simply note with you that when lots of jobs are lost, the effect is very clear — needs are unmet! So it is obviously untrue to think that work has *no* meaning! It *means* as we have said, culture and civilization!

Now, back to your job.

It is true that not many might notice if you did, or did not, show up for work. It is probably true that any number of other people probably could do whatever you are working at now. No one, they say, is irreplaceable, and that's probably so.

But that's not the point.

When you work, whatever your job is, something gets done. No matter if no one notices; no matter if any one else could do the same. You *do* the work! *You* do the work!

And what, then, does that mean?

It means that you add one thread, large or small, to the gigantic fabric which we call civilization. And without that fabric, we have already noticed, life as we take it for granted would be impossible.

And so we repeat: your work is the form through which you make yourself useful to mankind, by sharing in making the garment of civilization.

You may not think your efforts count much. Nobody has ever told you that they do. Fact is, though, that without the individual drops, there would never be a rain storm; without the individual flakes, there would never be a blizzard. And fact is, there are showers and snow storms only because the individual drops and flakes *are* there!

In precisely the same way, culture and civilization are possible only because individual workers are on the job — you included!

On the other hand, you might just be among those whose work is conspicuous — among the leaders of business and industry, the noted

and the named and the powerful. So you have no doubt of your importance, and perhaps assume that no one could really do your job in your
place. We do not detract from the importance of leadership jobs in
civilization. But we do observe that when you drive your car, there is
no way of knowing what contribution was made to its creation by the
president of the company and by the night-work custodian. All work,
finally, blends into the production of goods and services useful to
others. And thus all working has meaning, and gives meaning to the
life of the worker!

We think of it this way:

1) The farmer lays a blanket of seed upon his field...and, behold! a
harvest!

2) Labor lays a blanket of work upon the world...and, behold! a
civilization!

Work transforms your energies of head and hand into culture.

And that is how work gives meaning to your life!

Your Pay Check!

You, of course, like the rest of us, work to earn your living.

You think far more of wage or salary *for* working than of making
yourself useful to others *through* working. Yes, indeed. Don't we all?

And the pay check becomes the means for buying in on the goods
and services produced by others.

Exactly.

The more you earn, the more you can enjoy of all the things created
for you through the work of mankind.

And if you look at it closely for a while, you observe that in fact you
do enjoy far more of the things made by the work done by others than
you could ever provide for yourself alone.

If you doubt that, look around you for a moment from wherever you
are reading these lines.

How long, do you think, it would have taken you — alone — to make
the furnishings in your home, be they few or many? If, that is, you had
to start, say, the chair you are sitting on from scratch, and carry it
through to where it now supports you? Cutting the tree in the woods,
transporting it to the mill, getting it formed and finished in the shop,
while finding the ore and smelting the springs, and making the thread
for the fabric, and so on? Or think of how long you would be in as-
sembling your own automobile, piece by piece! To say nothing of

paving the streets you drive, creating the highways you use, erecting the stores you shop in, and so on, and on, and on....

True it is, indeed, that we need the pay check or bonus we earn to buy in on all we enjoy. But it's no less true that what we can make in wage or salary in a week goes to provide us with far more than we could ever have made for ourselves in the time it takes to earn the income!

Yes, there is something mysterious about it. Work gets congealed, as it were, in all kinds of goods. More precisely, workers themselves get congealed in all kinds of goods and services — because when you put your energies into working, you are putting yourself into what you share in making or doing. That is why you are weary at the end of the day — something of your self has gone out through the work of head or hand, and now belongs to whatever it is that you share in making or doing. The furnishings you see about you, right now, could tell you lots of stories of hard work, painful work, unnoticed work and worry in the shop, front office, and board room — if they could speak for each worker who has invested something of him or her self in what now serves you.

That's why we compare working with sowing seed.

Everyone knows that grain planted, multiplies itself. No one knows exactly how or why.

And we can know, if we are willing to look, that whatever we earn for working provides us with the use of far more than we could ever have made on our own. Perhaps no one knows exactly how or why, either.

We, however, believe that God opens His hand when the fields produce richly, and no less when the work of the world provides so many of God's children with more than they could otherwise enjoy.

The Bible sheds light on work, and the meaning which work gives to our lives.

Let's look and see.

The Word On Work

The Bible sets work in the light of divine revelation from countless perspectives. One of them is revealed through the following parable told by Jesus, as descriptive of the Last Day — that awesome Day when the world will be brought to final judgment.

The Lord says:

167

"When the Son of man comes in his glory, and all the angels with him, then he will sit on his glorious throne. Before him will be gathered all the nations, and he will separate them one from another as a shepherd separates the sheep from the goats, and he will place the sheep at his right hand, but the goats at the left. Then the King will say to those at his right hand, 'Come, O blessed of my Father, inherit the kingdom prepared for you from the foundation of the world; for I was hungry and you gave me food, I was thirsty and you gave me drink, I was a stranger and you welcomed me; I was naked and you clothed me, I was sick and you visited me, I was in prison and you came to me.' Then the righteous will answer him, 'Lord, when did we see thee hungry and feed thee, or thirsty and give thee drink? And when did we see thee a stranger and welcome thee, or naked and clothe thee? And when did we see thee sick or in prison and visit thee?' And the King will answer them, 'Truly, I say to you, as you did it to one of the least of these my brethren, you did it to me.' Then he will say to those at his left hand, 'Depart from me, you cursed, into the eternal fire prepared for the devil and his angels; for I was hungry and you gave me no food, I was thirsty and you gave me no drink, I was a stranger and you did not welcome me, naked and you did not clothe me, sick and in prison and you did not visit me.' Then they also will answer, 'Lord, when did we see thee hungry or thirsty or a stranger or naked or sick or in prison, and did not minister to thee?' Then he will answer them, 'Truly, I say to you, as you did it not to one of the least of these, you did it not to me.' And they will go away into eternal punishment, but the righteous into eternal life" (Matt. 25:31-46).

* * *

But what has this awesome account to do with work?

Work And Judgment

The parable quoted in the preceding section illumines work by the bright light of divine revelation.

You may not have read the parable that way. Perhaps it seemed to commend special acts of giving, charities we ought to be doing in our spare time?

It does that, no doubt. The Lord does not specify when, or where, the good deeds He blesses are done. But He obviously is speaking of more than avocational behavior, or pastime kindnesses. Why? Because He hinges our entire eternal destiny upon giving ourselves to the service of others.

And this, you will recall, is how we have already defined...work!

Did you notice, by the way, that the Day described in the parable might as readily be called the Day of Illumination as the Day of Judgment?

Do you recall when the sheep were separated from the goats? Was it after the Lord had pronounced His judgment upon all those assembled before Him? Did He, so to speak, add up accounts, and then pass judgment?

Not at all!

The separation of sheep from goat is not made *after* the Lord's judgment is announced. The awful separation has taken place *before* a word is spoken: "Before him will be gathered all the nations, and he will separate them one from another as a shepherd separates the sheep from the goats, and he will place the sheep at his right hand, but the goats on the left. Then the King will say..." (Matt. 25:32-34).

Before the Lord says a word, the separation has been made. The Judge does not designate some sheep and others goats. No, the sheep *came* as sheep; the goats *came* as goats. Those who arrived as "sheep" are guided to His right hand; those who arrived as "goats" are herded to His left! *Before*, mind you, a word is said!

Sheep and goats are gathered with their kind *first of all*, and then what happens?

Only then come the words of judgment.

No, not the words of judgment. Rather, the words of explanation! Words which shed light upon who each of us had made himself en route to that Last Day. Each is told what he or she has become — and how that took place! We will "see" at last what life has been all about.

What life has been "all about"?

Yes. We will "see" then, if we decline to look about us in the light of revelation now, that life is simply the process of becoming "sheep" or "goat".

And the dividing line in all such becoming is starkly obvious: the willingness (sheep) or the refusal (goat) to give of our selves to the service of others! This is exactly what the Lord teaches by the parable.

We become who we are, the parable shows us, through the spirit and aim of why and how we work!

"I Was..." And You...

In the light of the parable, let us "look" at your work in terms like these:

"I was hungry and you gave me food...."

The Lord is saying that He is present in human hunger. He waits there to be served. Yes, to be served by the work of those who perceive what work really is!

The Lord God is hungry! And you are serving Him *because* you:

—work in agriculture!

—work in wholesale or retail foods!

—work in kitchen or restaurant!

—work in food transportation or the mass production of food items!

—work in the manufacture of implements used in agriculture, or in any of the countless food-related industries.

—work in the innumerable support services and enterprises which together make food production and distribution possible!

The God whose bounties turn plantings into harvests waits on the energies of those whose work turns harvests into one of the basic elements of civilization. The gift of yourself to others through your work *is* the gift of yourself to God — and this is why your work has both temporal and eternal meaning, and gives such meaning to your life!

*   *   *

"I was thirsty and you gave me drink...."

Obviously, the Lord is getting at the basic necessities of human life. First, food, now water. And you serve Him, then, when your working contributes to the availability of water, be it for human consumption or the production of food. The Lord is "thirsty" and you serve Him, through the service of others, by:

—working in municipal or private water services!

—working in purifying water!

—working at the exploration for, or desalinization of, water!

—working in well-drilling, pipe-laying, plumbing installation or

170

maintenance!

—working in the manufacture or servicing of water-related equipment!

—working in the countless water-related goods and service industries!

The God whose cycle of evaporation and return replenishes the earth's water supply, waits on the service of those whose work refreshes the thirsty with life-giving water. The gift of yourself to civilized life through your work *is* the gift of yourself to God. A gift He will in due season — if your "aim" be to serve Him — reward at His right hand!

* * *

"I was naked and you clothed me...."

The third and last of the so-called basic necessities of life.

It is clear by now, if it was not so before, that the Lord is talking about far more than incidental charities in this parable. He is talking about the world's work! And the scope of the parable embraces all the work required to provide society with the basic physical necessities of life.

Here Jesus is saying, "I was in need of shelter and clothing, and you are working":

—in textiles!

—in building and repair of dwellings!

—in sales of clothing and shelter items!

—in fire and police protection of property!

—in real estate and insurance!

—in the, who knows how many, goods and service occupations related to clothing and shelter!

* * *

It becomes evident that the Lord's choice of the kinds of service which are instanced in the parable is a carefully calculated catalog of those fundamental physical goods and services without which human life would be impossible. The parable is not phrased at random. And it comprehends a vast number of jobs of mankind. The provision of food, drink, clothing, and shelter for the world is by no means pastime occupation.

Jesus is talking about our work!

"I Am . . . " And You . . .

You will notice a new tense in the caption.

In the previous section the title reads, "I Was...."

Now, it is, "I Am...."

Why the change?

To stress a point!

The parable is retrospective. From the parable's point of view, it's all over. Time has been rolled up like a scroll. All the world's clocks have stopped, the bells are silent, alarms sound no more. The trial period is ended. Life has been lived. Judge and the judged are looking back upon the irremediable. Sheep *are* sheep; goats *are* goats. Nothing left but finding that out.

Happily, for us it is not yet so!

We are still given time to "see" what the parable intends to illumine for us. Namely, that what we do indicates precisely what we are becoming.

The self we are sculpting is taking on the lineaments of..."sheep" or "goat" — there are no other options. Ours may be a very humble "sheep-like-ness' or a very elegant "goat-liness". No matter. What concerns us, here, is that every choice we make sculpts one form or the other.

The parable is meant to let us "see" this crucial aspect of what it means to live, right now.

It was not only yesterday that the Lord waited in the persons whom we can aim to serve through our work, but it is right now, today. "Now" is, in fact, all that time ever allows us. We may remember the past and anticipate the future, but we live only and always in the "now," the "today". And so the Apostle cautions us, "Today, when you hear his voice, do not harden your hearts..." (Heb. 3:15, quoting Ps. 95:7). Or, in the terms we have been using, *now* is the moment to "look" at your work anew, to focus or to refocus your aims in the light of revelation.

*   *   *

"Man does not live by bread alone" (Deut. 8:3; quoted by Jesus in Matt. 4:4).

Having blessed as done to Himself the work required to provide mankind with the basic physical necessities of life, the Lord turns to the other essentials of culture — so that, finally, the parable embraces the whole gamut of human labor.

* * *

Health is on the boundary between the physical and the mental, or spiritual. And the Lord says, "I am sick, and you...":
—work in medical services!
—work in counseling, visiting, healing!
—work in the making or selling of medicines, or in related research!
—work in health insurance!
—work in therapy!
—are serving others through working in any of the numerous health-related occupations.

* * *

Spiritual health is nurtured in communion with each other. To be human is to be in relation with others. Communion is the fruit of communication. Culture *means* togetherness. And togetherness is served by countless human occupations.

"I am a stranger," the Lord says, for all who seek communion through communication, "and you":
—work for a telephone company!
—work at delivering the mail!
—work in public or private charitable service!
—work at keeping cars moving, roads open, and commercial means of travel running!
—work in any of the innumerable avenues of service which keep people in communication with each other and the world!

* * *

"I am in prison...."
God chooses to be found among the "outcasts" of society, among those whom Franz Fannon called "The Wretched Of The Earth" — those literally imprisoned, and in those held hostage by ignorance, fear, exploitation, tyranny; "and you...":
—work in social services, professional or voluntary!
—work in law or the courts on behalf of justice!
—work in education!
—work in politics and government, or serve in the military!
—work at providing employment!
—work in human rehabilitation!

Including Your Own!

Have we missed the particular kind of work you do?

Not surprising. There are thousands of occupations.

Observe, though, that the parable includes your job.

First, we noticed, the Lord mentions the basic physical needs which civilization requires. Then He turns to specifically human interests — the need for health, for companionship, for concern and compassion.

Together these comprehend what man, as man, works for: the goods and services devoted to the body, and the goods and services devoted to mind and spirit.

Whatever it is that you work at, God waits to be served by your efforts!

What is done for others turns out to be done to God Himself!

It is in this revealed light that we can "see" why work not only has meaning in itself, but can give meaning to life.

We can now "see" why St. Benedict could say, "To work is to pray!"

And we may add, "To work is to love — both God and neighbor!"

For the "love" required by the Bible is the service of God through the service of man.

Some work, of course, violates the laws of God and man. Such work makes only "goats".

Intention

If to work is to love, what then is the basis of the Lord's separation between "sheep" and "goats"?

Did only the "sheep" work?

That is hardly likely.

The crucial difference between "sheep" and "goat" is one of purpose, of intent, of aim in life.

"Sheep" differs from "goat," say in "set of sail" or "point of compass" or, simply, "what am I really *after*?"

It is obvious from the parable that there is surprise on both sides of the glorious throne on that Day of Illumination.

The "sheep" are not surprised to discover that they had indeed been of service to others. This, apparently, was clear to them as they worked. Rather, the sheep are surprised to discover Whom they were serving in the work which placed themselves at the service of others.

They served God Himself!

"Goats" are surprised, too.

Why?

Because it never occurred to them that refusing to "see" work as the gift of self to another was refusal to serve God! How were they to know that working solely with their own self-interest in view was robbing God Himself!

Let us attend thoughtfully to what is being taught us about our own destiny by this same parable.

First, the simple facts:

1) Those on the Lord's right hand put themselves there by serving the needs of others. What surprises them is that in so doing they were serving God Himself.

2) Those on the Lord's left hand put themselves there by refusing to do their work with the aim of thus serving the needs of others. What frustrates them is the belated perception that it was God whom they robbed in their single-eyed concern for their own self-interest. They will have an eternity to reflect upon their temporal blindness!

In a word: the evidence is plain, and not denied on either side. "Sheep" *aimed* to serve others; "goats" *aimed* to serve themselves.

As applied to work, this follows: those who "see" their work as giving themselves to the service of others, *aim* to play the constructive role of weaving their small threads into the fabric of civilization — and discover, soon or late, that they are thus serving God. While those who *aim* only at the pay check, which they intend to spend only upon themselves, do in fact serve God's purposes in history — but only as against their own intent, and therefore without divine approbation or reward.

It is highly likely, too, that those whose "set of sail" or "point of compass" is outward, toward and for others, "aim" also at the integrity of a job well done. And it is equally likely that those whose only concern is the pay check are not always too scrupulous about how well they earn it.

If our lives are patterned by not only "me first" but "me alone," our aims are shaped accordingly. If, on the other hand, we choose to join our work with that of all other workers in knitting the garment of civilized life, God takes note — with intent to reward.

To "see" this is to *know* that life gets its temporal meaning from our working — a meaning made eternal as we "see" that our own work serves God by serving man.

At issue, therefore, is our "aim" in the light of what we can "see".

The Lord makes no excuse for voluntary blindness. Those on His left hand *could* have seen life as finding meaning in the service of others. That they declined so to see, and so to live, becomes their own judgment upon themselves. And the Lord simply assigns "goats" to the place where "goats" could alone belong — among their kind, in the alienation from each other and from God that they practised in life. This is, by the way, the theme of Dante's great poem, *The Divine Comedy*. We go, the great poet teaches, for eternity, exactly where we have been "aiming" to go all our lives — to the blessed union with others and with God to which we have been giving our selves, or to the alienation from God and others which we have so consciously practised.

Ratio

We've been suggesting all along that work has meaning, as work, whatever your particular job may be.

We, of course, rate some jobs as far more important than others. And we tend to forget that the fabric of civilization, like a chain, is as good as its smallest fiber. The mosaic of culture has its beauty in the harmony of each tiny particle with the whole.

The poet Longfellow puts it this way:

> Nothing useless is or low;
> Each thing in its place is best;
> And what seems but idle show
> Strengthens and supports the rest.

The ratio of importance which divine revelation applies to work is not between one job and another, but between each worker's ability and the use he makes of it. Not, what *is* your job? But, how well do you do it?

This is taught us by another of the Lord's parables:

"For it is as when a man going on a journey called his servants and entrusted to them his property; to one he gave five talents, to another two, to another one, to each according to his ability. Then he went away.

He who received the five talents went at once and traded with them; and he made five talents more. So also, he who had the two talents made two talents more. But he who received the one talent went and dug in the ground and hid his master's money.

Now after a long time the master of these servants came and settled accounts with them.

And he who had received the five talents came forward, bringing five talents more, saying, 'Master, you delivered to me five talents; here I have made five talents more.'

His master said to Him, 'Well done, good and faithful servant; you have been faithful over a little, I will set you over much; enter into the joy of your master.'

And he also who had the two talents came forward, saying, 'Master, you delivered me two talents; here I have made two talents more.'

His master said to him, 'Well done, good and faithful servant; you have been faithful over a little, I will set you over much; enter into the joy of your master.'

He also who had received the one talent came forward, saying, 'Master, I knew you to be a hard man, reaping where you did not sow, and gathering where you did not winnow; so I was afraid, and I went and hid your talent in the ground. Here you have what is yours.'

But his master answered him, 'You wicked and slothful servant! You knew that I reap where I have not sowed, and gathered where I have not winnowed? Then you ought to have invested my money with the bankers, and at my coming I should have received my own with interest. So take the talent from him, and give it to him who has ten talents. For to every one who has will more be given, and he will have abundance; but from him who has not, even what he has will be taken away. And cast the worthless servant into outer darkness; there men will gnash their teeth'' (Matt. 25:14-30).

Ratio Continued

We can "see" things like the following in the light of the just quoted parable:

1) Whatever our talents are, they are sheer gift. We came into the world without our consent, and we arrived when and where God, through others, determined. And it is He, finally, who chose to endow us with whatever skills and abilities we possess.

2) To each of us, however, was given the task of discerning and developing and deploying for use such talents as we were given.

3) We are to use our abilities on the Lord's business, so that in the end we can present Him a return on His investment.

4) The Lord's business is, obviously, service. That is why each of the characters in the parable is called a "servant".

5) The faithful servant works, you noticed, at full capacity. That is the ratio God requires — full use of whatever talents we are given. Five-talent people are required to turn in a five-talent performance; so also with two-talent folk, and so on. His is the choice as to our talents; ours is the duty to use them well and to the full. The kind of talents we have defines the purposes for which He lends them to us, and broadly limits the kinds of work we can hope to do.

6) The crucial difference between jobs, then, is not *what* your talents qualify you to do — that's the Lord's business; the crucial difference is *how well* each of us does what we are at work to do — that's our business.

7) Notice, too, that in the eye of heaven the differences we think important don't seem to loom so large. Five-talent people may be very "successful," stirring their pride and our envy; one-talent people risk our contempt and their own despair. But in the Master's eye each is on the same level. The distinctions which loom so large among us, rate pretty much the same as seen from eternity: the Master pronounces the very same commendation upon the work of the two-talented folks as He does upon that of the five-talented: "Well done, good and faithful servant; you have been faithful *over a little*...." No ground for pride; no excuse for envy. What counts in the Master's sight is the ratio between gift and performance, whether at the level of five talents or of two.

How well are *you* doing what your job requires? How persistently are you reaching out to do it better? That's His concern. The question is one of ratio, between gift and performance.

8) Note also that each of the faithful servants received the same reward: "enter into the joy of your master." Work well done in the public eye, like that of famous and successful people, will receive its due reward at the Last Day. Work done in the most unknown of places by the most unrecognized of workers, will receive its due reward at the Last Day. The promise to each, and to all, is the same, the same glorious prospect opens for both: the "joy" of the Master: "Eye has not seen, nor ear heard, nor the heart of man conceived, what God has prepared for those who love him," the Apostle writes (I Cor. 2:9). The quality of the love made manifest in work is a matter of ratio between

talent and its use. Precisely the same commendation is given to all who use well whatever the Master entrusts to their care. It's all a matter of ratio. Remember it next time you are tempted by envy — or by pride!

9) And there is that third chap, the ground-digging type. Surly, unappreciative, afraid to venture the use of his skills lest he benefit someone else. No true worker, he. No intention of using his talent for the advantage of the Giver through the service of those where the Giver wills to be found. Able to make something of a case, from his perspective, too: why should I be using my energies for anybody else? What do I owe anyone? Why let another reap what he has not planted, and harvest any benefits from my efforts? Do you know the type? There are too many of them around, crouched over talents they might just as well have hidden in the ground. Goats in the making. Not *you*, surely!!

In summary, there's no room, come the Last Day, for pride or arrogance. What do you have that you were not given? There's no room, either, for discontent or envy. It's all in the ratio — between gift and giving, through work!

Executive Stewardship

An executive is one who makes and carries out decisions.

You are such an executive.

You noted, no doubt, that both "sheep" and "goats" arrive at the glorious throne without any baggage. No evidence of learning, of academic degrees, of wealth or power. All these have been left behind. Each executive comes bearing only what he has made of himself through choosing, moment by moment, "for" the service of others, or "for" the service of self. We are each stripped down to "who" we are — "sheep" or "goat". Nothing else matters any longer. All the world's distinctions are left behind.

The prophet Job puts it this way after he had lost much of his vast possessions, including his children: "Naked I came from my mother's womb, and naked shall I return; the Lord gave, and the Lord has taken away; blessed be the name of the Lord" (Job 1:21).

Dispossessed by death of all our accomplishments, we stand at last simply as selves on one side or the other of God's judgment seat.

How did we get to that one side or the other?

Through executive stewardship.

Executive? Yes, by way of our choices! We have taken note of that.

Stewardship?

That's the name for how we use, by way of our choices, all that God places on loan to us just for that purpose.

Did you suppose that your talents, be they few or many, are solely for your own aggrandizement? And do you imagine that a crumb or two tossed to those in whose needs God tests your stewardship of His gifts will settle accounts with the Donor?

There can be no more serious blunder!

The servant given five talents returned *all* his profits to his Master! And we are thereby taught that the executive stewardship required of "sheep" is the "aim" of making all talents *serve* man and God!

"Seen," then, in the light of the inspired Word of God, life for each of us is the practice of executive stewardship.

God endows each with certain talents. These guide us, finally, into the kind of jobs we have. What matters to the all-seeing eye always fastened upon us is what we do with what we have been given. Do we seek to serve God through the service of man? Do we seek to serve ourselves, giving grudgingly of our talents to the common good? An executive decision becoming real in every choice — and gradually shaping us into candidacy for the right or the left hand of the Lord.

That's what living, finally, comes down to:

Executive decision.

Don't make either one of two fatal errors:

1) Don't imagine that just because no one seems to notice, or to care, what you do with your talents, therefore God, too, winks at your work. He gave you the skills, whatever they are, which you use in working. In fact, He gave you the job you have, like it or not. Just to "see" how you would behave as executive! Work that way! He is always looking on! Always!

2) Don't suppose that just because success crowns your efforts, and the world fawns at your feet, all this adulation, wealth, and power reflects divine approval of your executive stewardship. All depends upon your "aim," you know! He sees our motives, and it is these which finally point the way our choices are taking us. Yes, God watches, and His judgment is according to the same standard set for us by the Lord Jesus: "Do not judge by appearances, but judge with right judgment" (John 7:24).

And within the scope of executive stewardship we find the place of the pay check — both as to who pays it, and as to how we use it.

Business and industrial leadership involves stewardship of income. Payment of wages and salaries is a part of that stewardship. Each employee "needs" what is required to equip him for the work he does, and the obligations he rightfully has to family and society. Each employer "needs" what is required to fit him for the heavy responsibilities of his job, and the obligations he rightfully owes family and society.

All is a matter of stewardship.

What the employer does with company income, and his own, and what the employee does with his pay check becomes a part of the pattern of executive stewardship judged, finally, by the kind of self it creates.

God's economics is an economics of conscience — and final judgment.

That is to say, an economics of executive stewardship!

Reward!

The Bible has a thing about double-dipping!

Not that God seems to be skittish about giving rewards for obedience.

No, unlike some child psychologists, God favors rewarding good behavior. He simply does not seem to like rewarding it twice!

Reward, yes: "Give, and it will be given you; good measure, pressed down, shaken together, running over, will be put in your lap. For the measure you give will be the measure you get back" (Luke 6:38). Bear that well in mind next time you force yourself to go to work! Whatever your job, whatever you give to it for the benefit of others, is being recorded — and will be over-repaid beyond measure when you enter the "joy" of your Master!

Unless, it seems, you claim your reward *now*! That is, unless you do your work solely for what you can get out of it, and aim entirely at what the pay check will buy for you. Then the pay check, the salary, the bonus, the profit — whatever form your reward assumes — is *all* you are going to get!

The Lord tells a parable to make this point:

It is the familiar account of the "rich man" who declined to serve the needs of a poor beggar named Lazarus, who lay at his gate until he died. The rich man died, too. And Lazarus was rewarded. For what? For testing the rich man's sense of executive stewardship!

Lazarus finds himself in heaven. The rich man finds himself in hell.

"Seeing" at last what he had been blind to in life, the rich man finally thinks of others. He asks Abraham, with whom Lazarus now shares the joy of his Lord, to send messengers to brothers still alive. He hopes to warn them to exercise obedient stewardship of the talents God has on loan to them.

Abraham declines. There is Word enough for men to "see" by, Abraham says. And then he adds an ominous warning: "Son, remember that you in your lifetime received your good things, and Lazarus in like manner evil things; but now he is comforted here, and you are in anguish" (Luke 16:25).

Ominous?

Indeed! Frightening!

Will all the good things each of us now enjoys be balanced off by anguish after the end?

No, not that. For Abraham himself had enjoyed great possessions — and finds himself in the comfort of his Lord. He had stewarded well what God had entrusted to him.

What is taught us, then?

This: God is infinitely generous, but always on the basis of executive stewardship.

Sum it up this way: God gives us *every* talent we have. God gives us life and time to use *them*.

If, now, we claim as our own what in fact we earn by the use of His gifts, *that* is our reward. Jesus says: "Beware of practicing your piety before men in order to be seen of them; for then you will have no reward from your Father who is in heaven" (Matt. 6:1).

What does this mean?

It means that whatever we claim as due to us for even our most pious deeds will not be rewarded again. You did it! You earned it! Right, and now you have it — the pleasure, the satisfaction, the honor, the reward. Enjoy it, then, for that is all the reward your use of God's talents is going to earn you. No double-dipping in the divine economy.

"Thus, when you give alms," Jesus teaches, "sound no trumpet before you, as the hypocrites do in the synagogues and in the streets, that they may be praised by men. Truly, I say to you, they have their reward" (Matt. 6:2).

The same principle. Whatever we claim as due to our own diligence, to our own largesse, to our own work, to our own generosity with what *we* have made — this is our reward.

So, too, with wage or salary or profit. If we claim it, and whatever it will do to satisfy ourselves, as ours by right and hard work, two things happen together: 1) this is all the reward we will get for the work we do, and 2) we have forfeited the right to look upon our work as a gift of our selves to others. We cannot "give" ourselves to others through work, and at the same time claim as "earned" the income we receive: "You cannot serve God and mammon" (Matt. 6:24).

God permits our enjoyment of whatever wage and income we need to use our talents well — so long as we acknowledge that He is the giver both of talent and of whatever it earns. And God will reward beyond our dreams the talent and its fruits that we consciously devote through work and generosity to the service of others.

Does He, then, bless the lazy, and short-change those who work hardest for what they have?

Not at all!

Talents Are For Use!

The Bible takes a hard line on the loafer.

Just as the Master did on the servant who hid his talent in the ground.

God invests in us for return! For 100% return, as we have already observed.

"If any one will not work," St. Paul instructs, "let him not eat" (II Thess. 3:10).

So much for those who foolishly presume that the world owes anyone a living, or that this is the implication of the love all are obliged to show others. No room in civilization for sluggards. Work or starve! God is no sentimentalist!

God does indeed display, throughout the Bible, great concern for the poor. But it is evident from St. Paul's instruction that divine care focuses upon the poor who are in need because they cannot find, or cannot do, work. Opening opportunity to work for all those who can work is one obligation of executive stewardship for all who can create jobs — an obedience which will enjoy its reward.

The Bible views refusal to work as theft: "Let him that stole steal no more but, rather, let him labor, working with his hands the thing that is good, so that he may be able to give to those in need" (Eph. 4:28).

Work can be twice gift: 1) of the self, in the working, to serve the needs of others; and 2) of the pay check, shared with those who have less.

To work is not an option.

Work is a duty.
Why?
Because God loans talents for the purpose of reaping return.

For Reflection And Discussion

1. *What is the common view of work? Is it yours?*
2. *What are the real losses involved in unemployment?*
3. *Illustrate how the pay check provides us with far more than we could make for ourselves in the time required to earn the check.*
4. *How does the parable of the Last Judgment teach us about work?*
5. *Why might this parable also be called that of the Day of Illumination?*
6. *Show how the parable deals with the basic needs of human life.*
7. *Explain these sayings: "To work is to pray," and "To work is to love".*
8. *Why are the "sheep" and "goats" both surprised, according to the parable?*
9. *Does this parable teach salvation by works? Does it explain St. James' teaching that "faith without works is dead"?*

Chapter 14.

FAMILY

I bow my knees before the Father, from whom every family in heaven and on earth is named.
Ephesians 3:14-15

THE FAMILY

TRUTH:
The family is the basic institution of society, and is modeled on the relation of God to His creation and of Christ to His Church. The family is protected by two of the Ten Commandments, and the Bible provides clear guidance for the roles of father, mother, and child.
RESPONSE:
The believer must strive to pattern the family of which he is a part after the Biblical model and mandates.
DISTORTION:
The substitution of individual "rights" within the framework of the family for the obligations each owes his role, husbands as despots, wives as heads, and children as independent agents.

What Is The Family?

The family is basic to society.
Strong, healthy families guarantee a strong, healthy social order.
Weak, undisciplined families assure a disintegrating society.
The human family enjoys this key role in civilization because it models the relationship God has chosen to structure between His creation and Himself. When the human institution is true to its divinely ordained model, a society is strong and progressive. When the human

family is a distortion of its divine model, society is the loser.

The believer thus has a double stake in shaping his family relations after God's precepts and example:

1) This is the obedience required of believers, and

2) Familial obedience gives rise to the kind of society in which believers want to live and raise their children.

Paul says that "every family in heaven and on earth is named" after God the Father.

There are, apparently, many families. And we often use the term "family" in ways that imply that kind of variety. We speak of "families" of stars, of organisms, of minerals, of nations, of ideas, and so on. In each case we mean "related" groups.

The relations which establish human families are, of course, marriage and the procreation of children.

And the terms which apply to the human family are illumined for the believer by the Bible.

It is a mistake to suppose that we first know by experience what a "father" is, for example, and then are able to interpret all that the Bible says about the Fatherhood of God. It is just the other way around. Wise and obedient parents first turn to the Scriptures to find our what God expects a "father" and a "mother" to be, and then strive to apply these models to their own family-building.

It is true that God as "Father" and the Church as "Mother" and fellow believers as "brothers" and "sisters" can mean little — and that perverted — to a child raised in a wretched home, where the Word of God is honored only in its breach. But this awesome fact only etches all the more boldly the responsibility which parents have to model their familial relationships on the Word of God.

Consider the consequence, on the Last Day, for the parent whose disobedience to divine mandate corrupted a child's response to the Fatherhood of God or to the mothering guidance of the Church! Jesus displays a peculiar sensitivity to children, and warns us that leading them astray will not go unpunished: "It would be better for him if a millstone were hung around his neck and he were cast into the sea, than that he should cause one of these little ones to sin" (Luke 17:2-3).

"Take heed to yourselves," the Lord continues — and it is in this sober spirit that we turn to "the believer in the family".

Let us learn as best we can why God has established the family as the heart of society, as He has made the Church the heart of civilization.

The Family In The Word

The family is given a prominence in the Bible which no other institution enjoys.

In ways like these:

1) Marriage is instituted at the outset of human history, and its sanctity is affirmed from the very beginning. Genesis relates that God first made man then formed his wife out of man's own body: "So the Lord God caused a deep sleep to fall upon the man, and while he slept took one of his ribs and closed up its place with flesh; and the rib which the Lord God had taken from the man he made into a woman and brought her to the man. Then the man said, 'This at last is bone of my bones and flesh of my flesh; she shall be called Woman, because she was taken out of Man.' Therefore a man leaves his father and his mother and cleaves to his wife, and they become one flesh" (Gen. 2:21-24).

2) This, writes St. Paul, "is a great mystery, and I take it to mean Christ and the church..." (Eph. 5:32). The union of man and woman at the dawn of history foretells the coming of the Son of God in human flesh. For Jesus is one with His Church through having become one with us by taking on human flesh through the virgin Mary. Marriage models itself upon the awesome mystery of Christ's union with the Church. The believer enters upon marriage in awe, and strives to live it in obedience.

3) The family is protected by two of the Ten Commandments: a) "You shall not commit adultery" (Ex. 20:14) preserves the purity and priority of the marriage relation, and b) "Honor your father and your mother" (Ex. 20:12) bulworks the unity of the family.

4) While God did permit polygamy in the life of Israel, for whatever reasons, the ideal of monogamy was established from the beginning. It was enforced by the seventh commandment, against adultery, and reaffirmed by Christ Himself: "For your hardness of heart Moses allowed you to divorce your wives, but from the beginning it was not so. And I say to you: whoever divorces his wife, except for unchastity, and marries another, commits adultery" (Matt. 19:8).

It would obviously be impossible for the Christian to take the family too seriously. And the alert believer recognizes in every modern trend that weakens the family a threat to society, because such trends violate the will of God. Scrutinize very, very carefully whatever "advice" you receive about parenting, or child-raising — always checking out with God's Word and in His Church the courses of action suggested on every hand in the press, on the air, and through modern literature and behavior.

The Bible has much to say about every aspect of the family. We will summarize some of that teaching, now, and urge you to hear sermonizing, and to read the Word, with an ear and eye open to what God is teaching about your own position, whatever it is, in the family where He has placed you. Remembering that the family is based upon the form in which God has chosen to relate to us, and to develop us in relation to other believers.

The Father

Why can Paul say that God as "Father" is the one "from whom every family in heaven and earth is named" (Eph. 3:15)?

Because God initiates and sustains and rules all things.

Fatherhood implies 1) initiation, 2) support, and 3) authority.

The father is the biological head of his family, as God is the creator of the cosmos. The father has the initiating role in the conception of children, as God took the initiating role in the creation of man. The families of all kinds which can be observed in God's creation owe Him their creation and preservation. In parallel manner, the human family owes its initial existence and continuing sustenance to the father of the house.

The intrusion of sin has warped and twisted family relationships in many ways, but the basic parallel of the human family to the structures instituted by God for His whole world remains. "Father" means "in the image of God" — "Then God said, 'Let us make men in our image, after our likeness; and let them have dominion over the fish of the sea, and over the birds of the air, and over the cattle, and over all the earth, and over every creeping thing that creeps upon the earth" (Gen. 1:26).

The age-old theory of the "divine right of kings" rested upon the parallel between a monarch, as "father" of his people, and God as "Father" of the human race. But we have generally come to believe that this monarchical conception was mistaken. Why?

Because after man's fall, the status of the father in the family was no longer entirely parallel to the relation of God to the universe. And a fallen mankind all too commonly corrupted "fatherhood" into tyranny.

The role of the husband in the family is modeled by the Bible, now, on the relation of Christ to His Church. Fatherhood is still a headship, but its authority must be validated by self-sacrifice as Christ's headship was confirmed.

St. Paul puts it this way: "Wives, be subject to your husbands, as to the Lord. For the husband is the head of the wife as Christ is the head of the church, his body, and is himself its Savior. As the church is subject to Christ, so let wives be subject in everything to their husbands. Husbands, love your wives, as Christ loved the church and gave himself up for her....Even so husbands should love their wives as their own bodies. He who loves his wife loves himself. For no man ever hates his own flesh, but nourishes and cherishes it, as Christ does the church, because we are members of his body" (Eph. 5:21-30).

No longer — since Adam's fall — is the husband head of the family as God is head of all His creation. That parallel was shattered.

As father, the husband still initiates the conception of children. As provider, the father still is obliged to support his family. And, in the pattern of Jesus Christ, the father still is final authority in the home, but not as independent agent!

The Christ who now models the role of the believing father comes to fulfill the Law of God: "Think not I have come to abolish the law and the prophets; I have come not to abolish them but to fulfill them" (Matt. 5:17). This Paul confirms: "Have this mind among yourselves, which you have in Christ Jesus, who, though he was in the form of God, did not count equality with God a thing to be grasped, but emptied himself, taking the form of a servant, being born in the likeness of man. And being found in human form he humbled himself and became obedient unto death, even the death of the cross. Therefore God has exalted him..." (Phil. 2:5-9).

Living after the pattern displayed in the Christ, the father does lead the home, and the buck does stop with him. But his leadership begins and ends in obedience to the law of God, and his authority extends only to enforcing that law in his household. There is no ground in the Scriptures for fatherhood as tyranny — for love and tyranny exclude each other.

There is simply the pattern established by God in Christ: first, the self-sacrifice, and then the authority it entails. Christ empties Himself to assume our flesh; Christ lives in obedience to His Father's commands; Christ finally surrenders His own life that we might live. And then, exalted by God to the Father's right hand, Christ rules in His

Church. Fathers who struggle to mold their headship in the family after this pattern — a headship predicated upon complete self-sacrifice for the good of the family — may expect one day to be "exalted" too, in reward of their self-denying leadership. Yes, both: self-denying! but leadership! Only a believer will understand, from experience, how these two roles exactly complement each other! Too little leadership makes the father the family's doormat instead of its head; too little self-denial makes the father the family dictator instead of its leader.

Another way to express this Biblical projection is to observe that the father is head of the family as "husband," that is as of one flesh with his wife — and no one, St. Paul says, can be hateful to himself, or despise his own flesh.

Mother

Adam called his wife "Eve," meaning "mother of all living" human beings (Gen. 3:20).

But the descendants of Eve lost, through the disobedience of Adam and herself, the life communicated by the indwelling Spirit of God. And to be re-born into eternal life, each believer has needed a new mother — the Church: "But the Jerusalem above is free, and she is our mother," Paul writes to us via the Galatians (Gal. 4:26).

God the Father initiates the birth of believers, and schools them toward sainthood, by means of the Church.

In history the Church is pictured by the Scriptures as the Body of Jesus Christ (Eph. 5:23), a body subject to all the ills of the human body after which the analogy is drawn. And it is by comparison to the Church as Christ's Body that the role of the wife in marriage is set before us, in the passage from Paul's letter to Ephesus already quoted.

The image shifts when the Bible looks ahead to eternity. In heaven the Church will appear, not as Mother, but as Bride: "Husbands, love your wives as Christ loved the church and gave himself up for her, that he might sanctify her, having cleansed her by the washing of water with the word, that he might present the church to himself in splendor, without spot or wrinkle or any such thing, that she might be holy and without blemish" (Eph. 5:25-27).

On that day, after the Last Day, the Mother of us all, the New Jerusalem, the Church cleansed in the blood of the Lamb of God, will be given the Son as His Bride: "And I saw the holy city, new Jerusalem, coming down out of heaven from God, prepared as a bride adorned for her husband..." (Rev. 21:2). "And the angel said to me, 'Write this: Blessed are those who are invited to the marriage supper of the Lamb'" (Rev. 19:9).

The true mother, here and now, will be transformed with the Church into the spotless Bride of the Christ she has faithfully served in the life of her family. Her model today: the Church. Her model forever: the Bride of the Lamb!

Just as the Church now obeys the Word of her Lord, so the mother is bound to abide by that same Word as applied to the life of the family by the obedient father. And just as such obedience in the Church will one day be rewarded "more abundantly than all that we ask or think" (Eph. 3:20), so such cooperation in the home will lead the way to that marriage feast above.

It was a virgin of Nazareth who restored the model besmirched by Eve. Mary said, simply, "Behold, I am the handmaid of the Lord; let it be to me according to your word" (Luke 1:38). Mothering embodies the same obedience "according" to God's Word.

Paul sums up God's instructions to both husband and wife: "...let each one of you love his wife as himself, and let the wife see that she respects her husband" (Eph. 5:33).

Motherhood introduces the "feminine" into history. The feminine cushions mankind against disaster with the strength of resilience — the ability to bend without breaking. The feminine is God's ally against despair, God's partner in hope, God's messenger of love.

How tragic a thing that the feminine too often aspires, nowadays, to the masculine. What an irreparable loss to human life wherever that succeeds.

The Biblical imagery is clear: the Church, always patient, always hopeful, always there with helpful hand outreached, always ready to forgive, never willing to give up — is portrayed in motherhood!

Of course!

In motherhood mankind approaches most nearly its own redemption.

The strength of the Church in the world reflects the reality of motherhood in the family. The perfection of motherhood in the home reflects the influence of the Church in the life of the believer.

Parents

Taken together, father and mother, when joined by children, are parents.

All of the obligations laid by the Word upon fathers bear fruit, first of all and most of all, in the lives of their children.

All of the obligations laid by the Word upon mothers bear fruit, first of all and most of all, in the lives of their children.

The gravest disobedience a parent, as parent, can commit is neglect of the child.

Such neglect can take several forms:

1) Simple disregard. Treating the child as unwanted, one of the nuisances of life. To say nothing of child-abuse — so far off the fringes of Christian behavior as needing no condemnation here.

2) Substitution of gifts for sharing of the self. Love exists as between persons, not as between children and things. No amount of stuff, no extension of an allowance, compensates for parents absent most of the time in pursuit of "success"!

3) "It takes a heap of livin'," wrote Edgar Guest, "to make a house a home." He's right about that, and the "livin'" he has in mind must be done through *being in* the home! Only the severest necessity could account for — not excuse! — the mother's absence when children are growing up, and coming home from school. Or father's habitual absence in the evenings and on weekends and holidays.

4) Neglect roots in forgetting that, compared to all other obligations, the proper raising of the child ranks without comparison. Only the child, of all that one can learn or acquire, will outlast time! "Train up a child in the way he should go, and when he is old he will not depart from it" (Prov. 22:6). The time for such training fleets by. Days lost will not return. The hurt of neglect cannot be erased by intermittent surges of gifts and sporadic moments of attention.

Most of all, parenting requires consciousness that the relation between husband and wife is, for the child, model of that between Christ and His Church. Long before the impressionable self of childhood is aware of what is being imprinted upon it, the atmosphere of the family is indelibly writ on the soul. How will the young learn what the "Fatherhood of God" and the "Motherhood of the Church" *mean* if the parents display total indifference to the obligations these impose upon their behavior? As parents, too, there is the awesome warning: "Be not deceived; God is not mocked" (Gal. 6:7)! He has not made you parents of His children by mistake, nor is His eye ever closed to how you fulfill the obligations of Christian parenthood!

The commandment obliges children to do honor to both father and mother (Ex. 20:12). No difference between them!

This obliges parents so to relate to each other, as prescribed by the Word, that the love of the child for the one is love for the other, and the responsibility of the child to the one is that given the other.

There is no room in the family for favorites — neither of children for parents, nor of parents for children.

Parenting is God's first order of business in the life of the family.

This is no doubt why He structures His relations with His creation and with mankind on the model of the family.

Children

Children are God's gift (Ps. 127:3) to husbands and wives who, on receipt of these gifts, become fathers and mothers. We have already noticed with what frequency, and significance, the Bible uses these two terms.

Under the influence of Parent Effectiveness Training (PET) and similar fads, children are apt to assume — and parents apt to grant — certain "rights" in the family circle. But the Bible does not know of a child's "rights" as against his parents. Parental respect for children is due them because they are God's — and the duties of parents are defined and required by the Scriptures in terms of obedience to God's laws governing His gifts. What the parents owe the child is defined by the Word, not by the child's presumed innate rights.

What children owe their parents is also defined by God's Word, beginning with the fourth commandment: "Honor your father and your mother, that your days may be long in the land which the Lord your God gives you" (Ex. 20:12). St. Paul elaborates on this fundamental law: "Children, obey your parents in the Lord, for this is right. 'Honor your father and mother' (this is the first commandment with promise) 'that it may be well with you and that you may live long on the earth'" (Eph. 6:1-2).

The Bible sets no age limit upon the extent of childhood. Children are not relieved of the obligations toward their parents at any fixed age. But the Bible does declare that when "a man leaves his father and mother" to be married "and cleaves to his wife, they become one flesh" (Gen. 2:24), and this new relationship obviously supplants that of child to parent. The wise parent hesitates to intrude with any attempt to show authority upon the new family. The wise newly-weds profit all they can from the experience of parents.

The rest home and retirement benefits enable parents to live apart from grown children and their families. A great deal of social friction is thus eliminated. But grandchildren lose the time which grandparents could give them, were both in the home; grandparents lose the companionship of both children and grandchildren. Believers seek ways in which these disadvantages of separate living can be made up.

The child's obligations toward parents surface again if the mother is left a widow: "If a widow has children or grandchildren, let them first learn their religious duty to their own family and make some return to their parents; for this is acceptable in the sight of God" (I Tim. 5:4). Including as Paul does, here, the term "parents" as the object of the child's "religious duty" indicates that the widower, too, may need — and must be given — the child's aid.

In the relations between children and parents familiar Biblical terms come into use: children are to "honor" their parents (Deut. 5:16); children are to "obey" their parents (Eph. 6:1; Col. 3:20). Fathers are not to "provoke your children to anger" but are "to bring them up in the discipline and instruction of the Lord" (Eph. 6:4). The family grows best, in short, in an atmosphere characterized by love. For those who love, obedience is a delight, and discipline an opportunity. The loving child relates to the parents as they relate to God and His Church; and loving parents relate to the child, as God and the Church care for them.

In an age of universal education, parents are likely to leave all instruction of their children to other agencies. This the Bible does not encourage. Long ago the Lord instructed His Church through Moses that parents should themselves reflect upon God's blessings to themselves and their families, and should teach their children what the Lord has done: "And these words which I command you this day shall be upon your heart; and you shall teach them diligently to your children, and shall talk of them when you sit in your house, and when you walk by the way, and when you lie down, and when you rise" (Deut. 6:6-7).

No other gift which a parent can make to a child compares with the worth of what Moses here commands. The child raised from the mother's knee into a familiarity with the Bible acquires a heritage never to be lost. The father whose faith is the substance of mealtime table talk lends a dignity of his status to the open confession of Truth.

Children must be loved as highest of the Lord's gifts.

Parents must be honored as being those to whom such gifts are entrusted.

For Reflection And Discussion

1. *Why is the family so important?*
2. *What are we taught by the Bible's modeling marriage after Christ's union with the Church?*
3. *How is the family protected in the Ten Commandments?*
4. *What does the Bible imply with the term "fatherhood"?*
5. *Why is self-sacrifice the key to Christian family relationships?*
6. *How does the Bible compare motherhood to the Church?*
7. *How do you understand the role of the "feminine" in history? Illustrate.*
8. *Give some examples of child neglect.*
9. *Why do you think that the commandment to "honor your father and mother" is followed by a promise? What does such "honoring" mean? When is the child released from it?*

Chapter 15.

LOVE

...and the greatest of these is love.
I Corinthians 13:13

LOVE

TRUTH:
Love is at the heart of all creation, for God is love; and is the goal of the Christian life. The Bible views love as centered in the will, not in the feelings or emotions. As illumined by the parable of the sower, love consists in doing God's will. Love requires justice, and is not at odds with punishment or the just war. Love emerges in good works, and is the goal of Christianity.
RESPONSE:
The believer is to make love the aim of the Christian life.
DISTORTION:
Confusion of love with sentimentality, and the neglect of the works of obedience in which love flourishes.

Love

All that God does for us is summed up in one word: *love* — "For God so loved the world that he gave his only Son, that whoever believes in him should not perish but have eternal life" (John 3:16).

All that we owe God in return for His love is: *love!*

The Son whom the Father sent in His love sums up His Father's will for us as follows: "You shall love the Lord your God with all your heart, and with all your soul, and with all your mind, and with all your strength...You shall love your neighbor as yourself" (Mark 12:30-31;

quoting Deut. 6:5, and Lev. 19:18).

So central is love to the very essence of all things that God is called love: "God is love" (I John 4:8). So writes the Apostle whose three epistles are a veritable textbook to the meaning of love.

The same Apostle writes: "Beloved, let us love one another; for love is of God, and he who loves is born of God and knows God" (I John 4:7).

What does the Bible mean by *love*?

Careful now! Don't take it for granted that you already know!

When dealing with a term so basic, we must avoid the error of supposing that we know from our own experience what love is, and can bring that knowledge to interpreting the Scripture. It's the other way around!

The term "love" is indeed on everyone's lips. It is the stuff of popular lyrics, of plays and novels, of news talk. There is "falling in" and "falling out" of love, and "we're in love" is sometimes used to justify premarital and illicit sex.

Amidst all this use, and ab-use, of the term, what are we to understand the Bible to mean when it speaks of *love*?

Before we turn to the Bible, however, let us carefully guard against certain misunderstandings of what we will read there.

Misunderstandings like these:

1) Confusing "love" with feelings, and then reading the Bible as if it did so, too. (It doesn't!).

We almost instinctively read the word "love" in terms of our own feelings. Warm feelings denote love; feelings of aversion imply love's opposite.

That may seem to fit, too, in understanding some Biblical passages. It is easy to associate feelings with the Biblical instruction given husbands to "love your wives" (Eph. 5:25) — of course, feelings run deep and vibrant there.

But thinking of "love" as emotion or feeling runs into difficulty with another instruction: "But I say to you, Love your enemies..." (Matt. 5:44). If love is a feeling, then an "enemy" generates within us exactly the opposite of love. What can the Lord mean by such impossible prescription — if by "love" He means warm emotions?

If we confuse love with feelings, the command to love our neighbors as we do ourselves is even apt to create problems. Our feelings about ourselves are not always warm and rosy. There are days when we feel like giving ourselves away. Besides, there are any number of human beings who repel feelings of warmth even when we think highly of ourselves.

No, it would be a serious mistake to think that what the Bible calls "love" refers to how we feel or what our emotions are. These often do embroider love, as lace embraces a lovely table cloth, but feelings in themselves are *not* what the Bible views as "love"!

2) As a matter of fact, if the Bible viewed "love" as dwelling in the region of our feelings, we would often have difficulty in distinguishing our feelings for people from those we have for ice cream or spinach. How many people do you know who gushingly say, "O, I just *love*...!" almost anything! Even our emotional reaction to Jesus might be hard to discriminate, in kind, from our feelings about a favorite food or entertainment. You often cannot tell, watching the emotion-stricken face of a singer on television whether he or she is singing rock or gospel! Even the emotions stirred within us by Bach or Mozart might be attributed (mistakenly) to "love" for the Son of God!

3) Of course, the hope of salvation is surrounded with an aura of feeling. We do *feel* boundless appreciation for all that God the Father, God the Son, and God the Holy Spirit have done, and are doing, to save us. All we are saying is that such feeling is not what the Bible means by "love".

When the Word commands us to "love," it is *not* even concerned with our feelings, even those feelings that may well accompany, or stimulate, love.

Love gets confused with feeling because all too easily we use "love" and "like" as being the same. And then, by "loving" our neighbors we think of liking them, as we do our friends. And by Jesus' command to "love" our enemies, we understand the Lord to be instructing us to create feelings of "liking" toward them — akin to a little girl's mother telling her that she *must* learn to like spinach, right now!! "Try it!" Do you suppose that Jesus is thinking that we could learn to love our most disagreeable neighbor, one little taste at a time?

What, then, does the Bible mean by "love"?

Love And Will

The key to understanding the Bible on "love" is to remember that everywhere love comes as a command! We are ordered to "love...!" If love can be commanded, as the Lord obviously does command it, then His use of the word must have reference to our wills. For the feelings are notoriously un-controllable. We may endure emotions, and may indeed stimulate them, but we can no more command ourselves to feel happy, or to like a toothache, than we can fly to the nearest treetop.

Yes, as already said, love may be bathed in emotion, as the love of husband and wife is laced with soft delight.

But the Biblical command, "husbands love your wives," is not intended to arouse gentle feelings. A command is directed to the will.

And the role of the will in life is to govern behavior.

We might point out in passing that the Bible has a very simple psychology. It views man spiritually as made up of mind, will, and emotions. The Word views the mind as setting options before the will, after examining the alternatives. The mind will also learn what the Word has to say on whatever the choice to be made is. Having weighed with the mind what course of action to take, the self acts through the will. The will frames and executes decisions arrived at in the light of the mind or understanding. The emotions may (but need not) surround mind and will with enthusiasm for action. No one, it is said, goes to battle for a syllogism; that is to say, some actions may require stimulation by more than intellect, like, say, propulsion by feeling — or, for the believer even more powerful, a divine mandate!

The Bible uses "love" to focus, then, on the will, on what we are to do, not on the emotions, or how we are to feel.

Indeed, some of the things we are called to do — like "loving" our enemies — may run hard against our feelings and carry a great deal of distaste with them. The Bible pays no attention to that.

The obedience which is love may occasionally set us at the opposite pole from pleasant emotions and warm fuzzies. God doesn't seem to care.

St. John puts it plainly enough: "For this is the love of God, that we keep his commandments" (I John 5:3). Like it or not!

We are reminded at once of the Lord Himself, who says, "He who has my commandments and keeps them, he it is who loves me" (John 14:21).

Notice carefully how the Biblical sentences just quoted are phrased. St. John puts it very exactly: the love of God "is" keeping His commandments. Jesus says the same: having and keeping His commandments "is" loving Him.

Remember the Lord's parting command to His Church? The Great Commission is His instruction to teach believers to "love" Him, when He says: "teaching them to *do* all that I have commanded you..." (Matt. 28:20). To do what the Lord requires *is* to love Him!

We may now understand an otherwise puzzling thing. It is this: God reveals His will for our wills in the Ten Commandments. These Commandments require obedience. Yet when the Lord Jesus quotes Old Testament summaries of the two tables of the ancient Law, He uses the word "love": you shall love...! Meaning, You shall do...!

Why should Jesus use the term "love" for the Law unless to love is to obey the Law?

Which is exactly how St. Paul understands it: "Owe no one anything, except to love one another; for he who loves his neighbor has fulfilled the law. The commandments, 'You shall not commit adultery, You shall not kill, You shall not steal, You shall not covet,' and any other commandment, are summed up in this sentence, 'You shall love your neighbor as yourself.' Love does no wrong to a neighbor; therefore love is the fulfilling of the law" (Rom. 13:8-10). Take careful note, in passing, that it is St. Paul, the apostle of salvation by faith, who requires believers to obey the law.

Looking back, we can see that when the Bible says that "God is love," and that He "so loved the world" as to give His only Son to save us, the Word does not mean that God simply entertained warm feelings toward us. Such feelings He may have, but His "love" *is* what He did for the world. And the love He requires of us in return is a *doing* also! "And by this we may be sure that we know him," St. John says, "if we keep his commandments" (I John 2:3).

And now we can understand the striking contrasts which St. Paul draws between love and other virtues we are apt to think of equal importance: "If I speak in the tongues of men and of angels, but have not love, I am a noisy gong or a clanging symbol. And if I have prophetic powers, and understand all mysteries and all knowledge, and if I have all faith, so as to remove mountains, but have not love, I am nothing. If I give away all that I have, and if I deliver my body to be burned, but have not love, I gain nothing" (I Cor. 13:1-3).

We may be sure that the inspired writer is not urging upon us a desperate effort to generate strong feelings and warm emotions. He is saying that the Bible knows no substitutes for obedience.

None at all!

Love Is All — All Is Love!

Love is at the center of the Christian life. Love is basic to the whole of creation.

What else could it mean, really, when we are told, "God *is* love"?

Because He is "love," God wills only the good for all that He makes. And that means that He demands obedience — which is "love" from our side — to His will. Why? Because to be what we are meant to be, we must do His will.

To be what they are meant to be, all things must do God's will. The love of God which called all things into being demands the love which is obedience, in return.

Nature does obey the commands of God.

The universal order which we call "natural law" is simply the uniform obedience of nature to her Creator's ordinances. The "laws" of nature reflect nature's "love" for God!

Because stars and atoms obey the Creator's will, we can fashion theoretical science into all its practical consequences. Because God exacts obedience from His creation, we are able to create civilization based on "natural law". Love is at the foundation of all things!

We are told that the stars in their courses obey God's will. He "brings out their host by number, calling them all by name" (Is. 40:26). *Therefore* we can count on the sun's rising on schedule — it, too, being a star! Don't let the unbelief of secular science rob you of that insight! It is God who "covers the heavens with clouds, he prepares rain for the earth, he makes grass grow upon the hills. He gives to the beasts their food, and to the young ravens when they cry...He gives snow like wool; he scatters hoarfrost like ashes. He casts forth his ice like morsels; who can stand before his cold? He sends forth his word, and melts them; he makes his wind to blow, and the waters flow" (Ps. 147:8-9, 16-18). As the prophet puts it, "He makes lightnings for the rain, and he brings forth the wind from his storehouses" (Jer. 10:13).

To all who are blind to these manifestations of the "love" of nature for her Creator, the same prophet aptly says, "Every man is stupid and without knowledge; every goldsmith is put to shame by his idols; for his images are false, and there is no breath in them" (Jer. 10:14). Never permit those who have made a self-serving idol of natural science impose their idolatrous stupidity upon you! All who fail to see the "love" of God for and in His creation are "without knowledge"!

In sum, it is because God is love that He commands our obedience to His will.

Why? Because such obedience is the only way in which we can become what He means us to be! God's Law is our only key to true self-realization!

But man was not made like the elements of nature. Our obedience is not automatic. We are not creatures of "natural" law — though scientism tries to treat humans as things!

Made free, as we know, man fell! Adam plunged himself and all mankind into the bondage of disobedience.

To restore all who believe to the possibility of obedience, and thus to provide us with the capacity to love Him again, God sent His Son into the world. Jesus liberates all who believe from whatever might prevent our obeying Him. Only God could "save" us from the awful burden of guilt, and free us from the crippling effects of sin. God does so.

Why? So that we can once again, however poorly, respond in love to His love. That is, so we can will to become who we are meant to be by willing to do His will.

That is the gospel!

God inspires His Word so we may learn that only in the life of love, the life of obedience, do we become truly human beings. Believing this, we find the joy and peace of the ordered life now, with the promise of everlasting life hereafter.

All this is illustrated in one of Jesus' most familiar parables:

What About Soil?

Hear, now the parable of the sower:

> And when a great crowd came together and people from town after town came to him, he said in a parable: 'A sower went out to sow his seed; and as he sowed, some fell along the path, and was trodden under foot, and the birds of the air devoured it. And some fell on rock; and as it grew up, it withered away, because it had no moisture. And some fell among thorns, and the thorns grew with it and choked it. And some fell into good soil and grew, and yielded a hundredfold.'
>
> As he said this, he called out, 'He who has ears to hear, let him hear.'
>
> And when his disciples asked him what this parable meant, he said, 'To you it has been given to know the secrets of the kingdom of God; but for others they are in parables, so that

seeing they may not see, and hearing they may not understand. Now the parable is this: The seed is the word of God. The ones along the path are those who have heard; then the devil comes and takes away the word from their hearts, that they may not believe and be saved. And the ones on the rock are those who, when they hear the word, receive it with joy; but these have no root, they believe for a while and in time of temptation fall away. And as for what fell among thorns, they are those who hear, but as they go on their way they are choked by the cares and riches and pleasures of life, and their fruit does not mature. And as for that in the good soil, they are those who, hearing the word, hold it fast in an honest and good heart, and bring forth fruit with patience'" (Luke 8:4-15).

The same Word! Cast into the world by the lips of God's ambassadors.

Decisively different receptions!

Only one kind of hearer profits by what he hears.

It is not the Word that changes. All depends upon the kind of hearer the Word encounters. This leads to an important question: how does one become that fruit-bearing kind of hearer? Or, how does one respond to the Word in *love*? Or, how can we avoid being among that other three? How avoid not-loving?

We may at first seem to go in a circle, now, but the answer is this: only he who loves can hear; and only he who hears can love!

The crucial difference among the various "soils" as revealed by their different receptions of the Word is the most fundamental of all human distinctions. It is a distinction made in time, but with eternal consequence. It may seem that differences in wealth, or power, or fame, or recognition count most of all in life. Lots of people think so, and live accordingly. But such people provide the first three kinds of soil mentioned in the parable!

The parable is told us just to correct such a mistake.

The parable of the sower repeats, in another form, what we have already heard Jesus saying about the two ways and two gates: the wide gate and broad way leading to destruction, found by many (say, three as contrasted here to one?) and the narrow gate and hard road of obedience leading to life eternal as found by few (say, one as contrasted here to three?) — Matt. 7:13-14.

Divine Husbandry

What does divide those into whose ears the Word is spoken? Why are some "rock," others given to the production of brambles, and only a few, it seems, the kind of soil that is productive of fruits of obedience?

The Bible answers this crucial question in various ways:

1) St. Paul writes of those "who by their wickedness suppress the truth" (Rom. 1:18). In short, one way to avoid being good soil for the reception of God's Word is to disobey it. It is not, then, so circular after all, to say that only those who love can hear, and those who hear do love.

2) The Bible tells us that disobedience does turn the unbeliever's heart to stone — one kind of soil mentioned in the parable. The prophet Zechariah is commissioned by God to show Israel, and us, how to become the soil we are meant to be: "Render true judgments, show kindness and mercy each to his brother, do not oppress the widow, the fatherless, the sojourner, or the poor; and let none of you devise evil against his brother in your heart." Here are the ingredients of soil characterized by love! But Israel refused to listen, "and made their hearts like adamant lest they should hear the law and the words which the Lord of hosts had sent by his Spirit through the former prophets" (Zech. 7:9, 12). It is upon hearts made stony through the will to disobey that the Word seeks in vain for productive lodgment.

God has confronted all mankind, always, with a witness to Himself, one which can prepare the human soil for reception of the Word: "For what can be known about God is plain..., because God has shown it. Ever since the creation of the world his invisible nature, namely, his eternal power and deity, has been clearly perceived in the things that have been made. So they are without excuse; for although they knew God they did not honor him as God or give thanks to him, but became futile in their thinking and their senseless minds were darkened. Claiming to be wise, they became fools, and exchanged the glory of the immortal God for images resembling mortal man or birds and animals or reptiles" (Rom. 1:19-23).

God offers everyone the means to become a receptive hearer of His spoken Word. But many refuse to undertake the tilling of self this natural witness calls for: "they did not honor him as God or give thanks...."

Let's not be misled, now, into referring this only to primitive peoples who suffer under the scourge of one form or another of idolatry. They are included, of course, among those who fail to honor God in His self-revelation by way of creation. But there are many who would consider themselves highly civilized and quite un-primitive who suffer the same delusion!

"The heavens are telling the glory of God," the Psalmist cries out, "and the firmament proclaims his handiwork. Day to day pours forth speech, and night to night declares knowledge. There is no speech, nor are there words; their voice is not heard, yet their voice goes out through all the earth, and their words to the end of the world" (Ps. 19:1-4).

And what does the reigning idol of modern scientism see or hear, or permit its devotees to see or hear, of all this divine magnificence, of all this vocally voiceless majesty? Is it only the primitive who fails to acknowledge that the seasons change by divine decree, that the wind and the rain are God's messengers, that the glory of springtime and the beauty of autumn cry out God's name? Not at all. It is more likely to be those who consider themselves most highly sophisticated. The primitive man will often be nearer to sensing the presence of God in His creation than the modern sophisticate!

The soil which receives the Word in ways that stifle the production of obedient fruits has already shut out the divine witness. And the soil which hears the Word but permits it to be crowded out by mundane concerns only doubles its guilt.

How, in this light, can men prepare themselves to receive the Word for fruitful tillage?

By pausing to listen, over and again, to the "word" which the heavens declare, and to see ever more clearly the witness that the intricate structure of God's world displays.

God foretells the fruitless reception of His Word among those who decline to hear it, through His prophet Ezekiel: "As for you, son of man, your people who talk together about you by the walls and at the doors of the houses, say to one another, each to his brother, 'Come, and hear what the word is that comes forth from the Lord.' And they come to you as people come, and they sit before you as my people, and they hear what you say but they will not do it; for with their lips they show much love, but their heart is set on their gain. And, lo, you are to them like one who sings love songs with a beautiful voice and plays well on an instrument, for they hear what you say, but they will not do it" (Ezek. 33:30-33).

Exactly so. It is the same story, told under the same inspiring

Spirit, as that revealed in the parable of the sower.

The key is not only "hear," but also "do"!

And the soil divides among those who come to the Word in love, *willing* both to hear and to do, and those who may listen, but have no intention of doing!

This is the basic principle of divine agriculture!

Self Love?

We are commanded to love God above all, and the Lord adds, "You shall love your neighbor as yourself" (Matt. 19:19).

That is a tempting comparison: to "love" the other as I am commanded to "love" myself? So then, the believer is supposed to "love" him or her self? How convenient.

A good deal of pop psych gets brewed to this little recipe: learn to love yourself!

Not hard to do, really, it comes so naturally. Taking good and tender care of ourselves is never far from first priority. And now we are told that the Bible even requires it?!

Before being taken in by this subtle heresy, consider:

1. What does this admonition to "love our selves" mean by: a) self, and b) love?

2) Which "self" is it, do you suppose, that God's commandment has in view? Is it the "old" self inherited naturally from Adam, tainted with disposition to rebellion? Is that the "self" we are to love as we should love our neighbors? Bad luck for our neighbors, if so, because that "old" self is the one we are commanded to have no traffic with. The "old" natural self is precisely the self we are called upon to deny; our Lord expressly says: "If any man would come after me, let him deny himself and take up his cross and follow me" (Matt. 16:24). We can't "love" and "deny" the same "self" at the same time. It is obvious that the commandment to love neighbor as self does not mean loving the natural, tainted self we are required to deny, that is to repent of and replace — by grace — with another.

3) Are we, then, to "love" that new self we are becoming? If so, what is meant by "love"? To love, as God requires love is, as we have been learning from the Word, to do God's will, to keep the Lord's commandments. What then would be "loving," that is keeping the Lord's commandment as regards our new selves? Well, we have already heard one form of it: "take up his cross and follow me." If we "love" the new

self we are trying to mature, the form such loving requires is to oblige that self to shoulder a cross — and we have seen what that involves. This is not the kind of self-love those who abuse the commandment seem to have in mind.

4) Let's not make the mistake, then, of following Pied Pipers singing songs of self love, until we know (and they know) what "self" they have in mind — then we will know what they mean by "love". And then, *if* they mean denial of the "old" self and cross-bearing for the "new," we can of course hear their teaching.

5) Calvin says that the reason God phrases the second great commandment in the form of loving our neighbors *as we love ourselves* is not to promote some cult of self-worship. Not at all! God puts it that way, Calvin says, because by nature we always put our selves first, even as we move along toward sainthood, and the Lord is simply saying that Christians must give others that same priority. We think Calvin is right. The Lord utters no sentimentality about loving our selves. Our calling is to obedience, which is self-love enough because it alone leads along the narrow road to eternal beatitude.

A particularly insidious argument for self love goes like this: you must think well of yourself, Jesus did — He thought enough of you to die for you! What this glib distortion perverts is the solemn fact that we did, indeed, bring Christ to the cross as God's means of lifting the guilt of our sins. We cost the Lord His life, not because in ourselves we are a pretty prize. To the contrary, we cost Jesus the cross because we are otherwise so hopelessly perverse, so much children of the Devil, that only by the death of God can we receive the new selves we must be if God is to avoid destroying us. God loved what we can be, purged by grace and through faith of all that made us hateful to Himself. "God shows his love for us," St. Paul writes, "in that while we were yet sinners Christ died for us" (Rom. 6:8). The Lord does not die for us because we are so lovable; He died for us because, being sinners, that is the only way we could become lovable once more. That is what cost the blood of our Savior. Not some divine super evaluation of what in our natural selves we are. "I know," says Paul, "that in myself dwelleth no good thing" (Rom. 7:18) — not much to "love," this self of ours. Take care to avoid blasphemy.

Love And Justice

The Bible takes a hard line on disobedience.

God does so in the Old Testament. His Son does so in the New Testament.

Moses says to Israel: "Take heed lest you forget the Lord your God, by not keeping his commandments and his ordinances and his statutes...."

But what if Israel does forget? What if the people turn out to be, in practice, hard and rocky soil?

Moses gives the Lord's answer: "And if you forget the Lord your God and go after other gods and serve them and worship them, I solemnly warn you this day that you shall surely perish. Like the nations that the Lord makes to perish before you, so shall you perish, because you would not obey the voice of the Lord your God" (Deut. 8:11, 19-20).

Do you suppose that this is but Old Testament "legalism" which can threaten us no longer now that the New Testament has dawned? Has grace taken away the curse of the Law, and are we free from threats of punishment upon disobedience?

Let the Apostle of salvation by grace set us right, immediately, about that fatal blunder. St. Paul, whom we have quoted to this effect before, writes in the very epistle which lauds grace, the letter to the Galatians: "Be not deceived; God is not mocked, for whatever a man sows, that he will also reap. For he who sows to his own flesh will from the flesh reap corruption..." (Gal. 6:7-8). Again, the metaphor of sowing. Here the Apostle is saying that all of us sow, either in obedience to the will of God or in the service of our own self-interests. And the harvest of sowing to self-interest will be the future of the fleshy field for which we have labored: the body is destined to die. So will all the seed sown in its interests!

Jesus warns more often, and more sharply, against being unfruitful hearers than does anyone else in the Bible. Hear Him: "Every tree that does not bear good fruit is cut down and thrown into the fire" (Matt. 7:19).

Can He be serious? When salvation is not by works but by faith?

Yes, the Lord is serious. For salvation by faith is validated by obedient works!

Recall the parable we have already explained, that of the Day of Illumination. To those who bore no fruit, He will say, "Depart from me, you cursed, into the eternal fire prepared for the devil and his angels..." (Matt. 25:41). Have you heard someone suggest that all this is but figurative language; how could we imagine Jesus being so cruel?

Well, that can be suggested — but it isn't so!

Why should the Lord preserve His very words for us to hear, if He did not mean what He said?

It is Jesus who foretells the punishment of the fruitless in frightening language: "The Son of man will send his angels, and they will gather out of his kingdom all evildoers, and throw them into the furnace of fire; there men will weep and gnash their teeth" (Matt. 13:41-42). He it is who speaks of "...hell, where the worm does not die, and the fire is not quenched" (Mark 9:47-48), and of everlasting "outer darkness; there men will weep and gnash their teeth" (Matt. 22:13).

We might multiply similar warnings, but the point is clear: God's moral order does not change from Old Testament to New Testament. The obedience He required of the Old Testament believer is rooted in the anticipated incarnation and sacrificial death of the Christ; the obedience He requires of the New Testament believer (like ourselves) roots in the accomplished sacrifice of our Lord. The claim is the same. The reward of the will to obey is the same. The punishment promised the unwilling is also the same.

And of importance to us here is that God, who is love, has no problem with meting out punishment for disobedience.

Neither should we in our systems of law and justice.

The refusal to punish violation of law is not love, is not modeled after the God of love. It is sentimentality, rooted in the feelings.

It may well be that besides punishment, and during punishment, a criminal may be led to rehabilitation. But this desirable objective in no way affects the necessity of punishment for the violation of the civil or the criminal law.

For the courts to fail here, as so commonly occurs, under the pressure of sentimentality, is to threaten the very social fabric which makes peaceful life possible.

Still more, the persistent failure of the courts to administer justice by way of appropriate punishment invites the emergence of a dictator who promises the nation that he will make the streets safe by making crime unpopular. Through such a tyrant the Lord can bring His punishment upon a democratic people who forget that God is a God of love, not of sentiment, and who requires punishment for disobedience, in the societies He preserves for the common good.

Love And War

It is easy to imagine that love forbids war. Some people say so, very loudly — if not belligerently!

Easy to say, until you reflect a little upon the Lord's guidance of Israel into the promised land.

All of Israel's trek from Egypt to Palestine was littered with the ravage of war. God's people fought their way to the good land they were promised, and fought for their right to stay there.

We have already observed that it is productive of misunderstanding to think in terms of an "Old Testament" God and a "New Testament" God. That won't hold up.

It does not hold up in terms of punishment for disobedience.

It will not hold up, either, in terms of war.

Love has no quarrel with rightful war. Christians are not required by their faith to be peaceniks! Not at all! They are, rather, forbidden to promote peace at any price! By the fact that they must love!

Love is only at odds with the unjust war, the obvious war of aggression — not because love forbids war, but because love abhors injustice!

It is true that the believer must himself be willing to suffer injustice rather than to retaliate.

But that is a *personal* ethic.

The fact that the believer must willingly suffer injustice to himself must be carefully discriminated from his attitude toward injustice suffered by others. He may not, for instance, impose injustice upon another, saying that as a Christian that injured person should suffer in silence.

So yes, you, as believer, must struggle to endure injustice, to turn the other cheek, to love *your* enemies! So you are commanded to do.

But love forbids your trying to stand aloof while injustice is done to anyone else! Cowardice, or indifference, or not wanting "to get involved," is not love! Letting another suffer on the ground that you would be willing to do so yourself is the very opposite of love. Love rises at once to the defense of the oppressed. Love takes up arms to defend the freedom of others! Always!

When injustice is done anyone else, immediately your duty to the neighbor enters. And one aspect of that duty is to provide in every way for the neighbor's good: "...do good to all men," Paul instructs us (Gal. 6:10). How could one obey this injunction if he lifted no finger when evil is done his neighbor?

It may be that *you* could live under the tyranny of a totalitarian state rather than go to war. *You* could!

Well enough, but you have no right to stand aside and let such a state impose its violence upon anyone else! To call such cowardice or indifference "love" would be cynical. To try to justify it by the command to "love" our enemies would be absurd!

This is why the Christian is instructed to let the state decide when the threat upon its welfare is a call to arms: "Let every person be subject to the governing authorities. For there is no authority except from God, and those that exist have been instituted by God. Therefore he who resists the authorities resists what God has appointed, and those who resist will incur judgment" (Rom. 13:1-2). This may not be popular instruction in an age so widely dedicated to "doing your own thing," with no concern for others doing the same. But it is the Word of God!

When the state decides that war is essential to its survival, the believer has the inescapable obligation to obey the call to conscription.

Of course, at all times, and especially in an age of nuclear possibility, the Christian has every obligation to seek peace among nations with all his heart. This, too, is love.

But this does not extend to "sitting out" response to threats designed to bring down the state in which the Christian enjoys his freedoms.

Nothing in the Bible ever confuses love with sentimentalism. God does not want us to make that mistake, either!

Love calls upon the believer to be willing to sacrifice himself and his own self-interests whenever so doing would protect his neighbor from injury or injustice. Even when this call extends to military service.

We are aware that the question of when, and whether, a given war is indeed a "just" war has long been debated within and outside the Church. But we dispute the individual citizen's right to determine for himself when the state engages in "just" or "unjust" war. Citizens are not Lone Rangers!

"Make Love Your Aim"

This is the instruction with which Paul concludes his great hymn to love from which we have already quoted (I Cor. 13; the text is from 14:1).

Faith is exercised through love, for, the Apostle says, "love believes all things".

Hope is exercised through love, for, the Apostle says, "love hopes all things" (I Cor. 13:7).

The Christian life itself finds its goal in love, for, the Apostle says, "make love your aim"!

All the strands of the Christian life come to focus in love.

Or, to put it another way, love unifies all that the Christian is busy trying to do and to be.

Love is, and must be, the organizing principle of the believer's behavior — of his thought, desires, hopes, belief, and conduct.

Love must set the pattern of our lives as the magnet draws metal filings into contours subject to its lines of force.

And now, if we set all this in the light of how the Bible defines "love," we come at last to the final resolution of the age-old question of faith or works, grace or merit. It is not, as we have frequently pointed out, a matter of "or" at all. It is *both*, and together as one!

To *love* God IS, we have now seen, to *obey* Him!

And such obedience *is* the doing of His will.

And the doing of His will is what the Bible repeatedly calls *good works*!

Would it be surprising, then, if every aspect of what the Bible teaches us to do, and to be, has its aim in our doing *good works*?

It is so!

Every facet of Christianity has as its object our doing "good works" — not, we repeat, as a means of earning salvation. No, but as the means of becoming the self we have been "saved" to be!

Let us be very clear about that, by summing up what the Bible teaches:

1) God makes us in love, meaning in His overflowing desire to share His beatitude with others.

2) God requires love from us in return.

3) The love He asks *is* obedience to His will, as that will is revealed in the Bible and summarized in the divine Law.

4) Why? Because it is only by the exercise of such love that we can become the true persons He designed us to be.

5) The primary beneficiary, therefore, of our obedient good works is not the recipient of them. It is ourselves. God could, if He wishes, feed all the hungry, clothe all the naked, comfort all the lonely, do justice for all the oppressed. But He leaves these tasks to us to do, *so that* we can find innumerable ways of obedience all around us; indeed, so that

the cry for "love" resounds everywhere in our ears! No one, come the Last Day, will be able to excuse disobedience by saying that no one needed his love! Or that no one challenged him to become the person who, before the Fall, he was meant to be.

6) And God sends His Son to liberate us, through faith, from the crippling guilt derived from Adam and multiplied through our own sins. Jesus thus "saves" believers for service in obedience to God's will. And God provides in every kind of human need opportunities for all the service we could possibly do.

7) Everything, therefore, in the Christian life comes to its focus in *love* — that is, in obeying the will of God through the doing of what the Bible calls "good works".

Everything in the Scriptures has this as its aim:

1) *God Himself wants our good works:*

"For we are his workmanship, created in Christ Jesus *for good works*, which God prepared beforehand, that we should walk in them" (Eph. 2:10).

2) *Christ does:*

"If a man loves me, he will *keep my word*, and my Father will love him, and we will come to him and make our home with him. He who does not love me does not keep my words; and the word you hear is not mine but the Father's who sent me" (John 14:23-24).

3) *The Holy Spirit does:*

"But the fruit of the Spirit is *love* (!), joy, peace, patience, kindness, goodness, faithfulness, gentleness, self-control..." (Gal. 5:22-23).

4) *The Bible does:*

"All scripture is inspired by God and profitable for teaching, for reproof, for correction, and for training in righteousness, that the man of God may be complete, equipped *for every good work*" (II Tim. 3:16-17).

5) *The Church does:*

"Go therefore and make disciples of all nations, baptizing them in the name of the Father and of the Son and of the Holy Spirit, *teaching them to do* all that I have commanded you; and lo, I am with you always, to the close of the age" (Matt. 28:19-20).

6) *Faith does:*

"For in Christ Jesus neither circumcision nor uncircumcision is of any avail, but faith *working* through love" (Gal. 5:6). "So faith by itself, if it has no works, is dead" (James 2:17).

7) *Missions does:*

"Wherefore, O King Agrippa, I was not disobedient to the heavenly vision, but declared first to those at Damascus, then at Jerusalem and throughout all the country of Judea, and also to the Gentiles, that they should repent and turn to God and *perform deeds* worthy of their repentance" (Acts 26:19-20).

8) *God gives talents for good works:*

"And he who had received the five talents came forward, bringing five talents more, saying, 'Master, you delivered to me five talents; here *I have made* five talents more.' His Master said to him, 'Well done, good and faithful servant; you have been faithful over a little, I will set you over much; enter into the joy of your Master'" (Matt. 25:20-21).

9) *We will be judged by:*

"For he will render to every man *according to his works:* to those who by patience in *well-doing* seek for glory and honor and immortality, he will give eternal life; but for those who are factious and do not obey the truth, but obey wickedness, there will be wrath and fury. There will be tribulation and distress for every human being who does evil, the Jew first and also the Greek, but glory and honor and peace for every one who does good, the Jew first and also the Greek. For God shows no partiality" (Rom. 2:6-11).

The message conveyed by the above is summed up by Jesus Himself in His teaching about the religious leadership, the scribes and Pharisees, of His own day. Jesus says to His disciples, and to us: "For I tell you that unless your righteousness exceeds that of the scribes and Pharisees, you will never enter the kingdom of heaven" (Matt. 5:20). Serious business for every believer!

What, then, was — in the Lord's eyes (which today behold us!) — the fault of the scribes and Pharisees? Hear it in His own words: "Then said Jesus to the crowds and to his disciples, 'The scribes and Pharisees sit on Moses' seat; so practice and observe whatever they tell you, but not what they do; for they preach, but do not practice'" (Matt. 23:1-3).

In summary: "You see that a man is justified *by works* and not by faith alone" (James 2:24).

The whole of the Christian life is unified by love. That's how God made us!

And what the Bible calls "love" is obedience to God's will accomplished in good works, done through faith by the indwelling strength of the Holy Spirit.

Love completes the circle rent by the Fall.

In love, God's original intention is moving steadily toward that Great Day when all the imperfections wrought by sin upon man and universe will be done away, and God will be one with those who love Him, forever.

"Then I saw a new heaven and a new earth; for the first heaven and the first earth had passed away, and the sea was no more. And I saw the holy city, new Jerusalem, coming down out of heaven from God, prepared as a bride adorned for her husband; and I heard a great voice from the throne saying, 'Behold the dwelling of God is with man'" (Rev. 21:1-3).

Love has come at last to its fruition!

For Reflection And Discussion

1. *What are some of the misunderstandings of the Biblical meaning of "love"?*
2. *How is love related to will?*
3. *Does Christ in the summary of the Law show a different divine attitude toward the Commandments than when they were first given?*
4. *Explain: "love is at the foundation of all things".*
5. *What does the parable of the sower teach us about love?*
6. *How does love affect the administration of justice?*
7. *What does the Bible teach about our duties toward government?*
8. *Is the Christian allowed to bear arms? To do military service?*
9. *How do you understand the text: "Make love your aim"?*
10. *How does the Bible relate love and good works? Give examples.*

Chapter 16.

WITNESS

You shall be my witnesses....
Acts 1:8

WITNESS

TRUTH:
God demands that believers witness for Him to the world in both word
and works, with stress on word-witness (preaching) by the Church and
on works-witness (love) by the individual believers — who form a
"kingdom of priests" in the self-sacrifice of obedience. Such witnessing achieves the goals which Christ, the Church, and the Scripture set
for the believer in the Word.
RESPONSE:
The Church is to be ardent in proclamation, diligent in missions for the
planting of churches, and a school for believers whose faith must be a
"light" to the world through their devotion to doing the will of God
according to His Word.
DISTORTION:
For the Church to neglect preaching, confine it to select parts of the
Scriptures, or focus upon "salvation" to the exclusion of obedience
among the believers. For believers to rest content with a "witness" of
word not embodied in the deeds of total devotion to Christ by keeping
His commandments.

What Is Witnessing?

We are always "witnessing"!
That is to say, our behavior always speaks for us.

Every thought we entertain, every word we utter, every deed we do — each bears "witness" to whose kingdom we belong, to whom we pay allegiance: to God or to His Adversary, the Devil.

To live is to "witness" — though we may rarely think of it that way.

"Witness" is the "show and tell" of life.

The Greek term "martyr" is sometimes translated in the Bible as "witness". A martyr is one whose behavior in word and deed loudly proclaims who his Master is: "you shall be *my* witnesses!"

What is "witnessing," then?

It is revealing by word or deed whom we serve.

Everyone's behavior testifies, less obviously than martyrdom but no less surely, to whose servant he is.

And Christianity is in the world to make us into the Lord's witnesses. That is what the Lord means by, "You shall be MY witnesses"! That is, your behavior, in every observable respect, must testify to your allegiance to God as Lord and your love of neighbor as yourself. To create such "witnesses" is the goal of Christianity.

Jesus puts it this way: "For no good tree bears bad fruit, nor again does a bad tree bear good fruit; for each tree is known by its own fruit. For figs are not gathered from thorns, nor are grapes picked from a bramble bush. The good man out of the good treasure of his heart produces good, and the evil man out of his evil treasure produces evil; for out of the abundance of the heart his mouth speaks" (Luke 6:43-45).

Our words are telltale witnesses. Especially the words we utter without premeditation. The words we speak from the heart. "Thy speech betrayeth thee."

Our everyday words, and those that rise to our lips under tension or in anger and frustration, reveal far more than we realize about whose servants we are. And that is why the Lord can say, "I tell you that on the day of judgment men will render account for every careless word they utter; for by your words you will be justified, and by your words you will be condemned" (Matt. 12:36-37). Jesus no doubt means by "every careless word" the unpremeditated word, the things we say when we are most unguardedly ourselves. These are the truly revealing -- witnessing — words. And because they betray a citizenship, it is by these that we will be judged.

We can see why the Lord rejects pious talk put on as counterfeit "witness". There will be those, Jesus warns us, who on the day of judgment will plead: "Lord, Lord, did we not prophesy in your name, and cast out demons in your name, and do many mighty works in your name?'' These were the "witnesses" of the bold front, capable of stage-acting a considerable show of piety in the name of the Lord. How impressed some may have been who did not really know the self behind the mask. But the front was counterfeit, as their "careless" everyday speech no doubt revealed. Looking through the pious facade, the Master says: "I never knew you; depart from me, you evildoers" (Adapted from Matt. 7:22-23).

Yes, we are always "witnessing" by word and by deed.

It is the everyday "witness," that we display in the home, at our work, in our treatment of others who work for or with us, in what we like to talk about, where our interests lie — it is this "witness" that reveals what "god" we honor, and who our "lord" truly is.

In calling believers "His" witnesses, God does not mean that "witnessing" is something we add to our usual behavior. He means that our daily conduct itself must proclaim that we are His servants, citizens in His kingdom. You, He says, "shall be MY witnesses"! Your life declares your allegiance to Me!

The goal of salvation is to transform us, through faith, from doers of evil to doers of good, and thus from witnesses for the Devil to witnesses for the Lord. You are Mine!

The gospel has been given to make us into "good trees" or "fertile fields" which produce the fruits the Lord accepts as true witness to being His.

The call to "witness," then, is not the Lord's command to be something we normally are not. No, witnessing is inescapable. We do that by every word we speak, and every deed we do.

The call to "witness" is the call to believe the gospel, to cry out for the indwelling of the Holy Spirit, to devote ourselves to learning and doing the will of the Lord — knowing that witnessing for Him will follow. We can hope to be His witnesses in no other way: "Make the tree good, and its fruit good; or make the tree bad, and its fruit bad; for the tree is known by its fruit" (Matt. 12:33).

The fruits of our hearts, harvested in the words of our lips and the works of our hands, reveal who (and whose) we truly are: Christian or worldling!

Witness is made by word and by deed. Both are required of the believer and of the Church. But the Bible stresses Word witness by the Church, and works witness by the believer. Indeed, God demands word witness by the Church, and deed witness by the believer.

Let us hear God's Word on both.

Who Does What?

The call to be the Lord's witness is addressed, as we have already noted, to both the Church and the individual believer.

God is speaking to His Church, and to His followers, when He says "you" are My witnesses.

To avoid confusion and disobedience, we must carefully distinguish between the witness required of the Church and that required of the individual.

Whatever the Lord says to His Church is, of course, indirectly addressed as well to each Christian believer. We are, all of us taken together, the Church. But we must not confuse the whole with ourselves. What is required of the Church becomes the duty of the Church.

It is hard, of course, to think of "the Church" as being one Body because of the countless divisions which mar the face which the Church presents to the world. But the Church's countless forms do not annul the truth of our own confession, expressed in the Apostles' Creed: "I believe a holy, catholic church...." We do not, and could not rephrase that into "holy, catholic churches...." We confess "a" — one — Church, in the world but not worldly (holy), divided in structures, but universal (catholic).

As St. Paul writes: "There is one body and one Spirit, just as you were called to the one hope that belongs to your call, one Lord, one faith, one baptism, one God and Father of us all, who is above all and through all and in all" (Eph. 4:4-6). All believers share in this oneness, and should therefore claim the Church, in all its diversities and divisions, as their own.

For this reason, we must recognize that the call to witnessing laid upon the Church is not addressed to a something "out there" and away from us as individuals. The Church is each of us and all of us taken together. The witness demanded of the Church, and done by the Church, is witnessing done by ourselves — in the form of the Church. There can be no "competition" between the Church's witness and that of the believer. There is only a difference of form in which that witness is made. God is as much served by one form of witness as by the other. Indeed, it is God who has made the distinction between them.

This is not to say that you "are" the Church. Nor does it in any way imply that the authority and duties of the Church become those of each of us.

Therefore, the obligation which the Lord has laid upon the Church (as His Body in history) to "bear witness" is not identical in form with the witnessing required of each believer, but is an obligation which the believer fulfills through his membership in the Body.

Rejoice, therefore, in all the Church's missions, and in all evangelistic enterprise undertaken by the Church universal — in all its different denominational forms — and see that in the Church's action *you* act! In the Church's witnessing, you are witnessing. In the Church's proclamation of the Truth you are speaking. In the Church's obedience to her Lord, you are serving Him.

How is this possible?

Because there is only one Lord, one Father, one Body, one kingdom of heaven among men. Entrance to that Body is the same for every believer — via faith through baptism.

We cannot make the one Body into many; we cannot form our own Body. Either we are in Christ's Church through faith, or we are in unbelief, outside the kingdom. Either what the Church does, we are doing, or we are not living members of that holy communion.

The witness required of the Church will differ, then, in form from the witness required of you as believer. Yet *you* obey the call addressed to the Church in the witnessing that the Church does.

Lift up your eyes, often, and behold "your" communion of saints in action all over the world! Whatever the Church is doing, right now, be it in missions and evangelism (two names for the same activity, really) be it in prayer, in worship, in good works, in the struggle for human justice, — *you* are doing! IF you are, indeed, a true believer!

The call to "witness" is addressed, as we have been stressing, in different forms to the Church and to the individual believer.

Let us listen, first, to what is asked of the Church, resolving as we do so to throw our weight behind that universal witness in thought, prayer, service, goods, talents, money, and in every other way we can.

And let us be resolved never to set our witness in competition with that laid upon the Church.

For it is God who defines, in His Word, the forms of witness He will call "His". Let us try to hear what He is saying.

The Witness Of The Church

We begin with the witness which the Bible requires of the Church.
The Church has been called to be God's "witness" across the ages.

221

The Old Testament:

The Old Testament Church begins with Adam, and in structure is limited largely to God's chosen people, Israel.

From its beginnings, the people of Israel were pointed to a mission for all the world. God says to Abraham, Patriarch of Israel and "father of the faithful" (Rom. 4:16), that, "...by you shall all the families of the earth be blessed" (Gen. 12:3). And God adds how such blessing shall take form: "And in your seed shall all the nations of the earth be blessed, because you have obeyed my voice" (Gen. 22:18).

Who is this promised "seed" of Abraham?

Paul says: "Now, to Abraham and his seed were the promises made. He does not say, And to seeds, as of many; but as of one, And to your seed, who is Christ" (Gal. 3:16).

In the Christ, and through His Church, God's blessing is destined to expand until it includes all the nations of the earth.

How? Through the Church's "witness"!

Israel's prophets anticipate that time when the promises made to Israel will ring in the ears of all peoples (including, remember, us): "Behold, you shall call nations that you know not, and nations that knew you not shall run to you, because of the Lord your God, and of the Holy One of Israel, for he has glorified you" (Is. 55:5). And again: "I am coming to gather all nations and tongues, and they shall come and see my glory" (Is. 66:18). Gather how? Through the Church's "witness"!

The prophet Micah: "...and many nations shall come, and say: 'Come, let us go up to the mountain of the Lord, to the house of the God of Jacob; that he may teach us his ways and we may walk in his paths'" (Mi. 4:2). Why will they come? Because they have heard the Church's "witness"!

Witnessing, the "outward reach," was inherent in God's plans for the Church from her beginning.

And today, as in the time of Abraham, the role of the Church in the world is to be channel for the Lord's blessing, especially through her obedience as witness.

In The New Testament:

The witness required of the Church is made specific by the Head of the Church Himself.

Jesus' parting summary of the Church's duties, given to His disciples as representatives of the New Testament Church, is commonly called the "Great Commission" — "All authority in heaven and on earth has been given to me. Go therefore and make disciples of all nations, baptizing them in the name of the Father and of the Son and of the Holy Spirit, teaching them to observe all that I have commanded you; and lo, I am with you always, to the close of the age" (Matt. 28:18-20).

And how is the Church to "make disciples"?

St. Mark's account of the "Commission" supplies the answer: "Go into all the world and preach the gospel to every nation" (Mark 16:15).

The purpose of the Church's call to "witness" is discipling. How is the Church to witness?

By preaching the Word of God!

Discipling, done through preaching, incorporates all who believe into the Church through baptism, thus taking them under instruction to learn to do *all* that the Lord has commanded.

And what is this "all" that Jesus has commanded?

It is, of course, all that is commanded in His Word, the Bible. The Church trains disciples by bringing all who believe under the discipline of the Word of the Lord. For a disciple is one who lives, and desires nothing else than to live, under the teaching of a Master.

The primary *form* of witness required of the Church is preaching the gospel.

The primary *purpose* of such witness: to train disciples of Jesus in obedience to all that He requires of those who believe.

God sent His Son, in the words of old Simeon spoken at the time of Jesus' dedication in the temple, to be "a light for revelation to the Gentiles" (Luke 2:32).

And the Church, the Body of the risen Lord through which He acts in history, is called to "witness" — by preaching — to that divine light. Indeed, it is for such witness that the Church is first of all sustained by God against all her enemies.

As the Church performs her preaching witness, you, as believer, share in it through your living membership in the Body of Christ. All the more so as you promote the Church's missionary witness through your interest, your prayers, and your support in goods and money.

The Imperatives

The Church "witnesses" first of all through preaching.

The New Testament stresses such witness time and again.

Jesus says: "This gospel of the kingdom will be preached throughout the whole world, as a testimony to all nations; and then the end will come" (Matt. 24:14).

Note with what words the Lord praises the woman who anointed Him with a costly ointment just before His last Passover in Jerusalem: "Truly, I say to you, wherever this gospel is preached in the whole world, what she has done will be told in memory of her" (Matt. 26:13). The form of witness prescibed for the Church is universal proclamation of the gospel.

Luke phrases the "Great Commission" this way: "...and that repentence and forgiveness of sins should be preached in his name to all nations" (Luke 24:47).

Jesus unites "preaching" (which He has already commanded) with "witnessing" in His last words before ascending to heaven: "...and you shall be my witnesses in Jerusalem and in all Judea and Samaria and to the end of the earth" (Acts 1:8). How, witnesses? Through preaching, of course.

The first and greatest of the Church's itinerant preachers, or missionaries, writes of his witnessing: "And this is from God, who through Christ reconciled us to himself and gave us the ministry of reconciliation; that is, God was in Christ reconciling the world to himself, not counting their trespasses against them, and entrusting to us the message of reconciliation. So we are ambassadors for Christ, God making his appeal through us. We beseech you on behalf of Christ, be reconciled to God. For our sake he made him to be sin who knew no sin, so that in him we might become the righteousness of God" (II Cor. 5:18-21).

The Church performs her witness through a ministry trained and ordained for that purpose. And when she sends a ministry abroad, she calls these ordained preachers her "missionaries" — for they are on a mission. Their mission is to "witness" through preaching, for the purpose of establishing churches wherever that preaching is blessed with believers. And so churches are planted, which themselves carry on the Word witness from obedient pulpits.

There are some things to note now:

1) Paul speaks of the preaching ministry as "ambassadors". No

"ambassador" is ever self-appointed. Nor are God's ambassadors. Paul received his commission from the ascended Lord, beginning on the Damascus road (Acts 9:3-19). The Apostles received their appointments from the lips of Jesus.

2) After the Apostolic era, missionary witnesses were appointed by the Lord's Body, the Church. So they are today. They come, preaching, as sent by God through the Body He has authorized to commission them.

3) The Bible does not know of "free lance" evangelism, carried on in independence from the Church. Self-appointed "ambassadors" lack the reality of the Lord's credentials. They may speak as if commissioned by the Lord, but only the Church is called to preach, only the Church is authorized to baptize in the name of the Trinity, and only the Church can undertake to school those who believe in a lifelong course of discipline leading to a fruitful discipleship. And therefore only the Church can commission the Lord's representatives.

4) All of the Biblical mandates to witness through preaching are addressed to the Church. She chooses and ordains those able to witness for Jesus in the Church's name.

5) The gospel becomes a witnessing power through preaching, because it is through preaching that a saving faith is created in the believer: "So faith comes from what is heard, and what is heard comes by the preaching of Christ" (Rom. 10:7). The goal of mission is, therefore, the establishing of congregations where the pulpit is sustained to create faith, where the sacraments are administered to nourish faith, and where discipline leads to true discipleship in all who believe. These are the marks of the true Church.

The primary form of witnessing required of the Church is preaching the Word of God.

We turn, now, to the form of witness required from the believer.

The Believer As Witness

We have heard how the Church answers her call to witness.

How do you, as a believer, answer your call to witness?

Jesus thought of that question, and answered it, very early in His earthly ministry.

Here is what He says to us: "Let your light so shine before men, that they may see your good works and give glory to your Father who is in heaven" (Matt. 5:16).

It is obvious how the witness of the Church leads into the witness required of the believer: show through your behavior that you are being "discipled" by Christ through the ministry of His Church.

This is the form assigned the believer's witnessing.

We can see how the form given the Church's witness is adapted to the form required of the Church member.

Jesus has a "commission" for His Church. We have heard it.

He has a "commission" for each of us, too.

And Jesus has told us what that commission is: "Let your light so shine...!"

St. Peter repeats the believer's commission: "Maintain good conduct among the Gentiles, so that in case they speak against you as wrongdoers, they may see your good works and glorify God on the day of visitation" (I Pet. 2:12).

The Church, as Body of Christ, is of course required to do good works through her diaconate, acting for the membership. And the believer, as believer, is required to witness by word as well as in deed, as we shall see. But the basic word witness of the Church flows into the basic works witness of the believer, by divine design.

Does the Lord's basic "commission" to believers seem, at least at first, less dramatic than the "Great Commission" given the Church? Many of us have an itch to be out and sharing the Good News with our lips, like the missionaries and evangelists commissioned by the Church. Some see no reason for not hearing the Church's commission as their own.

But, as we have seen, the Lord's command to witness bears a different form for the Church than it does for the believer — while the believer also shares, as a member, in the Church's witnessing.

It soon becomes evident, too, that the believer's "commission" is no less challenging than that given the Church — and is no easier. May even seem harder, perhaps? (Of course, evangelists and missionaries are "believers," too, and so share the believer's obligation to do works witness as well as the Word witness required of them by the Body.)

What kind of "light," do you suppose is asked of you as believer? How about this: "But I say to you, Love your enemies and pray for those who persecute you, so that you may be sons of your Father who is in heaven; for he makes his sun rise on the evil and on the good, and sends rain on the just and on the unjust...You, therefore, must be perfect, as your heavenly Father is perfect" (Matt. 5:44-45, 48). Does anyone imagine that the witnessing life is an easy life? Or that he can do without the Church's instruction and discipline and go it on his own?

Add this, as a required way of shedding "light" into the world: "...if your enemy is hungry, feed him; if he is thirsty, give him drink; for by so doing you will heap burning coals upon his head" (Rom. 12:20). The inspired writer is not speaking of being nice to our friends. He does not consider this much of a witness. He is not urging us to be especially thoughtful of fellow believers. This obligation he thinks we know. He is setting a far higher standard for our "witness," and testing its quality: how do we treat those we count, or who count us, as "enemies"? That is where "perfection" witnesses to its presence...or absence!

And Paul is here only echoing the words of Jesus: "For if you love those who love you, what reward have you? Do not even the tax collectors do the same? And if you salute only your brethren, what more are you doing than others? Do not even the Gentiles do the same?" (Matt. 5:46-47). Witness is more than being nice; witness is hard work!

The forms of witness required of true believers are indeed so difficult that we may quite unconsciously prefer the seemingly easier task of "speaking a word for Jesus" — and are eager, therefore, to hear that the Church's mandate is laid also upon individual believers. And there is of course occasion for individual oral witness, as we will observe, but our words are never a substitute for the "light" gleaming from obedient behavior. *Saying* "Lord, Lord" is no substitute, Jesus says, for doing the will of God, which is our required witness (Matt. 7:21).

We have seen, now, that Word "witnessing" is one basic reason why the Church is in the world.

We have seen, too, that works "witnessing" is why believers are "saved" out of the kingdoms of the world.

It is, indeed, in the combination of Word and works "witnessing" that the gospel comes full circle.

Shall we see how?

From Witness to Witness

The witness of the Church finds its goal in the witness of the believer, as we have already briefly noted.

But this is so important that we repeat it: the "word" witness of the Church, through preaching, finds its goal in the "works" witness of the true believer, done in obedience to the Word!

We do not propose this as our opinion; we repeat it as the truth of

God's Word, revealed through St. Paul: "For we are his workmanship, created in Christ Jesus for good works, which God prepared beforehand, that we should walk in them" (Eph. 2:10).

The whole "scheme" of salvation (from Word witness to works witness) is summed up in these inspired words:

1) The believer's faith is not his own creation: "we are his workmanship...."

2) Paul stresses that our salvation is by grace just before the passage we have quoted: "For by grace you have been saved through faith; and this is not your own doing, it is the gift of God — not because of works, lest any man should boast" (Eph. 2:8-9). The inspired Word lays to rest here (and elsewhere) any notion that we "save" ourselves.

3) Our salvation is "in Christ Jesus...." This is the gospel.

4) But we are "saved" in Christ for a purpose.

5) God's purpose in "saving" believers is "for good works...."

6) In short, although we are not saved *by* good works, we are saved *for* them! Doing good works fulfills God's purpose in saving us.

7) God also has already determined what good works we are to do; He has prepared before our arrival what kind of witness we are to make.

It is evident from Paul's teaching that the goal of the Church's preaching witness is found in the believer's works witness.

Let us examine further Biblical teaching that fills out the outline just given.

Light!

The good works required of the believer are called "light". Jesus says, we recall: "Let your light so shine before men that seeing...."

Reading only this far we could start speculating as to what "light" means.

What could I do that would be seen as a "light" by others?

By my words? By my success? By my stylish elegance? By my fame? By my reputation for "soul-winning"? By my social, economic, or political clout? In short, by my becoming something men take notice of?!

The Lord does not define "light" in any of these ways. And no doubt we can guess why not: the gospel is not focused on what is eye-catching by everyday worldly standards.

Jesus says: "Let your light so shine before men, that they may see your good works...." (Matt. 5:16).

Ah, that's it! "Good works" shed light. It is by such works that we shed the light which becomes the believer's "witness" to his faith and to his Lord.

If you are wondering, incidentally, whether or not Jesus has some prejudice against the options we first proposed — talk, success, elegance, etc. — we may infer by the measure He proposes: do the options proposed compel people to "give glory to your Father..."? Or to *you*! Are they "good works" as defined by God's Law, or by popular acclaim?

Our word witness, in company with our works witness, may indeed help focus the "light" our works shed. St. Peter writes about that. What if someone wants to know why, for example, you are doing good to an "enemy"? Peter says: "...be ready always to give an answer to every man that asks you a reason of the hope that is in you, with meekness and fear" (I Pet. 3:15). The good works shed the light; our words may help others to "see" better what that light reveals about the Author of our faith. First, works; then, words!

But how do good works shed "light"?

We can answer that important question in several ways:

1) Our good works testify to our being "in Christ". Paul writes, for each believer: "I have been crucified with Christ; it is no longer I who live but Christ who lives in me; and the life I now live in the flesh I live by faith in the Son of God, who loved me and gave himself for me" (Gal. 2:20). Good works, then, are simply the evidence that the believer is "in Christ". But what does Christ call himself: "I am the light of the world; he who follows me will not walk in darkness, but will have the light of life" (John 8:12). Good works can be said to shed light, then, because they reflect our being in Him who is light. Our works do not themselves possess light-giving power; they reflect the light of Him whose presence we proclaim in the works we do.

2) Again: good works can be said to give light because they in-carnate God's Word. Good works provide the Word with "flesh" through our obedient behavior. And God's Word is spoken of as "light" — as "a lamp to the feet" of each believer, and "a light upon the path" of the obedient. Walking in that light reflects light — which others, seeing, credit to the Source of the Word, God Himself.

3) The Bible always contrasts good with evil as light with darkness. Believers who know God's will, and do it in the form of good works,

know whom they serve and why they do as they do. Unbelievers stumble in the confusion of fad and fashion, unaware of their slavery to God's Enemy. Amidst the chaos of conflicting unbeliefs, the works of believers are as the sober among the drunken, as light shining in the shadows.

Jesus is the world's "light". The reconciling purpose for which He assumed our flesh is accomplished through every believer who obediently incarnates "all I have commanded you" in good works. Those who "see," and understand, will then return thanks, not to us, but to God.

The cycle of witness is then complete: God gives all that we have and are, and creates a saving faith within us; we use our talents in good works; God receives the praise.

Full Circle!

When the Word witness of the Church achieves its goal in the works witness of the believer, then the power of the gospel has come full circle. This is true for:

The Church:

The Church achieves the purpose for which she is commissioned in the believer's witness through good works.

For the "Great Commission" under which her Lord sends her out into the world requires teaching believers "to do all that I have commanded you" (Matt. 28:20). Her "pupils" demonstrate the Church's success in carrying out the "Great Commission".

The Church completes the mission of her witness in the good works witness of her membership.

The Bible:

The Word of God also achieves its goal in the good works witness of believers. For this is the purpose for which the Word was "breathed" into being by God the Holy Spirit, as we have already heard St. Paul explain: "All scripture is inspired by God and is profitable...."

God does not send His written Word into the world aimlessly, nor simply to increase by one the stock of books upon the world's shelves. Nor is He concerned to augment our supply of information, or to provide occasion for theological speculation.

No, God has a certain "profit" in mind, His and ours: "...and is profitable for teaching, for reproof, for correction, and for training in righteousness...."

This is why the Church takes the Bible as her textbook for teaching believers to do all that their Savior has commanded. The Bible is God's own training manual. The Church serves as the believer's teacher. "All who would have God as their Father," writes John Calvin, "must have the Church as their mother" — from spiritual birth to physical death.

Why, then, did God inspire the Bible?

Paul finishes the instruction we have been quoting: "...for training in righteousness, that the man of God may be complete, equipped for every good work" (II Tim. 3:16-17).

The Bible, too, achieves the end for which it was inspired in the light shed by the good works of believers trained in the Word.

The Christ:

Jesus achieves His mission in the good works witness of believers. For He says, "I am come that they (His sheep) may have life, and have it abundantly" (John 10:10).

And what, according to our Lord, is life: "And this is eternal life, that they know thee the only true God, and Jesus Christ whom thou hast sent" (John 17:3).

"Knowing" God is manifest in the witness of good works: "Did not your father eat and drink and do justice and righteousness?" the prophet Jeremiah asks Israel (and us), "Then it was well with him. He judged the cause of the poor and the needy; then it was well. Is not this to know me? says the Lord" (Jer. 22:15-16). The "knowing" of God which is eternal life *is* the doing of good works! So the Lord teaches through His prophet.

The Lord Jesus comes to give believers "life". The "life" He offers consists in "knowing God" through "keeping His Word".

The believer's witness in good works shows that in him Jesus has accomplished what He came to do for him.

Through our good works each of us witnesses that he is saved, by faith, by Jesus Christ.

For such salvation Jesus took human flesh and died for our sins.

All comes full circle when the witness of the Church becomes the witness of the believer.

That is what Christianity is in the world to do!

Priests

The believer's obligation to witness by means of good works is further driven home by the Scriptures in yet another way.

Citizens of the kingdom of heaven — that is, all who believe — are spoken of in the Bible in a unique way — as a *kingdom of priests:* "made...a kingdom of priests unto God..." (Rev. 1:6). St. Peter says to us: "But you are a chosen race, a royal priesthood, a holy nation, God's own people..." (I Pet. 2:9).

The prophet Isaiah foretells: "But you shall be called the priests of the Lord, men shall speak of you as the ministers of our God" (Is. 61:6).

And all this echoes the Lord's word to Israel: "...and you shall be to me a kingdom of priests and a holy nation" (Ex. 19:6).

What is a priest?

A priest, from the beginning of the Church of Israel, is one who sacrifices.

Why, then, is the Church so often called a "kingdom of priests"?

First, because membership in the Church is citizenship in the kingdom of heaven. The Church is a "kingdom" of believers, those loyal to the King, Jesus Christ, saved and led by Him.

Second, the true believer is called "priest" because he is required to do sacrifice, the *sacrifice of himself*! That is, to do good works! Paul chooses just this language of priesthood to require of us self-sacrificial obedience in the form of good works: "I appeal to you, therefore, brethren, by the mercies of God, to present your bodies as a living sacrifice, holy and acceptable to God, which is your spiritual worship" (Rom. 12:1) — and then for this and the next three chapters of this inspired letter, Paul specifies the kind of good works which the self-sacrifice he has in mind requires (Rom. 12-15).

O yes! True believers constitute a kingdom of priests! For they do priestly business: sacrifice! of themselves!

The priesthood of believers rests upon a command which we have heard Jesus lay upon all who would follow Him, namely to assume for themselves the symbol of His own self-sacrifice, a cross: "If any man would come after me, let him deny himself and take up his cross and follow me" (Matt. 16:24). Let the believer, that is, truly don priestly vestments — with himself as the offering he presents to God, in the form of the witness of good works!

Just how serious the Lord is about this kind of priesthood emerges in what He goes on to say: "For whoever would save his life will lose it, and whoever loses his life for my sake will find it" (Matt. 16:25). Obedience has no options: either self-sacrifice now, or the ultimate loss of life in the hereafter!

Yes, believers are a kingdom of priests — but only because we perform the kind of self-sacrifice which the Lord demands!

*　　*　　*

The priesthood of all believers is sometimes misunderstood as an office wielding authority, or authorized to share witness in the form required of the Church.

There is such a priesthood.

But it is not the priesthood of self-sacrifice imposed upon all who would be citizens of the kingdom of God.

There are, in the Church, appointed priests. So it was in Israel; so it has been from the beginning of the New Testament Church, though not now an acknowledged office in all communions.

Entrance upon this priestly office is by appointment, made by the Church through channels long established for the purpose. This priesthood is not common to all believers, nor assumed by anyone upon his own initiative.

Even Jesus Himself, God's chosen "high Priest," did not seize His office, but was called to it by His Father: "So also Christ did not exalt himself to be made a high priest, but was appointed by him who said to him, 'Thou art my Son, today have I begotten thee'" (Heb. 5:5). And, following divine precedent, "every high priest chosen from among men is appointed..." (Heb. 5:1). And this appointment is by the Church, where the appointing God is now represented among men.

The priesthood of self-sacrifice required of *all* believers is one we enter upon through faith. The office of priesthood in the Church is open only to those whom the Church herself appoints.

Be sure never to confuse the two.

And do not use the phrase "priesthood of believers" to self-appoint yourself to an "office" of "witness" which only the Church may fill. You might fool yourself, and perhaps fool others by seeming to be doing notable (and noticeable) work for the Lord, but "Be not deceived; God is not mocked, for whatever a man sows, that he will also reap" (Gal. 6:7). The fruits of disobedience are not the harvest anyone wants to reap. Don't sow them!

Nothing To Do?

You may be wondering, now, if the believer, as believer, has nothing to do for Jesus in missions and evangelism. Nothing to say? No faith to share? No souls to save?

O yes, there are words to be said, and ways to point the lost toward home. But we do find such questions surprising.

Nothing for the believer to be doing, really, for Jesus if your lips be not busy? Is it nothing to seek the "perfection" we have already heard Him demand: "You, therefore, must be perfect, as your heavenly Father is perfect" (Matt. 5:48)?

Nothing to do in the Church except as missionary or evangelist? Is it nothing to set out on a course of training under the Word calculated to school yourself toward achieving what Jesus requires the Church to accomplish, namely "teaching them to do *all* that I have commanded you" (Matt. 28:20)? Will any of us ever really even come close?

Nothing to do in the face of the Lord's commandments, summarized in the two obligations: "You shall love the Lord your God with all your heart, and with all your soul, and with all your strength, and with all your mind; and your neighbor as yourself" — a summary of the Law which Jesus endorses: "...do this, and you will live" (Luke 10:27-28)?

Can any believer *really* think that, as a believer, the Lord asks of him but little to do, so little that in order to serve obediently he must also undertake some of the tasks laid upon the Church?!

Have you been reading the Bible seriously enough? Or finding the Word preached clearly enough? Should we not rather be asking, with St. Paul: "Who is sufficient for these things?" (II Cor. 2:16).

But we may ask: does not the "doing" which the Lord requires at least include witnessing by word, even though it rejects substituting word for deed?

Of course, the prospect of our "saving a soul" is so attractive that doing good works of any other kind may look unimportant by comparison.

That seems so obvious that we wonder why we, and not the Bible, perceive it. Why doesn't the Word of God put witnessing by word at the top of the requirements laid upon believers as it does upon the Church?

For the Bible obviously requires "soul-saving" of the Church. Just as the Bible empowers the Church to baptize, and obliges the Church to train those who are being saved. And just as the Bible prescribes "preaching" as the mode of creating faith, and restricts the authority to preach to those "sent" by the Church. Why?

God alone knows "why". But He clearly joins preaching, baptism, and lifelong training of believers together — and assigns all to the

Church!

That is evident from the "Great Commission," were it taught no-where else in the inspired Word — though, as we have seen, it clearly is.

But the believer, as believer, is indeed asked to speak a word for the Lord.

As believer, however, and not as self-ordained witness of the Body!

Believers are to bear oral witness in several contexts:

1) Jesus heals a man "with an unclean spirit," the victim of demon-possession. The grateful believer then wants to go with Jesus there-after. But the Lord lays upon him, and so upon all who recognize that by faith they are liberated from the tyranny of the Devil, this obliga-tion: "Go home to your friends, and tell them how much the Lord has done for you, and how he has had mercy on you." Obedient, the man did as he was asked: "And he went away and began to proclaim in Decapolis how much Jesus had done for him; and all men marveled" (Mark 5:2-20). Believers have an account to give of what Jesus does for us! Being sure, of course, that our stress is always on *Jesus* and not only on *us*! There is ever the risk that our oral witness turns out to be what "I" have done for Jesus.

2) And we must be aware, of course, that such witness can easily slip into some assertion of our own unusual piety. The Lord objects to that: "Beware of practising [shall we say 'advertising'] your piety before men in order to be seen by them; for then you will have no reward in heaven" (Matt. 6:1).

3) Rather, observe the advice of St. Paul: "Conduct yourselves wisely toward outsiders, making the most of the time. Let your speech always be gracious, seasoned with salt, so that you may know how to answer every one" (Col. 4:5-6).

4) Because you know that faith is wrought in the believer by the Word preached, and confirmed by baptism, an important part of your oral witness can consist of urging others to come to Church. This is a pattern established among those who became Jesus' first disciples: "One of the two who heard John speak, and followed him, was Andrew, Simon Peter's brother. He first found his brother Simon, and said to him, 'We have found the Messiah' (which means Christ). He brought him to Jesus. Jesus looked at him, and said, 'So you are Simon the son of John? You shall be called Cephas' (which means Peter)" (John 1:40-42). Just as Andrew brought his brother to the living Lord, so we are to bring others to that Lord's living Body, the Church, where that

Lord's living Word, the Holy Scriptures, is faithfully preached. And He will do the rest!

Again, after Jesus had said to Philip of Galilee, "Follow me," Philip found Nathanael, and said to him, "'We have found him of whom Moses in the law and also the prophets wrote, Jesus of Nazareth, the son of Joseph'" Nathanael is sceptical, as any of our hearers may be, and Philip provides us with a response: "Come and see."

This is the word laid upon the lips of the believer who engages in evangelism: *Come! See* for yourself...in the Church!

And those who do come may discover, as did Nathanael, that the Lord has known them all along: "Jesus saw Nathanael coming to him, and said of him, 'Behold, an Israelite indeed, in whom is no guile!'"

Nathanael is surprised to discover that the Lord had "seen" him before he saw Jesus: "How do you know me?"

"Jesus answered him, 'Before Philip called you, when you were under the fig tree, I saw you.'"

Wherever anyone's fig tree may be, whatever his condition, whoever he is, the Lord "sees" him — and waits upon his coming into the orbit of the Church. Your word, like Philip's, can issue the invitation.

"Nathanael answered him, 'Rabbi, you are the Son of God! You are the King of Israel!'" (Adapted from John 1:43-49). Philip's invitation had achieved its purpose! So can yours!

Of course, believers can, and must, witness with words: come!

And thus lead others to the Word who saves!

5) We have already heard the command issued to us through Peter: "Always be prepared to make a defense to any one who calls you to account for the hope that is in you, yet do it with gentleness and reverence..." (I Pet. 3:15).

Such an accounting requires the knowledge of the Scriptures which the Church exists to teach, and we are to acquire by persistent study, besides, so that when asked we can witness by our answer.

No doubt the Lord is thinking, here, of the question roused by the witness of those good works which draw attention because they gleam like a light in the world's dark selfishness and passion. And when someone asks, "But why?" — why so thoughtful, so kind, so unselfish, so loving, so quietly helpful: "Always be prepared..." to answer by pointing the questioner to the Lord and His Church!

6) Never forgetting: "So neither he who plants nor he who waters is anything, but only God who gives the increase" (I Cor. 3:7). A "witness" is one who reports, not about himself but about Another.

And More

There is still more witnessing the believer can do.

Witness by giving your weight to the Church, in:

1) Prayer.

"Pray, therefore, the Lord of the harvest, that he will send forth laborers into his harvest" (Matt. 9:38).

This is the answer to St. Paul's question: "And how are they to hear without a preacher? And how can men preach unless they are sent?" (Rom. 10:14-15).

The Church is supported by the prayers of believers who call upon the Lord of the harvest to "send" through His Body the church-building mission which the world needs.

Believers play their role, their oral role, in prayer.

2) In prayer backed up by generosity:

St. Paul writes to Timothy: "Let the elders who rule well be considered worthy of double honor, especially those who labor in preaching and teaching; for the scripture says, 'You shall not muzzle an ox when it is treading out the grain,' and, 'The laborer deserves his wages'" (I Tim. 5:17-18; he is quoting Deut. 25:4, and Luke 10:7).

The "double honor" which the Apostle has in mind is, no doubt, a) the respect due God's appointed representatives, and b) the support in money and goods they need while serving the Church. Paul has used the quotation before about permitting the ox to eat of the grain it treads. He writes to Corinth: "Is it for oxen that God is concerned? Does he not speak entirely for our sake? It was written for our sake, because the plowman should plow in hope and the thresher thresh in hope of a share in the crop. If we have sown spiritual good among you, is it too much if we reap your material benefits?" (I Cor. 9:10-12).

Believers witness to their participation in the mission and evangelism of the Church by their financial support of the Body. This is not an optional form of witness; it is required, as we have just heard.

*   *   *

And finally, always bear clearly in mind that the obligation of witness is laid upon all, Church and believer alike; but that the form prescribed for witnessing differs: the priority of good works in your witness as believer, and the priority of preaching in the witness of the Church.

Recall every day that the witness of the Church reaches its God-given goal in your witness as believer.

So the Word of God clearly teaches.

One more thing: to the Church, not the believer, has been entrusted the ultimate responsibility for the destiny of those to whom her witness is made: "And I tell you, you are Peter, and on this rock I will build my church, and the powers of hell shall not prevail against it. I will give you the keys of the kingdom of heaven, and whatever you bind on earth shall be bound in heaven, and whatever you loose on earth shall be loosed in heaven" (Matt. 16:18-19).

This is the Word of the Lord!

Let no individual dare lay claim to that awesome responsibility!

And let the Church never shirk its implications!

For Reflection And Discussion

1. *How are we always involved in witnessing?*
2. *In what primary form is the Church required to witness?*
3. *Indicate how this is already evident in the Old Testament.*
4. *What is the primary form of witness required of the believer?*
5. *What relation does the Bible establish between evangelism and good works?*
6. *What does the Bible mean by "a kingdom of priests"? Are you one of them?*
7. *How can believers bear word witness?*

PART FOUR

GOD'S BLESSING

Chapter 17.

HOPE

We have been born anew to a living hope.
I Peter 1:3

HOPE

TRUTH:
Hope is the work of the Holy Spirit, and illumines the Christian life by anchoring the believer's future within heaven itself.
RESPONSE:
The believer nourishes hope by constant recourse to the Word of God and persistent meditation upon its countless promises.
DISTORTION:
Effort to substitute the "seen" for the "unseen", to ground hope in knowledge instead of in faith.

HOPE

Faith, hope, and love form an inseparable trinity.

St. Paul makes it clear, in the thirteenth chapter of I Corinthians, that in the Christian life faith, hope, and love dwell in us together. Earlier in the chapter he says that, "Love...believes all things, hopes all things..." (v. 7). It is love, then, which unites faith and hope with itself into the essence of the Christian life.

In the light of all that has been said in this *Handbook* before, starting at the very outset with "God's initiative," we can now see that hope is not something we can acquire for ourselves.

Hope, like all that the Christian enjoys and uses, is God's gift.

But, like all other gifts from above, hope must be sought to be received.

Let us ask, first, what hope does and then how hope is created within us.

What Hope Does

Children live by anticipation, which is the natural form of hope. So do adults.

"Nothing to look forward to" is the curse of the meaningless life.

Even though our expectations may be for things quickly past, even events trivial in themselves, a day begun with nothing to fix the heart on is a day dull indeed. A life bereft of all anticipation, or haunted by fears unrelieved by any expectation of good, is temptation to suicide.

Anticipation — the natural hope of something that pleases, definite or indefinite, great or small — underlies the mood in which we face the passing hours. The day derives its color from the brightness or dullness of our expectations.

Hope embroiders life with "tone," often called optimism; its absence shrouds us in pessimism — as is so plainly evident in children, and can easily be observed in ourselves.

Much of the restless going and coming so typical of our time reflects the desperate necessity to "look forward" to something in order to get through the day — even if we know from experience that doing whatever lent hope to the passing hours may turn out in itself to afford little real pleasure. We, like the child, are easily made victims of our emotions, and have to fix them on some anticipation to live with ourselves.

We know well enough through experience, then, what hope in the form of anticipation means.

Now, the hope of which the Bible frequently speaks lifts our natural experience of expectation into another dimension.

Our daily hopes suffer inevitably from the daily discovery that what we looked forward to is either not so much in itself or is cut short by the passage of time. Christian hope opens another horizon, not bounded by time, and not really subject to disappointment, though it may vary from hour to hour in strength and vividness.

The Scripture puts it this way: "We have this as a sure and stedfast anchor of the soul, a hope that enters into the inner shrine behind the curtain, where Jesus has gone as a forerunner on our behalf..." (Heb. 6:19).

With a beautiful figure of speech the Bible pictures hope as casting an anchor — taking sure hold — into heaven itself!

Our childish and natural anticipations point beyond and above themselves. They reflect a profound and desperate thirst of the self for anchorage in true hope. The expectation of a "treat" that brightens a child's day, or the anticipation of a call, or card, or visit that illumines the hours for a shut-in, bear God's own witness to His sure relief of the deep hunger of the self made in His Image for communion with Him.

Our daily desire for "something to look forward to" should be understood as reflecting our deep longing for a communion that passes not away — one we can in fact enjoy right now (!) through hope. A hope that, as the Apostle says, "enters" behind the curtain of time and space into heaven itself. And our disappointments in finding that whatever else we anticipated does not quite live up to expectation, or is quickly borne away in time's elusive theft — these disappointments are not meant to rob us of the daily pleasures of anticipation, but are intended to teach us that we must look above, and beyond, our daily expectations to the genuine and God-given hope of which they are but mirrors.

Christian hope transmutes the passage of time from a mockery of all our dreams into a pilgrimage walked in the light of timeless eternity.

Christian hope fills the emptiness left by life's last farewells with the sweet voice of eternity's first greeting, "Come, ye beloved of my Father...!" (Matt. 25:34).

The Stoic life, as taught and practiced by the ancient Roman philosophers, was a passionate effort to deprive life of all passion, and to silence expectation at its very birth in the self.

Christian hope does not smother our natural anticipations. It simply illumines what they mean.

Paganism peoples its temples with gods to justify otherwise unanchored hopes. The hold which the primitive medicine man and witch doctor has on his victims resides in his presumed control of things hoped for. Just as the lure of the gambling table, the vision of eventual success, and the challenge of the unknown all confirm the poet's "Hope springs eternal in the human breast" (Pope).

But, as Paul said to the Athenians about their worship of unknown gods, the Christian faith says to all the natural anticipations of mankind: "What therefore you worship as unknown, this I proclaim to you" (Acts 17:23).

Faith inspires the expectations that color our days with a hope that re-makes our lives! For the hope that springs from love will flower, as we shall see, in joy!

How Is Hope Obtained?

Hope is the work of the Holy Spirit: "May the God of hope," Paul writes, "fill you with all joy and peace in believing, so that by the power of the Holy Spirit you may abound in hope" (Rom. 15:13).

But hope is not to be sought by direct appeal to the Spirit. Hope is the fruit of faith which the Spirit works in us, as we have already described, through the Word. As Paul puts it: "For through the Spirit, by faith, we wait for the hope of righteousness" (Gal. 5:5). And, "whatever was written in former days was written for our instruction, that by steadfastness and by encouragement of the scriptures we might have hope" (Rom. 15:4).

Hope is the expectation, created in the believer through faith, of all things promised us in God's Word. Faith believes the Word to be true. Hope lifts up our hearts to the time when all that the Word says will be accomplished. Faith believes that God is, as the Word says, indeed our Father. Hope fully expects God to prove Himself, over and again, to *be* a Father — not indeed in giving us all that we may like, but in dealing with us exactly as we need to enter upon the joy of eternal life. Faith is thus the foundation of hope, while hope feeds our faith with echoes out of heaven itself.

The Word sums it up: "For in this hope are we saved. Now hope that is seen is not hope" (Rom. 8:24). That is to say, as we have already observed about daily expectations, hope sets the atmosphere, the environment, of the Christian life. Saints exude an aura of calm, of certainty, almost of living already in another world — an environment that is breathed into their lives by the Holy Spirit through hope. They have learned the wisdom of the prophet: "If it seem slow, wait for it; it will surely come, it will not delay" (Hab. 2:3). Such godly patience is the offspring of hope.

Faith which has given birth to hope underlies such an attitude toward life. The saint is no longer at the mercy of events; faith, fruitful in hope, has established the core of his life in the rock which is Christ — the winds and rains of life beat indeed, but what is built upon that rock is not shaken (thanks to faith) nor afraid (thanks to hope)! The hurts and the pains of life remain real, but are no longer devastating. Hope has lifted the eyes of the inner self above the ebb and flow of daily events. The surface of the sea of life may be agitated, sometimes boiling and boisterous, but hope calms the waters underneath.

So closely related are faith and hope that the terms may be used almost interchangeably in the Scriptures: "By his great mercy we have been born again to a living hope through the resurrection of Jesus Christ from the dead, and to an inheritance which is imperishable, undefiled and unfading, kept in heaven for you, who by God's power are guarded through faith for a salvation ready to be revealed in the last time" (I Pet. 1:3-5).

Here the inspired Word points to the already accomplished defeat of our "last enemy, death" (I Cor. 15:26), a defeat guaranteed the believer by faith, and enjoyed in hope. In the bright light of a hope created and nourished, through faith, by the Word, the believer joins Paul in the wildly joyous shout: "Death is swallowed in victory! O death, where is thy victory? O death, where is thy sting?" (I Cor. 15:54-55; quoting Is. 25:8, and Hos. 13:14).

The triumphant voice of hope comes to focus in thanksgiving: "But thanks be to God, who gives us the victory through our Lord Jesus Christ" (I Cor. 15:57).

If we seek hope, then, we must go again and again to the Word, as preached in the Church, and to the Word waiting upon our reading at our hand.

Yes, hope has its ups and downs.

But if we examine the "downs," we will find that they relate to neglect of the Word.

The hope we need from the Spirit, the hope we may expect from the Spirit, the hope we must have from the Spirit, itself waits upon our constant recourse to the Spirit's chosen vehicle: the inspired Word, the Holy Scriptures. We may paraphrase the great prophet: "Seek the Lord *where* he may be found, call upon him while he is near..." (Is. 55:6).

Our "dry" seasons, our hopeless moments, our spiritually cloudy days owe much of their monotony to our neglect of God's Word.

Do we lack hope?

Do we want hope?

Seek it where God wills that hope be found!

Make a close companion of your Bible! God will do the rest!

For Reflection And Discussion

1. *What does hope do for us?*
2. *Explain the Biblical use of an anchor for hope.*
3. *How do we obtain hope?*
4. *What is the relation between hope and faith?*
5. *How is childish anticipation a model of Christian hope?*
6. *What does hope do for daily living?*

Chapter 18.

JOY

These things have I spoken to you, that my joy may be in you, and that your joy may be full.
John 15:11

JOY

TRUTH:
Joy is a uniquely Christian term for a uniquely Christian experience, the byproduct of obedience, gift of the Holy Spirit, and foretaste of heaven.
RESPONSE:
Setting of the will upon the doing of God's will, and rejoicing in God's blessings.
DISTORTION:
The confusion of fun, pleasure, or hyped-up emotions with joy.

Joy

Joy is a uniquely Christian term for a uniquely Christian experience.

Pagan religions seek for ecstasy, a self-induced hypnosis, wild and unrestrained. The aftermath to ecstatic experience is the let-down. The self lacks the energy to sustain the "high" indefinitely.

Recreation aims at fun, by-product of the game. Fun wears out after a while.

Everyone seeks pleasure in whatever excites the senses. Success depends upon the resources of wherever pleasure is sought. Some pleasures end quickly, others endure. But, soon or late, all pleasures pall, worn out in themselves or having worn out the taste for them.

Only joy lasts, and grows.

This is because joy is foretaste of heaven.

Hope, we are told, casts an anchor into the precincts of God's presence. Joy is the pulse which flows back along the anchor-cable.

Joy cannot be defined. For those who know it by experience, definition is unnecessary. To those who yet have to receive it, definition is inadequate.

Joy is more exhilarating than fun, more pleasant than pleasure.

Joy flares. Joy fades. But having once experienced it, the believer knows that joy is the inexhaustible resource for the Christian life.

Joy stands at the decisive dividing-line between the "old" self which the believer is trying to crucify, and the "new" self we are trying to mature.

The "old" self comes to the Bible with its own interpretation of joy. It defines joy in terms of pleasure or fun, a self-indulgence we can achieve on our own. That is because the "old" self always lives in a world divided between the pleasant (to be sought) and the unpleasant (to be avoided). In that scheme, Christianity of course must belong to the "pleasant" and the "positive" — a kind of celestial pep-pill. That makes the "old" self a sucker for any presentation of the "gospel" which neglects cross-bearing, the narrow gate and the hard road.

But these lie, of course, at the very heart of the gospel. We have heard the Lord require those who would follow Him to take up their cross, deny themselves (and their pleasures!), and walk the narrow road of discipleship (see Chapter 3).

Only those will know the experience of joy!

A "gospel" which detours obedience, avoids hardship, and wreathes our faces in toothy smiles produces no joy! For such a "gospel" could not understand St. Paul's, "I am exceedingly joyful in all our tribulation" (II Cor. 7:4). Such a "gospel" would never produce the joy experienced by the early disciples who were first beaten and imprisoned for teaching in the name of Jesus, and then called before the Jewish council. The council "charged them not to speak in the name of Jesus, and let them go." And they, determined to go on speaking, "left the presence of the council, rejoicing that they were counted worthy to suffer dishonor for the name. And every day in the temple and at home they did not cease teaching and preaching the name of Jesus Christ" (Acts 5:40-42). The Apostles were re-joicing (which is joy multiplied) not because they got clean away, not because they had prevailed through the power of their positive attitude — no, because they had endured punishment and saw persecution ahead!

Joy always remains elusively out of reach of the "old" man, but his counterfeits for it are legion.

Joy Is Byproduct:

God endows the obedient with joy — the more difficult the obedience and the more stringent the self-denial, the greater the joy. Joy spins off from obedience. Like heaven, joy comes as surprise to those whose lives are full of thankful service to God and neighbor. This is why the saints can, indeed, and do, find joy in the hardships imposed upon them by living the Christian life. Only the saintly know experientially the truth of their Lord's severe prescription, spoken as the last of the Beatitudes: "Blessed are you when men revile you and persecute you and utter all kinds of evil against you falsely on my account. Rejoice and be glad, for your reward is great in heaven, for so men persecuted the prophets who were before you" (Matt. 5:11).

Consider: we as believers can experience what the prophets experienced!

But observe how carefully Jesus limits the cause for the opposition that promises joy to the victims of persecution: 1) The suffering must be on His account; and, 2) the charges must in fact be contrived, inaccurate, untrue.

The "old" self can invite enmity and opposition in many ways, none of them productive of joy. Pride may stimulate envy, hatred, adverse reaction: so may greed, selfishness, discrimination, indifference, brutality. But the opposition these provoke gives no occasion for joy. The Christian must always be sure that the hardship he suffers is in fact for obedience to that Lord, and not because his "old" self remains obnoxious! How can we judge that? By keeping before us the standards set for our conduct by the inspired Word. And by carefully discriminating the pleasure that opposition can stimulate in some characters from the joy that flows from suffering in obedience to the Truth.

Joy Is Gift:

We cannot reach out and lay hold of joy. Those who think so must be satisfied with fun or pleasure.

We can make ourselves eligible for joy — by obedience to the Word of the Lord.

So Jesus says: "If you keep my commandments, you will abide in my love, just as I have kept my Father's commandments and abide in his love. These things I have spoken to you, that my joy may be in you, and that your joy may be full" (John 15:10-11).

Into joy by way of obedience. This is the Lord's prescription. It is the route which He Himself followed: "...Jesus, the pioneer and perfecter of our faith, who for the joy that was set before him endured the cross, despising the shame, and is seated at the right hand of the throne of God" (Heb. 12:2).

Using the familiar analogy of sowing, the Psalmist repeats the same truth this way: "He that goes forth weeping, bearing the seed for sowing, shall come home with shouts of joy, bringing his sheaves with him" (Ps. 126:6). The divinely established pattern is ever the same. The easy life, on the broad way, attains only pleasure. The strenuous life, on the hard road of obedience, is crowned with joy. Samson put it in the form of a riddle, after he discovered that bees had filled with honey the mouth of a lion he had slain: "Out of the eater came something to eat. Out of the strong came something sweet" (Judg. 14:14). The prophet (for such Samson was) sums up what God provides in the life of the believer, what Christianity is really all about. Out of the crucified body and shed blood of the Christ, God makes nourishing food, exemplified in the sacrament. Out of the threats of the strong, and persecution of the weak, God brings forth the sweetness of joy.

"I will turn their mourning into joy," the Lord says, "I will comfort them, and give them gladness for sorrow" (Jer. 31:13).

How does God do so?

Through the gift of His Spirit, as we have seen in Chapter 9. For one of the "fruits of the Spirit" is *joy* (Gal. 5:22).

Everlasting:

Unlike fun or pleasure, we have said, joy is unending.

There are, indeed, as we have also observed, ebbs and flows in the tide of joy.

But joy endures because it is not of our attainment; joy is God's gift. We do not grasp joy; we become aware of it. C.S. Lewis, once called by *Time* magazine, "apostle to the sceptics," speaks of his own conversion as *Surprised By Joy,* the title of his autobiography.

God promises His saints joy without end, beginning now: "Instead of your shame you shall have a double portion, instead of dishonor you shall rejoice in your lot; therefore in your land you shall possess a double portion; yours shall be everlasting joy'' (Is. 61:7).

Unlike pleasure, joy is invulnerable. The believer knows that fears may come, anxieties seem to overwhelm, night obscure the day — but above and beneath such feelings burns the calm light of joy. Jesus' disciples sorrowed exceedingly over His departing from them, but the Lord says: "So you have sorrow now, but I will see you again and your hearts will rejoice, and no one will take your joy from you" (John 16:22). No one! Not even we ourselves can rob our selves of joy. Why? Because joy is foretaste of heaven! Joy is participation, now, in life everlasting. Joy sees even the tomb as an open door!

Re-joice:

St. Paul writes: "Rejoice in the Lord always; and again I say, Rejoice" (Phil. 4:4).

Rejoicing is joy enjoyed, joy re-lived, joy multiplied by itself.

Joy is a gift we must relish. Joy can nourish quiet moments, fill empty days, enlarge limited prospects, expand lowering horizons: "...and again, I say Rejoice"! Paul writes in the same letter: "I joy, and rejoice..." (Phil. 2:17). So should we! Joy and re-joy!

We are not to take, then, the set of our sail from the direction of the wind. We are never to suppose that joy, like fun or pleasure, is derivative from circumstances. Joy transcends daily events as the heaven overlays the earth.

In this light we can understand otherwise puzzling Biblical requirements, like these:

1) "Count it all joy, my brethren..." When? As you meet to "celebrate" salvation? As you pump up the emotions once more with peppy songs and selected slogans? No, "Count it all joy, my brethren, when you meet various trials, for you know that the testing of your faith produces stedfastness. And let stedfastness have its full effect, that you may be perfect and complete, lacking in nothing" (James 1:2-3). Joy emerges where pleasure flees. Do you find that surprising, in the light of all we've been hearing from the Word?

2) "We rejoice in our sufferings," Paul joins James in writing, "knowing that suffering produces endurance, and endurance produces character, and character produces hope, and hope does not disappoint us, because God's love has been poured into our hearts through the Holy Spirit which has been given us" (Rom. 5:3-5).

3) Peter joins James and Paul: "In this you rejoice, though now for a little while you may have to suffer various trials, so that the genuineness of your faith, more precious than gold which though perishable is tested by fire, may redound to praise and glory and honor at the revelation of Jesus Christ" (I Pet. 1:6-7).

All this is possible, by grace, because through hope and in joy the believer has possession of life eternal as portrayed by the greatest of the Hebrew prophets:

> For you shall go out in joy, and be led forth in peace;
> the mountains and the hills before you
> shall break forth into singing,
> and the trees of the field shall clap their hands.
> Instead of the thorn shall come up the cypress;
> instead of the brier shall come up the myrtle;
> and it shall be to the Lord for a memorial,
> for an everlasting sign which shall not be cut off.

Isaiah 55:12-13

REJOICE!

For Reflection And Discussion

1. *Why is joy uniquely Christian?*
2. *How can the Bible equate joy and tribulation?*
3. *How can we make ourselves eligible for joy?*
4. *Explain the title which C.S. Lewis chose for his autobiography: "Surprised By Joy".*
5. *What is the meaning of "rejoice"?*
6. *What do you see as the difference among: fun, pleasure, joy?*

Chapter 19.

VICTORY

But thanks be to God, who gives us the victory through our Lord.
I Corinthians 15:57

VICTORY

TRUTH:
The Christian life is a victorious life, not by the evasion of trials and hardships, but through the recognition of these as God's means for testing the believer's faith and thus maturing it, not in our strength but in His.

RESPONSE:
The believer is challenged to recognize God's hand in all that happens, and to perceive a constant testing of our faith not only by the world, the flesh, and the devil, and by life's tribulations but also in its blessings; and especially to perceive the tests of faith always at hand in the routines of everyday living.

DISTORTION:
To account blessings as our own achievement, and trials as somehow outside the providence of God; and to think of life's daily contacts as "little" no-account events.

Victory

The Christian life is a victorious life — not by detouring difficulties but by going straight through them! And not because *we* triumph, but because Christ triumphs for us, and we follow His leading — as He instructs us: "If any man would come after me, let him deny himself and take up his cross and *follow* me" (Matt. 16:24).

The Lord sums it up this way: "In the world you have tribulation; but be of good cheer, I have overcome the world" (John 16:33). Meaning, of course, if He, then we who believe in Him! The Christian life is, we repeat, the victorious life.

St. Paul can therefore teach us to say: "...we glory in tribulations also, knowing that tribulation worketh patience; and patience, experience; and experience, hope; and hope maketh not ashamed, because the love of God is shed abroad in our hearts by the Holy Spirit who is given us" (Rom. 5:3-5).

Notice carefully in what Paul's (and our) glorying can consist, not in what passes for great good fortune on the world's markets, but even "in tribulations"!

Indeed, Paul teaches us that, "all who desire to live a godly life in Christ Jesus will be persecuted" (II Tim. 3:12) — a sober warning to those who confuse the *Christian* life with the carefree, untroubled life!

Christian joy, as we have already observed, does not rise out of the placid waters of painless, popular, celebrative living — these can be the signs of counterfeit faith. No, true joy emerges from transcending, through the Spirit, the trials and tribulations of bearing the cross in word and deed witness to the Christ and His truth.

Testing

Why is tribulation or persecution so characteristic of the Christian life?

There are cultists who seek physical pain and spiritual suffering to prove themselves superior to others, or to purge themselves of desire.

Such masochism has nothing in common with Christianity.

Why not?

Because the hardships of the Christian life are never self-inflicted, nor sought in themselves. Rather, the believer knows that God chooses the trials and sufferings which believers must undergo, fitting them precisely to the individual's needs. The believer, through the Spirit, supplies the loyal effort to obey his Lord through thick and thin; the Lord, sometimes working through the Devil, supplies the testing of our faith through persecution and hardship. And, humanly speaking, to those who overcome the hardships, God gives the joy of victory. We say "humanly speaking," knowing that the initiatives are always God's. It is He who tries our faith, supplies the stamina which overcomes, and rewards the triumph.

God's testing of faith goes back to the beginning of human history. It is implicit in love. The love God asks of man is to be a freely given love, one that can transcend testing. The first Adam was forbidden to eat of the tree of the knowledge of good and evil, not because the fruit of that tree was in itself poisonous, but to test Adam's love through obedience (Gen. 2:15-17). And we are tested by God, through tribulation and temptation, for the same purpose: do we love Him freely, and strive to obey Him at all costs? Or is ours a fairweather love that alters with the climate in which we are?

Divine testing has always been the lot of the saints. God tests Abraham by asking him to sacrifice his only son Isaac, child of promise; and Abraham is ready to comply, the knife in his hand uplifted to kill the child, when the Lord stops him: "Do not lay your hand on the lad or do anything to him; for now I know that you fear God, seeing you have not withheld your son, your only son, from me" (Gen. 22:12). Didn't God *know* whether or not the faith of Abraham was genuine, and his willingness to obey unlimited? Of course, God knew — just as He knows the authenticity of our faith. But God wants Abraham himself to know the depth of his own commitment, a knowledge to be gained only through the experience of self-sacrificial obedience. So for Abraham; so for each of us! God tests. How do you respond? It reveals the measure of your faith — not for His sake, but for your own! So each can learn what God already knows!

God tested Israel on the forty year trek across the wilderness, to see who among them were truly His servants: "Then the Lord said to Moses, 'Behold, I will rain bread from heaven for you; and the people shall go out and gather a day's portion every day, that I may prove them, whether they will walk in my law or not'" (Ex. 16:4). How we handle blessings is a test.

Looking back, just before the people cross over into the promised land, Moses recalls: "And you shall remember all the way which the Lord your God has led you in these forty years in the wilderness, that he might humble you, testing you to know what was in your heart, whether you would keep his commandments or not. And he humbled you and let you hunger and fed you with manna, which you did not know, nor did your fathers know; that he might make you know that man does not live by bread alone, but that man lives by every word that proceeds out of the mouth of the Lord" (Deut. 8:2-3).

And after Israel had crossed the Jordan and begun under Joshua to possess the land promised them through Abraham, God says to the successors of Joshua: "I will not henceforth drive out before them any of the nations Joshua left when he died, that by them I may test Israel, whether they will take care to walk in the way of the Lord as their fathers did, or not" (Judg. 2:22).

The untested faith is, for the believer, an unknown faith.

The Christian life is one of tribulation for the purpose of testing belief, not for God's advantage but for the believer's. The risen Lord says, "Those whom I love, I reprove and chasten..." (Rev. 3:19). As He had already said through Solomon: "For the Lord disciplines him whom he loves, and chastises every son whom he receives" (Prov. 3:12; quoted in Heb. 12:6).

Jesus Is Tested

Even the Son of God undergoes testing:

"And Jesus, full of the Holy Spirit, returned from the Jordan, and was led by the Spirit for forty days in the wilderness, tempted by the devil. And he ate nothing in those days; and when they were ended, he was hungry. The devil said to him, 'If you are the Son of God, command this stone to become bread.' And Jesus answered him, 'It is written, "Man shall not live by bread alone."'

And the devil took him up, and showed him all the kingdoms of the world in a moment of time, and said to him, 'To you I will give all this authority and their glory; for it has been delivered to me, and I give it to whom I will.' And Jesus answered him, 'It is written, "You shall worship the Lord your God, and him only shall you serve."'

And he took him to Jerusalem, and set him on the pinnacle of the temple, and said to him, 'If you are the Son of God, throw yourself down from here; for it is written, "He will give his angels charge of you, to guard you," and "On their hands they will bear you up, lest you strike your foot against a stone."'

And Jesus answered him, 'It is said, "You shall not tempt the Lord your God."'

And when the devil had ended every temptation, he departed from him until an opportune time" (Luke 4:1-13).

The second Adam undergoes the encounter which felled the first

Adam, and comes out the victor! The Apostle can say of the Lord that He "in every respect has been tempted as we are, yet without sinning" (Heb. 4:15).

Jesus' three temptations no doubt symbolize our own: 1) the inducement to make stones into bread represents all the temptations of the flesh, of the passions, of the body which test believers daily; 2) the challenge to plunge from the temple symbolizes all the temptations of the spirit — pride, the lure of the occult, fame, honor and notoriety which confront us; 3) the offer of power and authority test the believer who is tempted to throw his weight around and to claim all his achievements as solely his own. Our bouts with temptation confront us with the lure of the world, the flesh, and the Devil.

God tests us, then, through blessings and through tribulations and temptations, so that *we* may know from experience how loyal we are to Him, and grow in the process.

Alongside

We never experience trial alone. God is always ready to help if we, in faith, call upon Him and recognize His presence: "Those who trust in the Lord are like Mount Zion, which cannot be moved, but abides forever. As the mountains are round about Jerusalem, so the Lord is round about his people..." (Ps. 125:1-2).

"Thanks be to God," Paul writes for us, "who in Christ always leads us to triumph, and through us spreads the fragrance of the knowledge of him everywhere" (II Cor. 2:14). Again, "We were buried therefore with him in baptism into death, so that as Christ was raised from the dead by the glory of the Father, we too might walk in newness of life" (Rom. 6:4).

From the Lord we take courage: "Let us run with perseverance the race that is set before us, looking to Jesus the pioneer and perfecter of our faith, who for the joy that was set before him endured the cross, despising the shame, and is seated at the right hand of the throne of God" (Heb. 12:1-2).

Fruits

Tests are never ends in themselves. Believers are tested for their own benefit, as we have already pointed out. Specifically God tries us:

1) *To stimulate obedience:*

"It was good for me that I was afflicted," writes the Psalmist, "that I might learn thy statutes" (Ps. 119:71). Our hardships may simply reflect disobedience and its fruits of pain and regret; we thus learn better to obey. Or our trials may awaken us to a larger obedience which we had hitherto left unobserved. Jesus Himself "learned obedience through what he suffered," the Apostle tells us (Heb. 5:8). If He, then surely we also.

2) *To expose pride:*

How readily we assume full credit for our blessings, take pride in our accomplishments, and forget that all we are and acquire comes from the hand of the Lord. God restrains our arrogance by setting us before limitations of health, strength, endurance, or resources that remind us how frail and dependent we really are.

3) *To expose hypocrisy:*

We may indeed seem to credit God for our gains, even carefully and often publicly giving a share to charity. But only the testing of adversity reveals to us, if not to others, whether our reliance upon the Lord is of the lip only. God's testing penetrates the cloak of our hypocrisies.

4) *To increase our patience:*

"Suffering produces patience," Paul reminds us (Rom. 5:4). So does unanswered prayer, or delayed achievement of goals which seemed within reach. So does persistent struggle with temptation. Patience rises out of the realization that nothing happens to us by chance. God is always at work, maturing His children for better citizenship in the Kingdom of Heaven, now and eternally.

5) *To help us comfort others:*

"Who comforts us in all our afflictions," St. Paul reminds us, "so that we may be able to comfort those who are in any affliction" (II Cor. 1:4). Those who have "been there" are the better able to help those who come under trial and temptation. The tested believer is qualified to stand by the believer undergoing testing, for he knows by experience that God indeed never does forsake His own: "With God shall we do valiantly; it is he who will tread down our foes" (Ps. 60:12). Those who have persevered know that "the God of peace will soon crush Satan under your feet" (Rom. 16:20).

Tactics

Experience teaches us that trials and temptations approach from the right or from the left. Things good and proper in themselves can be used by the Devil to tempt us, and thus by God to test us. From the right come such tests as riches, honor, and power, all these seeming to guarantee, as did the Devil to Christ, authority among men, with pride around the corner. From the left come such tests as poverty, loneliness, afflictions, and losses, tempting us to deny our hope and neglect our faith.

It is with these alternatives in view that the wise king says: "Give me neither poverty nor riches; feed me with the food that is needful for me, lest I be full and deny thee, and say, 'Who is the Lord?' or lest I be poor, and steal, and profane the name of my God" (Prov. 30:8-9).

It is important that the believer bear in mind that God's children are not "punished" through the trials — the punishment for sin was borne by Jesus Christ. The term is "chastisement" rather than "punishment" — God chastises those whom He loves: "It is for discipline that you have to endure. God is treating you as sons; for what son is there whom his father does not discipline? If you are left without discipline, in which all have participated, then you are illegitimate children and not sons" (Heb. 12:7-8).

The eye of faith distinguishes between chastising and punishing, and in so doing leads the believer from discouragement and despair to the joy of being tested, in love, by a Father. The disciples, called before the Jewish council for preaching in Christ's name, "left the presence of the council, rejoicing that they were counted worthy to suffer dishonor for the name" (Acts 5:41). The believer does not seek suffering, but when it comes he understands it as the maturing discipline imposed by God for his benefit. And this is why Christian joy emerges from what would otherwise be cause for worldly gloom.

Outcome

St. Paul sets trials, temptations, and all forms of testing in their final context this way: "This slight momentary affliction is preparing us for an eternal weight of glory beyond all comparison, because we look not at the things that are seen but to the things that are unseen, for the things that are seen are transient, but the things that are unseen are eternal" (II Cor. 4:17-18).

St. Peter writes: "But rejoice in so far as you share Christ's sufferings, that you may also rejoice and be glad when his glory is revealed" (I Pet. 4:13).

"He disciplines us for our good," the Apostle says, "that we may share his holiness" (Heb. 12:10).

Believers across the centuries have rejoiced, not by the evasion of God's testing, but by undergoing it.

"What then shall we say to this? If God is for us, who is against us?...Who shall separate us from the love of Christ? Shall tribulation, or distress, or persecution, or famine, or nakedness, or peril, or sword?...No, in all these things we are more than conquerors through him who loved us. For I am sure that neither death, nor life, nor angels, nor principalities, nor things present, nor things to come, nor powers, nor height, nor depth, nor anything else in all creation, will be able to separate us from the love of God in Christ Jesus our Lord" (Rom. 8:31, 35, 37-39).

The Psalmist knew this, too, and writes for all believers who know it: "I will both lie down in peace, and sleep; for thou, Lord, only makest me dwell in safety" (Ps. 4:8).

The Christian life *is* a victorious life, not by the evasion of God's testing, but because with the testing God gives victory to those who believe.

Footnote

We have been talking so far as if the tests which God sets before us are always the obvious, like illness, disappointment, failure, loss. And such, indeed, many of our testings are. Tests sometimes so severe that we say with the Psalmist, "But as for me, my feet had almost stumbled, my steps had well nigh slipped" (Ps. 73:2). The patriarch Jacob, when his son Joseph introduces him to the Pharaoh of Egypt, says, "Few and evil have been the days of the years of my life, and they have not attained to the days of the years of the life of my fathers in the days of their sojourning" (Gen. 47:9). Jacob's was the view of all of the patriarchs of Israel, namely that the life of the saint is the hard, the tested life.

But it would be a serious mistake to think of God's testing of our faith, to promote our growth in it, as always so obvious as to be unmistakable. This is not necessarily so. Not at all.

Consider:

1) How seldom we perceive blessings as also a part of God's testing. How the rich handle their wealth, how the powerful handle their authority, how the famous handle their "instant recognition," and so

on, is also God's testing. Again and again the believer is warned by the Word to acknowledge all that he is, and all that he has, as God's un-merited gift. Not because the believer does not work, and work hard, to achieve what God gives — no, God expects us to work as if all de-pended upon us for whatever we achieve in life. But rather because, *after* we have expended every effort we can, and used every talent God has given us (remember that: talents, too, are gifts!), *then* we are to acknowledge that whatever reward comes is still divine blessing, not our own earning. What a burden of testing there is in wealth, fame, power, genius.... How hard not to imagine that full credit for all the fruits born of these gifts belongs to whoever gets them.

There is, of course, the intertwining of our own effort with God's blessings. God gives the talents; we are to use them with all diligence in whatever calling they qualify us for. But the testing comes in our acknowledging that talent, time, life, and effort are all, finally, given and not earned, and so then are all the fruits they produce.

So it is, also, with beauty, and charm, and skills — all gifts, testing our ability to withstand pride and practise humility.

2) We are tested also by what we ought to see, and ought to hear, but may selfishly miss. Opportunities for service, challenges to wit-ness by word and deed, human needs at our doorstep — all await us as tests of our willingness to obey. Faith, like the Lord's miracles, we have already pointed out, opens our eyes to opportunity and to need, opens our ears to cries of distress. How well we see and hear is God's *test* of how real is our faith.

3) And then there are the little things. How we meet frustrations, how we control our tempers, how we deal with others either as employ-er or employee, or clerk or customer, or buyer or seller — tests of integrity, of patience, of endurance, of courage, of simple kindness. There are many more of these in daily life than there are, for most of us, of the easily recognized testings. Life is the gradual accumulation of the fruits of what seems to be very ordinary behavior. The test is whether or not we perceive God's hand in what we take to be unim-portant, even monotonous, daily living. This means that the primary testing ground is not on the stage of dramatic success, or startling loss. No one so lives most of the time. The primary tests of life are those which confront us in the home, at work, in our recreation, at school, and at play. There the Lord waits to mature our Christian life through our handling of one "little" thing after another — little things that finally come to compose the life of faith or the life of disobedience

(and therefore are not "little" at all!).

O yes! The Christian life *is* the victorious life!

If, indeed, we have the eye and ear of faith, and the living will to obey in every situation!

For then God will ever be at our right hand, and the triumph which the Word pronounces upon all who diligently strive to meet divine testing will surely be our own!

For Reflection And Discussion

1. *What is the basis for our assurance of victory now and forever?*
2. *May the Christian seek trials and hardships in order to enjoy the experience of victory over them?*
3. *Why does God test believers' faith?*
4. *Does God test us only through hardship? Explain.*
5. *What can we learn from the temptations of Jesus in the wilderness?*
6. *What are some of the fruits which God brings out of our victory over testing?*
7. *What does it mean that God's children are not being punished through their experience of testing?*
8. *Think of some of the not-so-obvious ways in which God tests us.*
9. *Would you want the un-tested life? Why or why not?*

Chapter 20.

ETERNAL LIFE

And this is eternal life, that they know thee the only true God, and Jesus Christ whom thou hast sent.
John 17:3

ETERNAL LIFE

TRUTH:
The believer can now enjoy life eternal, in "knowing" God, a knowledge that liberates us from the tyranny of the "now," and opens to us the doors of life renewed.
RESPONSE:
Through the Word, preached and studied, through obedience, prayer and the exercise of faith, the believer is ever to enrich "knowing" God.
DISTORTION:
Permitting ourselves to be misled as to the nature of life eternal, as to its assurance, and the experience of death in relation to it.

Eternity

What is meant by the common Biblical idea of "eternal life"?

We must not confuse eternal life with immortality, though the Bible uses that latter term also. We should, better, say that Christianity gives its own meaning to the common idea of immortality. In this way:

Immortal life is likely to be conceived as infinitely extended life. The immortals simply go on living, as we live now. The immortal "gods" of Greek mythology lived pretty much as humans do, only indefinitely. Such an idea is common to many religions and philosophies — living infinitely prolonged.

The Bible does not talk about eternal life in this way. We are told, for instance, that the new heaven and new earth promised to the faithful will have no need of sun or moon, nor will night enclose them ever again: "And the city has no need of sun or moon to shine upon it, for the glory of God is its light, and its lamp is the Lamb...and there shall be no night there..." (Rev. 21:23, 25). The march of days is over. Just what will take its place we do not know.

Eternal life, then, is not time infinitely extended, at least not time as we experience its passing now.

Rather, eternal life is existence in another dimension. Because this is so, eternal life is something we can enjoy now as foretaste of eternity. So the Lord says in the quotation at the head of this chapter: "And this is eternal life, that they know thee the only true God, and Jesus Christ whom thou has sent" (John 17:3). Not, notice well, "this *will be* eternal life..." but rather "this *is*..." NOW!

The great gift of God in Christ to the believer is liberation from the tyranny of the "now"!

We live, always, in the "now". We can no more retrieve yesterday than we can lay hold of tomorrow. *And* we can no more stop time at "now" than we can recover or run ahead of it. "Now" is all we ever have. Yet "now" is past even as we mention its name. "For what is your life?" asks the Apostle, "It is even a vapor that appeareth for a little time, and then vanisheth away" (James 4:14). This grim truth about our temporal existence underlies the despair so characteristic of unbelieving people and cultures. The Egyptian pyramids were built to evade the erosion of time. but those who built them followed those buried in them along the irresistible path of the passing "now". The anxiety, which certain philosophers describe with the German term *angst* grows out of our consciousness that the "now" is all we have, but is always passing out of our grasp. We stand on quicksand, and have no firm footing here. Nor does gaining a mass of possessions, material or intellectual, stem the ceaseless flow of the "now".

Poets reflect on that, comparing life to a swift-flowing river and our being caught upon its restless stream:

"We look before and after;
We pine for what is not;
Our sincerest laughter
With some pain is fraught."

So writes Shelley.

The disillusioned Macbeth, in Shakespeare's play by that name, having sought to find life's meaning in the "now," at last cries out:

> "To-morrow, and to-morrow, and to-morrow,
> Creeps in this petty pace from day to day,
> To the last syllable of recorded time;
> And all our yesterdays have lighted fools
> The way to dusty death. Out, out, brief candle!
> Life's but a walking shadow, a poor player,
> That struts and frets his hour upon the stage,
> And then is heard no more; it is a tale
> Told by an idiot, full of sound and fury,
> Signifying nothing."

The poets would not be mistaken, *if* our "nows" were all. How could we, unaided, ever escape them? Or stop their swift passage?

Praise be to God, His eternal life breaks into the stream of time from above. The vertical touches the horizontal; time opens to eternity, NOW! Suddenly the ever fleeting "now" becomes our point of contact with the eternal. As swiftly as time moves along on the horizontal, so swiftly the vertical keeps pace. It is precisely in the "now" that we hear the voice of God, what the Bible always calls "today," meaning every moment: "Today, when you hear his voice, do not harden your hearts..." (Heb. 3:15).

Eternity has broken in upon time; our "now" becomes the very moment when we can hear God's voice, and enjoy eternal life — a new dimension, into which we are born by faith, a new dimension in which we live our "nows" as described all along the way of this *Handbook*!

How does this come about?

Knowing God

Knowing God, we are told, *is* the life eternal which we seek among the swiftly passing "nows". Such knowing touches each moment with the light of life eternal. We need no longer cling to the passing, as if in it were the meaning of living; we need no longer long for the past, knowing that God has absorbed what we want saved of it into eternity; we need no longer rest all our anticipations upon future "nows" which will pass as surely as the present passes. All is different when we come to *know* God. The tyranny of the "now" is broken; the horizontal is illumined by the vertical.

But, what does it mean to "know" God?

How do we manage that? God, in fact, manages it for us; but we can talk as if we were the initiators — it is good self-discipline to assume responsibility for such knowing).

Because God is a person, we can think of knowing Him in terms of our knowing others.

We know other persons by way of their words, their deeds, and through our love for them.

Our Lord adds to the teaching we have been quoting, "that they know thee the only true God, and Jesus Christ...."

He might have put it this way: "that they know thee the only true God, *through* Jesus Christ...."

Why may we say that?

Because Jesus says so. His disciple Philip wanted very much to see God, and said to his Master: "Lord, show us the Father, and we shall be satisfied." Jesus replies, "Have I been with you so long, and yet you do not know me, Philip? He who has seen me has seen the Father..." (John 14:8-9).

This little exchange of words is very instructive.

Philip had been with Jesus from the outset of His ministry. He had seen Him day by day, walked, rested, talked with Him. Yet, Jesus has to chide Philip for not "knowing" Him. This means, for us, that the key to "knowing" Jesus, and the Father who sent Him, is not physical contact. We may suppress whatever envy we might have of those who lived when Jesus did. Only those really "knew" Him who were given the eye of faith — exactly the eye God gives to believers of all ages. And, given the eye of faith, we "see" the Master in the words of Holy Scripture which describe Him, report His sayings, and describe His doings. So "seeing" Jesus we also "see" God — Jesus says just that!

The way in which we "know" our friends by sight, then, is hardly the way in which we "know" God — but it points to that way. For we really know very little of our friends simply through seeing them. And, as to strangers, looks may be, as the old adage says, very deceiving. It is what friends — and everyone else — says and does that are keys to "knowing" who they are. And so it is with "knowing" God.

Once we really believe that the whole creation witnesses to the power and majesty of God, we "know" Him through His works. Once we understand that human history, and our own history, testify to the over-arching Providence of God, we "know" Him in the events of every "now" that passes swiftly by. And whenever we fully appreciate what it means that the Bible *is* the very Word of God, we enter, as it were, into conversation with Him as we take up the sacred book.

There, in the form of words, He lives and communes with us. When-ever we realize that in prayer our voice lifts itself up to God, we "know" Him as a Father who hears our every lisping syllable. And as the revelation of God in the Person of His Son grows more and more real to us through intimacy with His Word, we find Jesus a companion as real as all other persons are companions in the flesh — for He shares our fleshness, even now, at the right hand of His Father.

And in all these "knowings" of God, the passing "now" is touched with the light of eternity. We have come to live in two worlds, the one passing away and the other already our home with the Father.

Still more, "knowing" God discovers how intimately God "knows" us; hear how the Psalmist puts it:

"O Lord, thou has searched me and known me!
Thou knowest when I sit down and when I rise up;
Thou discernest my thoughts from afar.
Thou searchest out my path and my lying down,
And art acquainted with all my ways.
Even before a word is on my tongue,
Lo, O Lord, thou knowest it altogether.
Thou dost beset me behind and before,
And layest thy hand upon me.
Such knowledge is too wonderful for me;
It is high, I cannot attain it....
Thou knowest me right well,
My frame was not hidden from thee,
When I was being made in secret,
Intricately wrought in the depths of the earth.
Thy eyes beheld my unformed substance,
In thy book were they written, every one of them,
The days that were formed for me,
When as yet there was none of them.
How precious to me are thy thoughts, O God!
How vast is the sum of them!
If I would count them, they are more than the sand,
When I awake, I am still with thee" (Ps. 139:1-6; 14-18).

Even the "nows" that pass in our sleep are each of them touched with the light of God's "knowing" us. To "know" God, then, is to "know" that He also *knows* you!

Knowing And Marriage

The Bible presents marriage to us as symbolic of the believer's "knowing" God, and strictly requires loyalty to marriage as symbolic of the believer's allegiance to God.

Unless we "see" marriage in this light, there are some things which the Bible teaches us which we cannot understand.

Marriage rests upon sexual differentiation. Though man and woman differ in a number of ways, none is more distinctive than the sexual. Society is everywhere, and in all ages, permeated by sexual awareness and sexual difference — stimulating both the noblest and the most base forms of human conduct.

The Bible chooses sexual comparison to illumine what we have been discussing, namely what "knowing" God is.

The sexual intercourse which is productive of children is commonly referred to in Scripture as "knowing": "Adam knew Eve his wife, and she conceived and bear Cain, saying, 'I have gotten a man child with the help of the Lord'" (Gen. 4:1). This use of "knowing" appears not only in the Old Testament, but also in the New. After the virgin Mary conceived Jesus through the Holy Spirit, her husband Joseph, "knew her not until she had borne a son; and he called his name Jesus" (Matt. 1:25).

Why should sexual union be described as "knowing," and how does that usage assist in our understanding of what it means to "know" God?

On several grounds:

1) Sexual union makes of man and woman "one flesh". Jesus alludes to that: "But from the beginning of creation, 'God made them male and female. For this reason a man shall leave his father and mother and be joined to his wife, and the two shall become one flesh'" (Mark 10:8, quoting Gen. 2:24). In parallel fashion, by "knowing" God the believer enjoys a spiritual union described in the Bible as the indwelling of the Spirit, and dwelling in Christ.

2) Yet, the union symbolized by marriage does not dissolve the identity of either partner. Marriage is a "one flesh" of two persons, neither becoming less, but rather more, of a self in the unity — as mysteriously as the Christ was one in two persons, God and man; and as the Holy Trinity is one in the unity of Three. Indeed, when the bond between husband and wife is called "love," the relationship mirrors that within the Trinity where the Spirit is the bond which unites

Father and Son, these Three. Similarly, the believer is never more truly a person, never more wholly a self, than in the "knowing" of God. For it is God who not only creates and sustains you, but who makes of you the unique self you are meant to be. The believer never stands more firmly against unbelief, more courageously for righteousness, than when he perceives how profoundly he is known by the God who permits us to "know" Him.

4) Again, just as the sexual relation symbolized by the term "know" bears fruit in children, so our "knowing" God is fruitful in good works. "With the help of God," Eve cries, she bore a son. In the doing of justice and righteousness, God says, "Is not this to know me?" (Jer. 22:16).

4) The illustration of "knowing" God in terms of sexual intimacy explains what some find the rather embarrassing imagery of the Song of Solomon. The union of man and wife, poetically pictured there, is but the symbol in sensual language of the union of believer and God. Read the book that way, and discover the freedom from the "now" which we enjoy in the "knowledge" of God.

5) We can see, also, why the Bible places so high a premium upon fidelity in marriage, and rejects out of hand all abuse of sex. The seventh commandment ("You shall not commit adultery" — Ex. 20:14) reflects the thrust of the whole first table of the Law: "You shall love the Lord your God with all your heart, and with all your soul, and with all your strength, and with all your mind..." (Luke 10:27; quoting Lev. 19:18). The love "above all" which exists between husband and wife, and underlies sexual union, reflects the love "above all" which each believer is required to show to God. The integrity required for the symbol, marriage, reflects the absolute integrity required of the believer's allegiance to God by the divine Law. And that integrity focuses upon the symbolism of "knowing" by way of sexual union because that union symbolizes our "knowing" God. The ab-use of sex in our times (and in all times) reflects just how far the "natural" human being is from understanding, and enjoying, "knowing" God. "You shall have no other gods before me" is the reality underlying "you shall not commit adultery" (Ex. 20:3, 14). What may seem, by certain standards, "innocent" experiments in sex, lose all their innocency when viewed in the light of sexual intimacy as illumining the believer's "knowing" of God.

6) Sexual imagery also illumines illicit liason with the Devil and his lies. Babylon, symbol of the confusion of tongues made by God at the

time of Babel (Gen. 11:1-9), is called the "great harlot" (Rev. 17:1). Why? Because, just as through the true Word, both written and Christ, we "know" God, so through allegiance to false words we "know" Satan — both "knowings" symbolized by sexual union. Therefore, again and again, the prophets describe Israel's serving of idols as adultery, as breaking vows of chastity required by God.

7) We also understand, here, why Jesus Himself did not marry. He who was truth incarnate had no need of symbolism in His own behavior. He who knew God so intimately as to be Himself one of the Trinity need not symbolize the reality He Himself both enjoyed and is.

8) Explained here also is the Lord's otherwise disturbing teaching that the most precious of all inter-human relationships will not characterize the new heaven and earth: "For in the resurrection they neither marry nor are given in marriage..." (Matt. 22:30). When the shadows flee away, symbols will be needed no longer. The very intimacy which makes marriage so precious will be the blessed experience enjoyed among believers, themselves, and with their God.

9) Finally, we can understand why the sex drive is so potent a force in human life. It reflects, not the evolutionary concern for the survival of the race, but rather the hunger and thirst of the person for the knowledge of God. "Thou hast made us for thyself," writes St. Augustine, "and our hearts are restless 'til at last they rest in thee" (*Confessions,* 1:1). The sexual passion which is so easily aroused, and so readily abused, testifies to our hunger for that "knowing" God which unites time and eternity. And the countless forms in which sexual desire is illicitly pandered to and gratified bear testimony to man's natural alienation from his Creator. It is not without reason that warnings against sexual misdoing figure so prominently in the Bible and especially in the letters of St. Paul. Paul is not, as is so often foolishly argued, at enmity with the feminine; Paul is caught up in the vision of how the "knowing" of God is symbolized in both the sexual and the marriage relations.

In summary, through "knowing" God we are liberated from the tyranny of time, the bounds of the "now," and the horizons of our brief years. Every moment of our lives, waking and sleeping, passes at the intersection of eternal and temporal life: "For in him we live and move and have our being" (Acts 17:28).

Rejoice!

270

Death

What, then, of dying?

How can those who already enjoy *eternal* "life" die?

With the eye of faith, we perceive that in one sense we who enjoy eternal life do *not* die. Jesus says to Martha, sister of the dead Lazarus (and to us all, who believe): "I am the resurrection and the life; he who believes in me, though he die, yet shall he live, and whoever believes in me shall never die" (John 11:25-26). On the one hand, "though he die" — the physical demise that awaits all born of mankind; on the other hand, "yet shall he live" — the eternal life promised all who believe, and guaranteed them eternally: "shall never die"! Physical death, yes; spiritual death, not at all!

From the cross, Jesus declares to the repentant thief, "Truly, I say to you, today you will be with me in Paradise" (Luke 23:43).

Eternal life means just that: the life that cannot be lost, cannot be mislaid, cannot ever be exhausted — also not at the "now" of our physical death. The Psalmist foresaw that: "Yea, though I walk the valley of the shadow of death, I fear no evil; for thou art with me; thy rod and thy staff, they comfort me" (Ps. 23:4).

Death, for the believer, is transition. The Lord has made of the tomb an open door, from out of the gardens of this world — lovely as they are — into the New Jerusalem of eternity.

In his powerful hymn to our resurrection, St. Paul tells us why believers must lay aside the garment of their bodies in the experience of death: "I tell you this, brethren; flesh and blood cannot inherit the kingdom of God, nor does the perishable inherit the imperishable" (I Cor. 15:50).

None-the-less, the believer's apprehensions over death, and sorrow in the death of those who are beloved, is not without foundation. Man was not made to die. Death is a punishment upon the first transgression: "...sin came into the world through one man and death through sin, and so death spread to all men because all men sinned..." (Rom. 5:12). And, therefore, Paul speaks of death as the *last enemy*: "The last enemy to be destroyed is death" (I Cor. 15:26). And "enemy" death remains. The joy of eternal life does not reside in our being able to detour death. No, the joy of eternal life is this, that He in whom we have life eternal went through death, burst open the tomb, and thus set out a safe path for us and all who are His.

We mourn at the graves of loved ones, but we "grieve not as others do who have no hope" (I Thes. 4:13). We dread our own plunge in the icy waters of final dissolution, but we are certain that God "knows what you need before you ask him" (Matt. 6:8). This, too, is "knowing" God! And enjoying life eternal "now"!

The Bible is, therefore, full of comfort for those whom death leaves behind, grieving the loss of those gone on before: "Precious in the sight of the Lord," the Psalmist teaches us, "is the death of his saints" (Ps. 116:15). Jesus speaks of the beggar Lazarus as "carried by the angels to Abraham's bosom" when he dies (Luke 16:2). He tells His disciples (and us) that, "In my Father's house are many rooms...I go to prepare a place for you. And when I go and prepare a place for you, I will come again and will take you to myself, that where I am you may be also" (John 14:2-3). How could our own future be more soothingly portrayed, or that of those who travel that last road before us? St. Paul speaks of dying as means to being "at home with the Lord" (II Cor. 5:8), and of going to that home as "far better" than his living on earth (Phil. 1:23).

Believers are urged to share Paul's attitude. He reminds us of "our blessed hope" (Titus 2:13). We have, Paul says, "a building from God, a house not made with hands, eternal in the heavens" (II Cor. 5:1). And something of the glory of that eternal habitation is suggested in the description given in the book of Revelation of the New Jerusalem (Rev. 21). There, St. John says, "death shall be no more, neither shall there be mourning nor crying nor pain any more, for the former things have passed away" — and the God whom "now" we "know" by faith "will wipe away every tear from their eyes" (Rev. 21:4).

The "passing away" of the "former" things is the service death has been made, in the providence of God, to render — all that is sin's heritage slips away from us in the valley of the shadow. And with us, all the way, is the Lord who has made the way straight and plain before us.

There are some questions often raised about death's transition, like:

1) Where are the souls of those who have left their bodies behind in death? The Bible leaves no doubt as to the believers' being with the Lord: "We would rather be away from the body," St. Paul writes, "and at home with the Lord" (II Cor. 5:8). We have already heard Jesus promise that "today" the repentant thief would enjoy Paradise with Him. The Psalmist rejoices that, "Thou dost guide me with thy counsel, and afterward thou wilt receive me to glory" (Ps. 73:24). And Jesus prays just before His going to the cross: "Father, I will that they also whom thou hast given me be with me where I am, that they

may behold my glory" (John 17:24).

2) In what condition are the souls of the blessed? They await reunion with their resurrected bodies, already enjoying the full realization of eternal life. How this is to imagined is suggested by St. John: "After this I looked, and behold, a great multitude, which no man could number, from every nation, from all tribes and peoples and tongues, standing before the throne and before the Lamb, clothed in white robes, with palm branches in their hands..." (Rev. 7:9).

3) The Bible offers certain tantalizing glimpses of this intermediate state: "...that they may rest from their labors, for their deeds follow them" (Rev. 14:13). And, "they shall see his face, and his name shall be on their foreheads" (Rev. 22:4). "For now we see in a mirror dimly," Paul writes, "but then face to face. Now I know in part; then I shall understand fully, even as I have been fully understood" (I Cor. 13:12).

4) At the very end, the judgment: "Do not marvel at this; for the hour is coming when all who are in the tombs will hear his voice and come forth, those who have done good, to the resurrection of life, and those who have done evil, to the resurrection of judgment" (John 5:28-29).

From the Son, God receives the kingdom He has purged: "And then comes the end, when he delivers the kingdom to God the Father after destroying every rule and authority and power" (I Cor. 15:21).

From the Father the Son receives a feast: "Then I heard what seemed to be the voice of a very great multitude, like the sound of many waters, and like the sound of mighty thunderbolts, crying, 'Hallelujah! For the Lord our God the Almighty reigns. Let us rejoice and exult and give him the glory, for the marriage of the Lamb has come, and his Bride has made herself ready; it was granted her to be clothed with fine linen, bright and pure' — for the fine linen is the righteous deeds of the saints. And the angel said to me, 'Write this: Blessed are those who are invited to the marriage supper of the Lamb'" (Rev. 19:6-9).

The Son Jesus and His Bride the Church are united, at the end, for eternity — a life the believer begins to enjoy "now".

"The Spirit and the Bride say, 'Come'"

"And let him who hears say, 'Come'"

"And let him who is thirsty come, let him who desires take the water of life without price" (Rev. 22:17).

That is what this *Handbook* is all about!

Yes, more — much more: that is what life itself is all about!

For Reflection And Discussion

1. *What is the difference between the Christian conception of eternal life and the idea of immortality?*
2. *How does Jesus define eternal life?*
3. *What does it mean to "know" God?*
4. *How does the Bible use the sexual relationship between husband and wife to signify knowing God?*
5. *Why does the Bible place such stress upon fidelity in marriage?*
6. *Why did Jesus not marry?*
7. *Why do believers die physically even when already participating in life eternal?*
8. *What does the Bible teach about death as transition?*
9. *How is the end of this age described in the book of Revelation?*
10. *What does it mean that in the New Jerusalem there will be neither night or light of sun and moon?*

INDEX OF SCRIPTURAL REFERENCES

GENERAL INDEX

A

B

C

D

M

V

W